# Advance Praise for *The Digital Doctor*

"*The Digital Doctor* is the eye-opening, well-told, and frustrating story of how computerization is pulling medicine apart with only a vague promise of putting it back together again. I kept thinking, 'Exactly!' while reading it, and that is a measure of Wachter's accomplishment in telling the tale. This is the real story of what it's like to practice medicine in the midst of a painful, historic, and often dangerous transition."

—Atul Gawande
author of *Being Mortal* and *The Checklist Manifesto*

"As scientific breakthroughs and information technology transform the practice of medicine, Bob Wachter is one of the few people with the insight, credibility, and investigative skills to go from the trenches to the observation booth. *The Digital Doctor* is first of all a personal journey, as Wachter travels the country, meets with key players who are shaping our future, and wrestles with their views. His intimate narrative left me entertained, amazed, alarmed at times, but always engrossed as I came to a new understanding of my own profession as it is being reshaped by technology. Simply brilliant."

—Abraham Verghese, MD, MACP, FRCP (Edin)
Professor and Vice Chair for the
Theory and Practice of Medicine,
Stanford University School of Medicine;
author of *Cutting for Stone*

"A much-needed study of the moment in technological change we don't want to see: the in-between moment where technology is making things worse because we just assumed that 'adding it' would make things better. Wachter maintains his enthusiasm for the long view, but helps the reader see that getting there requires an understanding of medicine and technology and, most of all, of people and their needs. It requires thinking and caring; the hope for a magic bullet got in our way. Wachter deserves our gratitude for his clarity of vision and our support so that his views can become influential in policy circles."

—Sherry Turkle
Professor of the Social Studies of Science
and Technology, MIT; author of *Alone Together:
Why We Expect More from Technology
and Less from Each Other*

"I've long admired Bob Wachter for his skill and acumen as a physician and as a leader in the field of patient safety and healthcare quality, but this book has made me appreciate him in a new light. In *The Digital Doctor*, Wachter is our indispensable guide through the computerization of medicine—the rich history, the forces that impede progress, and the potential for today's technology innovations to transform every aspect of healthcare. Read this book and you will see the future of medicine."

—**Marc Benioff, Chairman and CEO, Salesforce**

"Noted physician-author Bob Wachter takes the reader on a fascinating journey of discovery through medicine's nascent digital world. He shows us that it's not just the technology but how we manage it that will determine whether the computerization of medicine will be for good or for ill. And he reminds us that the promise of technology in healthcare will be realized only if it augments, but does not replace, the human touch."

—**Captain Chesley "Sully" Sullenberger**
speaker; consultant; author of *Highest Duty* and
*Making a Difference*; pilot of US Airways 1549,
the "Miracle on the Hudson"

"With vivid stories and sharp analysis, Wachter exposes the good, the bad, and the ugly of electronic health records and all things electronic in the complex settings of hospitals, physician offices, and pharmacies. Everyone will learn from Wachter's intelligent assessment and become a believer that, despite today's glitches and frustrations, the future computer age will make medicine much better for us all."

—**Ezekiel J. Emanuel, MD, PhD**
Vice Provost for Global Initiatives and Chair,
Departments of Medical Ethics and Health Policy,
University of Pennsylvania

"In Bob Wachter, I recognize a fellow mindful optimist: someone who understands the immense power of digital technologies, yet also realizes just how hard it is to incorporate them into complicated, high-stakes environments full of people who don't like being told what to do by a computer. Read this important book to see what changes are ahead in healthcare, and why they're so necessary."

—**Andrew McAfee**
cofounder of the MIT Initiative on the Digital Economy;
coauthor of *The Second Machine Age*

"One of the best books I've ever read. Wachter's warm humor and deep insights kept me turning the pages without interruption. To make our healthcare system work, we need new models of care and new ways of managing our technology. *The Digital Doctor* brings us much closer to making this happen, which is why I finished the book far more optimistic than I was when I began it. It is a must read for everyone—patients, clinicians, technology designers, and policy makers."

—**Maureen Bisognano**
President and CEO, Institute for Healthcare
Improvement (IHI)

"An engaging, accessible, and terribly important book by one of our finest medical writers. The electronic health record not only is the most disruptive innovation in the history of healthcare, but will also prove to be transformative. In his inimitable mix of conversation, reporting, and insightful analysis, Bob Wachter explains to you why. A must read for healthcare professionals and the public alike."

—**Lucian Leape, MD**
Professor, Harvard School of Public Health and Chair,
Lucian Leape Institute of the National Patient Safety
Foundation

"*The Digital Doctor* truly defines today's epoch of technological transformation in healthcare. Wachter tells a gripping tale about the personalities and politics behind healthcare's digital revolution. With a sweeping view that takes us from the grand political battles in Washington to the subtle changes in the interactions between people when a computer enters the picture, Wachter offers surprising, often shocking insights into how technology changes the daily lives of clinicians and patients—sometimes for the better, sometimes for the worse."

—**Leah Binder, MA, MGA**
President and CEO, The Leapfrog Group

"In this brilliant and compelling book, Wachter provides us with a view from the balcony of the last decade of healthcare information technology. As one of the players, I'm amazed by the way he's captured the characters, the plot subtleties, and the triumphs and tragedies of the work we've done. This book is the definitive chronicle of our modern efforts to wire our healthcare system."

—**John Halamka, MD**
Chief Information Officer, Beth Israel Deaconess
Medical Center; Professor of Emergency Medicine,
Harvard Medical School

"Wachter not only has unmatched insider knowledge of healthcare but deeply understands technology as well. This breadth allows him to prescribe commonsense solutions to the problems emerging from the inevitable marriage between the fields, which he reveals as a more troubled union than many suspect. *The Digital Doctor* not only enlightens and awakens, but is a delight to read—rare for such an important book."

—Steven Levy
author of *Hackers* and *In the Plex*

"A fascinating and insightful look at the digital transformation of healthcare, thoroughly researched and brought to life by dozens of stories and interviews with practicing clinicians. Wachter plots a realistic road map for navigating the obstacles ahead, without the hype that frequently accompanies digital health solutions. It's an essential read for anyone involved in our healthcare system, from everyday providers in exam rooms to politicians and policy makers who shape the system."

—Kevin Pho, MD
founder and editor, KevinMD.com

"In a style that combines the best of storytelling, historical inquiry, and investigative reporting, Wachter takes us on the journey of how healthcare information technology is transforming healthcare, highlighting the risks along the way as well as the powerful future state we might achieve."

—Tejal Gandhi, MD, MPH, CPPS
President and CEO,
National Patient Safety Foundation

"This is a brilliant book: funny, informative, well written, and accessible. Wachter takes a very complicated subject and makes it understandable, giving new perspectives and insights, whether you are yourself an electronic health record user or you are a patient who has watched your doctor struggle to use one. Given how rapidly EHRs have moved into healthcare, all of us need to understand how technology changes medicine, and, even more important, how it doesn't."

—Richard Baron, MD
President and CEO, American Board
of Internal Medicine

# THE
# DIGITAL
# DOCTOR

# Also by Robert Wachter

*Understanding Patient Safety*

*Internal Bleeding: The Truth Behind America's
Terrifying Epidemic of Medical Mistakes*
(with Kaveh Shojania)

*Hospital Medicine*
(edited with Lee Goldman and Harry Hollander)

*The Fragile Coalition: Scientists, Activists, and AIDS*

# THE DIGITAL DOCTOR

## Hope, Hype, and Harm at the Dawn of Medicine's Computer Age

### ROBERT WACHTER

New York   Chicago   San Francisco
Athens   London   Madrid   Mexico City
Milan   New Delhi   Singapore   Sydney   Toronto

2 3 4 5 6 7 8 9 0   DOC/DOC   1 2 1 0 9 8 7 6 5

ISBN      978-0-07-184946-3
MHID      0-07-184946-7

e-ISBN  978-0-07-184947-0
e-MHID    0-07-184947-5

Library of Congress Cataloging-in-Publication Data

Wachter, Robert M., author.
  The digital doctor : hope, hype, and harm at the dawn of medicine's computer age / by Robert Wachter.
     p. ; cm.
  ISBN 978-0-07-184946-3 (hardback : alk. paper) — ISBN 0-07-184946-7 (alk. paper)
  I. Title.
  1. Medical Informatics. 2. Clinical Competence. 3. Clinical Medicine. 4. Physician-Patient Relations.
  R858
  610.285—dc23
                                                                    2015001206


McGraw-Hill Education books are available at special quantity discounts to use as premiums and sales promotions or for use in corporate training programs. To contact a representative, please visit the Contact Us pages at www.mhprofessional.com.

*To Katie*

# Contents

# Preface

In retrospect, we were bound to be disappointed. Our daily experience has taught us that all we need to do is turn on our iPhone, download an app, and off we go—whether we're buying a book, making a restaurant reservation, finding a favorite song, or getting directions to the nearest Starbucks. It was only natural for us to believe that wiring the healthcare system would be similarly straightforward. Perhaps if Apple had done it, it would have been.

But healthcare's path to computerization has been strewn with land mines, large and small. Medicine, our most intimately human profession, is being dehumanized by the entry of the computer into the exam room. While computers are preventing many medical errors, they are also causing new kinds of mistakes, some of them whoppers. Sensors and monitors are throwing off mountains of data, often leading to more confusion than clarity. Patients are now in the loop—many of them get to see their laboratory and pathology results before their physician does; some are even reading their doctor's notes—yet they remain woefully unprepared to handle their hard-fought empowerment.

While someday the computerization of medicine will surely be that long-awaited "disruptive innovation," today it's often just plain disruptive: of the doctor-patient relationship, of clinicians' professional interactions and work flow, and of the way we measure and try to improve things. I'd never heard the term *unanticipated consequences* in my professional world until a few years ago, and now we use it all the time, since we—yes, even the insiders—are constantly astounded by the speed with which things are changing and the unpredictability of the results.

Before I go any further, it's important that you understand that I am all for the wiring of healthcare. I bought my first computer in 1984, back when one inserted and ejected floppy disks so often ("Insert MacWrite Disk 2") that the machine felt more like an infuriating toaster than a sparkling harbinger of a new era. Today, I can't live without my MacBook Pro, iPad, iPhone, Facetime, Twitter, OpenTable, and Evernote. I even blog and tweet. In other words, I am a typical electronically overendowed American.

And healthcare *needs* to be disrupted. Despite being staffed with (mostly) well-trained and committed doctors and nurses, our system delivers evidence-based care only about half the time, kills a jumbo jet's worth of patients each day from medical mistakes, and is bankrupting the country. Patients and policy makers are no longer willing to tolerate the status quo, and they're right not to.

For decades, healthcare's immunity to computerization was remarkable; until recently, in many communities the high school was more wired than the local hospital. But over the past five years, tens of billions of dollars of federal incentive payments have helped increase the adoption of electronic health records by hospitals and doctors' offices from about 10 percent to about 70 percent. When it comes to technology, we've been like a car stuck in a ditch whose spinning tires suddenly gain purchase, so accustomed to staying still that we were totally unprepared for that first lurch forward.

▶    ▶    ▶

When I was a medical resident in the 1980s, my colleagues and I performed a daily ritual that we called "checking the shoebox." All of our patients' blood test results came back on flimsy slips that were filed, in rough alphabetical order, in a shoebox on a small card table outside the clinical laboratory. This system, like so many others in medicine, was wildly error-prone. Moreover, all the things you'd want your physician to be able to do with laboratory results— trend them over time; communicate them to other doctors, patients, or families; be reminded to adjust doses of relevant medications—were pipe dreams. On our Maslow's hierarchy of needs, just finding the right test result for the right patient was a small, sweet triumph. We didn't dare hope for more.

For those of us whose formative years were spent rummaging through shoeboxes, how could we help but greet healthcare's reluctant, subsidized entry into the computer age with unalloyed enthusiasm? Yet once we clinicians started using computers to actually deliver care, it dawned on us that something was deeply wrong. Why were doctors no longer making eye contact with their patients? How could one of America's leading hospitals (my own) give a teenager a 39-fold overdose of a common antibiotic, despite (scratch that—because of) a state-of-the-art computerized prescribing system? How could a recruiting ad for physicians tout the *absence* of an electronic medical record as a major selling point? Logically, we pinned the problems on clunky software, flawed implementations, muscle-bound regulations, and bad karma. It was all of those things, but it was also something far more complicated—and far more interesting.

As I struggled to answer these questions, I realized that I needed to write this book—first to explain all this to myself, and then to others.

What I've come to understand is that computers and medicine are awkward companions. Not to diminish the miracles that are Amazon.com, Google Maps, or the cockpit of an Airbus, but computerizing the healthcare system turns out to be a problem of a wholly different magnitude. The simple narrative of our age—that computers improve the performance of every industry they touch—turns out to have been magical thinking when it comes to healthcare. In our sliver of the world, we're learning, computers make some things better, some things worse, and they change everything.

Harvard psychiatrist and leadership guru Ronald Heifetz has described two types of problems: technical and adaptive. Technical problems can be solved with new tools, new practices, and conventional leadership. Baking a cake is a technical problem: follow the recipe and the results are likely to be fine. Heifetz contrasts technical problems with adaptive ones: problems that require people themselves to change. In adaptive problems, he explains, the people are both the problem and the solution. Leadership, he once said, requires mobilizing and engaging people around a problem "rather than trying to anesthetize them so you can go off and solve it on your own."

The wiring of healthcare has proven to be the Mother of All Adaptive Problems. Yet we've mistakenly treated it as a technical problem: simply buy the computer system, went the conventional wisdom, take off the shrink-wrap, and flip the switch. We were so oblivious to the need for adaptive change that when we were faced with failed installations, mangled work flows, and computer-generated mistakes, we usually misdiagnosed the problem; sometimes we even blamed the victims, both clinicians and patients. Of course, our prescription was wrong—that's what always happens when you start with the wrong diagnosis.

Making this work matters. Talk of interoperability, federal incentives, bar coding, and machine learning can make it seem as if healthcare information technology is about, well, the technology. Of course it is. But from here on out, it is also about the way your baby is delivered; the way your cancer is treated; the way you are diagnosed with lupus or reassured that you aren't having a heart attack; the way, when it comes down to whether you will live or die, you decide (and tell the medical system) that you do or you don't want to be resuscitated. It is also about the way your insurance rates are calculated and the way you figure out whether your doctor is any good—and whether you need to see a doctor at all. Starting now and lasting until forever, your health and healthcare will be determined, to a remarkable and somewhat disquieting degree, by how well the technology works.

▶   ▶   ▶

While this is a book about the challenges we're facing at the dawn of healthcare's digital age, if you're looking for Dr. Luddite, you've come to the wrong place. Part of the reason we're experiencing so much disappointment is that in the rest of our lives, information technology is so astonishing. I have no doubt that, even in medicine, our bungling adolescence will ultimately mature into a productive adulthood. We just have to make it through this stage without too much carnage.

Of course, if you picked up this book looking for breathless hyperbole, you won't find that here, either. We are late to the digital carnival, but there are barkers everywhere telling us that this or that app will transform everything, that the answer to all of healthcare's ills is being developed—even as we speak—by a soon-to-be billionaire twentysomething tinkering in a Cupertino garage. This narrative is seductive; some of it may even be real. But for now, despite some scattered rays of hope, the digital transformation of medicine remains more promise than reality. Lycra bike shorts that take our pulse, count our steps, and read our moods are pretty nifty, but they aren't the change we need.

What you'll find in these pages is an insider's unvarnished view of the early days of healthcare's transformation from analog to digital, with tales of modest wins as well as surprising obstacles. Notwithstanding the latter, the answer to what ails healthcare is not going to be found in romanticizing how wonderful things were when your doctor was Marcus Welby. We can—in fact, we must— wire the world of medicine, but we need to do it with our eyes open, building on our successes, learning from our mistakes, and mitigating the harms that are emerging.

To do so effectively, we need to recognize that computers in healthcare don't simply replace my doctor's scrawl with Helvetica 12. Instead, they transform the work, the people who do it, and their relationships with one another and with patients. Sorting out all these issues will take deep thought and hard work on the part of clinicians, healthcare leaders, policy makers, technology vendors, and patients. Sure, we should have thought of this sooner. But it's not too late to get it right.

# Chapter 1

## On Call

One must confess that whatever his mental and moral
deficiencies, and they are certainly great, as a machine, man
has no equal.

      —Dr. Will Mayo, cofounder of the Mayo Clinic, in 1915

In late June 2003, 27-year-old Matthew Burton began a residency in general surgery in Buffalo, New York. The first year of residency, commonly referred to as the internship, is a rite of passage so colorful, ethically fraught, exhausting, and ennobling that it has served as the backdrop for countless books, television shows, and movies. Among physicians, a surgical internship is considered the most taxing of all, but Burton was ready for it—particularly since he was a "mature" student, having taken a few years between college and medical school to work as a systems analyst for Otis, the elevator company.

I'm sitting with Burton in a conference room on the third floor of Brackenridge, one of the dozen or so buildings scattered around the Mayo Clinic's main campus in Rochester, Minnesota. It is here that Burton now works as a human factors expert, helping Mayo translate its billion-dollar investment in information technology into better patient care. He is telling me the story of the horrific night that set him on the path to leaving his chosen field of surgery—in fact, to leaving the practice of medicine altogether—to devote his career to making healthcare's computer systems work.

▶    ▶    ▶

August 2, 2003, was a warm Saturday in Buffalo. Only six weeks after gradu-
ating from the University of Michigan's medical school, Burton was on call
at Millard Fillmore Gates Hospital, one of several facilities affiliated with the
surgical residency program of the State University of New York at Buffalo. In
addition to seeing emergency room patients with potential surgical problems,
such as appendicitis, and covering the post-op patients on the surgical floor,
one of his duties was to carry the Code Blue beeper.

When somebody, usually a nurse, walks into a hospital room and finds a
patient *in extremis* (a Latin term physicians use that means "at the point of
death"), she pushes an emergency button on the wall or calls an internal 911-
like phone number. This pages the Code Blue team, usually made up of doctors, specially trained nurses, a pharmacist, and a respiratory therapist. Calling
a code is the hospital equivalent of summoning the cavalry.

You never know what you're going to discover when you rush to the scene
of a code. In addition to finding patients in full cardiac arrest (unconscious
with no pulse and no blood pressure), I've encountered patients unable to
move one side of their body as a result of a massive stroke, and patients with
arterial bleeders spurting like pulsating red geysers. Of course, I've also come
upon patients in a deep slumber who woke up wondering what all the fuss
was about (this situation is more than a little embarrassing). When the code
beeper goes off, your adrenaline spikes instantaneously. It is medicine's scariest
moment—certainly for patients (if they are conscious) and their families, but
for doctors, too.

When the Code Blue page shattered the calm of what had been an unevent-
ful evening on call, Burton ran to the patient's room. The nurse had discovered
that her patient, a man in his seventies recovering from an uncomplicated surgical procedure, was short of breath and confused, and had a dangerously low
blood pressure. Burton and the nurse worked on him, but the patient's condition spiraled downward; within a few minutes, he had lost both pulse and
blood pressure, and the team began full-bore CPR.

Burton wondered about the whereabouts of his senior resident, who also
carried the code beeper and would normally have been there to supervise the
code (as an intern, Burton was too junior to be given this responsibility on
his own). He quickly learned that his "senior" was stuck in the OR, operating
on an elderly woman with a dying bowel. It dawned on Burton that he was
the only doctor available to run the code. During his med school cardiology

rotation, he had carried one of the code beepers and had even started running a few codes before senior physicians arrived, an unusual experience for a student. *I can do this*, he thought as he worked through the protocol and tried to figure out what was wrong with the patient.

Just then, his Code Blue beeper went off again.

This time it was for a patient on another floor who appeared to be having a massive heart attack. Burton couldn't abandon the first patient, now receiving CPR and still a diagnostic mystery, so he tried to manage the second patient by phone, commanding the floor nurses to hightail the patient to the intensive care unit. At least there were nurses there who could start advanced cardiac life support, although without any physicians around, there were limits on what they could accomplish.

Keeping these two plates spinning—running the code for Patient 1 and orchestrating the code for Patient 2—was a remarkable test for this newly minted physician. It was hard to believe that things could get worse. But about 20 minutes later, they did: Burton's code beeper went off again, this time for a woman having a grand mal seizure. One saving grace was that she was on Burton's floor, so that he was able to toggle between the rooms of Patients 1 and 3, giving orders sequentially to the nurses and respiratory therapists in the two rooms like an army drill sergeant trying to keep two groups of new recruits in line—except that, in this case, the recruits were far more experienced in running codes than their leader.

Lest you think this was an average day at an American hospital, you should know that the situation Matt Burton found himself in is remarkably rare. A busy hospital might see a single Code Blue in a day; seeing two is rare, and in 30 years of hospital practice, I've never seen three in an hour; my 600-bed academic medical center averages about 300 Code Blues each year. In fact, the odds of having three codes in an hour are so low that Burton briefly entertained the possibility that something, or someone, was poisoning the patients.

The survival rate for in-hospital codes is about one in six, and those who make it depend on a physician arriving within moments and leading the team through the complicated CPR protocol effectively. While automatic defibrillators—the kind you now see in gyms and hotel lobbies—have made CPR seem easy, running a code in the hospital is much more complicated, since the deterioration is usually related to the patient's underlying illness, which also needs to be addressed. It's rarely a simple matter of applying the paddles, listening for the electronic whir to signify a full battery charge, and pushing a green button.

Burton steeled himself as he tried to figure out what to do. His instinct was to call for help. He contacted the doctor in the emergency room, only to learn that this physician had a "strict policy" never to leave the ER during a shift, come hell or high water. Burton knew there were a few other senior residents from his program stationed at nearby hospitals (and probably sitting with their feet up on their call room beds, watching TV), but there was no way to get information out of the paper medical record to them. Without that information, and without any ability to order treatments remotely, they couldn't be of much help. Counting the patients, family members, clinicians, and support staff, at that moment Burton was sharing the Gates Hospital building with some 250 other people. Yet he had never felt more alone.

Incredibly enough, as Burton worked to revive Patients 1 and 3, checked in to see whether Patient 2 had made it to the ICU, and struggled to tamp down his swirling emotions, his Code Blue beeper went off yet again. At that point, all that the overwhelmed intern could do for the fourth patient—who, like Patient 2, was on a different floor—was to enjoin this patient's nurses to rush him to the ICU. And hope.

By the time the dust settled, three of Burton's four Code Blue patients were dead, as was his senior resident's patient in the operating room. It was the kind of death toll that an unlucky intern might expect in an exceptionally bad month. Not in an hour.

▶   ▶   ▶

Matt Burton is now 39 years old. With his shaven head, handsome, unlined face, and neat goatee, he bears a passing resemblance to a young Bruce Willis. His broad shoulders are clues to his athleticism; in his Bloomington, Indiana, high school, he was a defensive tackle, a shot-putter, and a champion weight lifter who still holds a few school records. I notice his build, but I can't see the scars covering his thighs, remnants of the fourth-degree burns he suffered when a high school chemistry experiment went awry. His botched treatment by a local surgeon—he should have been referred to a specialized burn center but wasn't—triggered his decision to devote his professional life to improving the healthcare system.

It is no surprise that Matt Burton found his way to the Mayo Clinic, even if his path to southeastern Minnesota was not exactly straight. The Clinic, the most storied brand in healthcare, was founded by the two Mayo brothers, Will and Charlie, in 1889 on a simple principle: patients deserved the world's best care, and they could receive it only from physicians working in high-functioning teams, embedded in a system that supported their efforts.

The practice of medicine is all about information, from making a diagnosis to picking the best medication to offering an accurate prognosis. Unsurprisingly, Mayo has been home to many of the critical innovations in information management. The idea of a centralized medical record and patient registration system was developed there, as was a remarkable network of pneumatic tubes for moving paper charts and x-rays around. At its height, Mayo had some 10,000 tubes traversing more than 10 miles, including one tube that was nine blocks long, connecting the two main campuses.

The year 2003—when Burton had his call night from hell—was iconic in the world of medical training. Following a report by the Institute of Medicine that estimated that nearly 100,000 Americans were dying each year from medical mistakes, regulators had limited the number of hours that residents could work to 80 a week. However, in most training programs, the volume of work was not pruned; it was simply compressed. "Now we were doing 120 hours' worth of work in 80 hours," Burton recalled. "But I realized that most of my time was spent moving information from one place to another, doing what we in computer science would call 'simple transforms'"—like transforming the fact that a patient was on insulin, which lived on a medication list, into "diabetes mellitus" on a different page, the problem list. With Burton's background as a computer expert, he knew that information technology could help with this kind of task, but in the hospitals and clinics he worked in, computers either were absent or, when they were around, often made things worse through their frequent crashes, rigid work flows, and dreadful user interfaces.

During Burton's years working at Otis, he had learned an important lesson: although his work was ostensibly about computers, cables, and controls, solving the technical puzzles wasn't nearly as hard, or as important, as fixing the underlying business, cultural, and political problems. That's what really determined how well the system worked.

In 1997, Burton began medical school in Ann Arbor, where he was quickly pegged as a computer geek ("Oh, you know how to write *code*!") and ended up on several technology-related committees. One of his projects was to write a program to deliver the pathology curriculum to his fellow students. "I wasn't learning histopathology," he realized. "I was learning how to develop good software, and how to engage users in the design." Burton enjoyed the computer work but regarded it as a future hobby, for he had decided to be a surgeon, a career that demands slavish devotion. "I loved surgery," he said wistfully when recalling his first few times in the operating room. "I loved the adrenaline. I thought it was the coolest thing in the world."

And now, six weeks into his surgical training, he had faced a trial that few physicians experience over a lifetime of practice. I asked him how he felt on that August night, once the code beeper finally, mercifully, went silent; when all that was left to do for his three patients was remove their IVs and call the next of kin. "I was a deer in the headlights," he said. When the senior resident finally emerged from the operating room, Burton gave him a playback of the astonishing events of the prior few hours. "He and I were, like, '*What* just happened here?'" As Burton described this night to me, using the dispassionate shorthand that doctors often employ when talking to colleagues ("My senior was in the OR with the lady with the mesenteric artery embolus . . ."), something happened that I was not prepared for. He began to cry.

▶   ▶   ▶

A few months after that terrible night, Matt Burton sat down with the director of his surgical residency program. To the program's credit, Burton had not detected any finger-pointing aimed in his direction. Quite the opposite, in fact—he got mostly sympathy, and even a little street cred, for having lived through a night so awful that none of the old-timers had seen its like.

He and his program director talked about what had happened, and, while they touched on the medical issues, both of them recognized that the real breakdowns were those of the system: a system that placed too many residents where they weren't needed and too few where they were; a system that missed the early signs of patient deterioration whose recognition might avert a Code Blue; a system that did not allow an overwhelmed young physician to summon help; a system that made it impossible for clinicians to access patients' information or order treatments remotely. In Burton's world, all these systems were nonexistent or had been slapped together. Yet not only were the technologies to support them available, they were already being used in other industries. "There are tens of thousands of people who can be surgeons," his program director told him. "But there aren't tens of thousands of people who can help solve these problems."

Burton finished his internship and then left the practice of medicine. I asked him how he could make such a monumental decision, one I can barely imagine for myself. "Medicine is the most information-rich, knowledge-intensive human activity, probably ever," he said. "I was angry, because I knew that there were technological solutions to these problems, and we weren't using them." After receiving advanced training in informatics[1] at the Regenstrief Institute in Indianapolis, he took a position at Mayo, where he is now one of dozens of doctors, nurses, and pharmacists working to bridge the worlds of clinical medicine and information technology.

▶    ▶    ▶

These should be glorious times for the Mayo Clinic. President Obama highlighted the Clinic time and time again during the run-up to healthcare reform. The patient safety movement has cast a bright light on the need for effective healthcare delivery systems, and nobody has a better one than the folks in Rochester. Today, instead of charts whooshing their way through pneumatic tubes, there is a computer in every hospital room, in every operating room, and in every clinic, placing information at the fingertips of doctors and nurses. Telemedicine is coming of age—Mayo physicians now deliver care to patients who are hundreds, even thousands, of miles away. And we can now test new ways of improving care through the magic of sensors and big data analytics.

It is Burton's job to ensure that these great ideas make the jump from polished PowerPoint presentations to the big, messy realities of the wards without stumbling along the way. In one of his first studies, he asked nurses and doctors how they organized their work. Many told him, "We're managing to the plan." He asked them to show him this "plan." "They said stuff like, 'Well, it's kind of in the note, and it's kind of on this piece of paper, and it's kind of in our conversations,'" Burton recalled. In other words, this central piece of knowledge—what computer scientists refer to as the "information artifact"—was everywhere. And nowhere.

Burton and his colleagues followed a few nurse practitioners on the colorectal surgery service. One of the NPs' jobs was to gather the relevant data during a ritual we call prerounds. So they tracked what the NPs actually did on these early-morning expeditions. At Mayo, a lack of resources usually isn't the problem—private jets ferrying billionaires from Dubai swoop in with metronomic regularity. "There is a downside to being flush with money," Burton said, "because you end up throwing resources at any problem that you have."

Burton's observations on the surgery service reflected this haphazard abundance. The NPs had to log in to *11 different information systems*—an OR sched-

---

[1] Informatics is the field of medicine that concerns itself with "the interactions among and between humans and information tools and systems." In 2013, it became an official specialty, like cardiology or obstetrics, with its own board certification.

uling system, a separate clinic scheduling system, an outpatient medication system, and so on—to gather what they needed. This digital Easter egg hunt required more than 600 clicks, accompanied by more than 200 screen transitions. Besides the sheer insanity of the enterprise, the problem is that with each screen flip, your brain must process the new visual information—which generates the neuronal equivalent of the brief static you sometimes see on the TV screen when you're channel surfing—and before long, all of your cognitive bandwidth is exhausted. He recalled a few cases in which the NPs missed obvious things, like a significant fall in the blood count, because "all they're doing is foraging for information, writing it down, not even paying attention."

Burton and his team developed a patient summary screen that the NPs could fill in with just 25 clicks. This dramatically reduced the amount of time they spent completing their prerounds—from 35 minutes to less than 5. Not only did this free up huge chunks of their days, but it also liberated tons of cognitive space to actually think about the patients. As a result, the NPs made fewer mistakes.

► ► ►

Mayo's computer systems were built by some of the best companies in the business, including household names like GE and IBM (the latter runs a large facility in Rochester) and specialized healthcare companies like Cerner. Knowing how crucial it is to observe how real people actually do their work in order to design functioning computer systems, Burton is irritated by how little attention these vendors have given to the plight of frontline clinicians and their patients. Having worked for a healthcare computer vendor and for Mayo, he knows why this is: the systems that support clinical care are inseparable from the systems that send out the bills, and the latter often trump the former on the priority list. "The vendors are selling to a CEO," he said, not to doctors and nurses.

I asked him about the massive federal push to get these vendor-built systems installed in doctors' offices and hospitals, a push enlivened by $30 billion in incentive payments doled out between 2010 and 2014. I expected that this physician—a man who gave up a promising surgical career to commit himself to the computerization of healthcare—would be enthusiastic, perhaps even ecstatic, about this turn of events. I was wrong.

"They are mandating the use of snake oil," he said, his voice a mixture of frustration and sadness.

# Chapter 2

# Shovel Ready

By computerizing health records, we can avoid dangerous
medical mistakes, reduce costs, and improve care.
—President George W. Bush, State of the Union
address, January 20, 2004

President George W. Bush was discouraged, and more than a little envious. The year 2003 had begun well enough for Bush and his administration, starting with March's "Shock and Awe" campaign to launch the Iraq war, followed two months later by the exuberant "Mission Accomplished" speech on the deck of the U.S.S. *Abraham Lincoln*. But by summer, the security situation in Iraq had frayed badly, and Bush realized that the war would not yield the quick, painless victory he had hoped for. Particularly with a reelection campaign just over the horizon, the president was eager to pivot to domestic affairs and anxious for an easy win—in an area that was not too politically contentious.

As Bill Clinton learned in 1993 (and Barack Obama would learn in 2009), a U.S. president looking for a bipartisan domestic triumph would be wise to give healthcare a very wide berth. But there was a portion of the healthcare landscape that was ripe for change and appeared to have the support of both parties, particularly in light of the growing national anxiety about medical mistakes and the skyrocketing costs of care.

At a summit meeting in 2003—around the time that Matt Burton was beginning his internship—British prime minister Tony Blair bragged to the American president about his new $16 billion "Connecting for Health" initiative, designed to wire the United Kingdom's entire healthcare system. After Bush returned to Washington, he pressed his policy team to come up with a similar program. It did, and in his 2004 State of the Union address, Bush called for a comprehensive effort to computerize American healthcare. Three months later, in a speech in Minnesota, Bush articulated an ambitious goal: every American would have a personal electronic health record within a decade. Days later, he announced the creation of a new Office of the National Coordinator for Health Information Technology (ONCHIT, later shortened to ONC) and selected David Brailer to lead it.

The 44-year-old Brailer was an intriguing choice for America's first health information technology czar. A study in contrasts, he grew up in Kingwood, West Virginia, population 500, after being born in the 22-bed hospital where his mother worked for decades as a nurse. Brailer trained as a physician, but also received a PhD in economics from the Wharton School at the University of Pennsylvania. Before assuming his job at ONC, he was an academic, an entrepreneur, and a CEO. And he is an openly gay man who served in a very visible position in a very conservative administration. He may well be healthcare's version of the "Most Interesting Man in the World."

Brailer had a twinkle in his eye as he told me the story of President Bush's decision to focus on wiring healthcare. "Policy initiatives that bring nations into the modern era sometimes represent nothing more than petty rivalries between global leaders," he said.

▶   ▶   ▶

For someone who was assuming a role as a Washington bureaucrat, Brailer's politics tilted in a decidedly libertarian direction. In fact, he opposed the formation of the very office he was asked to lead. "I thought it would be bad for the standing bureaucracy to have a role overseeing something as innovative as technology," he said. While he felt that the federal government had a place in setting standards; in convening communities of clinicians, payers, policy makers, and vendors; and in banging the drum for healthcare computerization, he wanted the government to use a light touch, being careful not to overwhelm a nascent and fragile healthcare technology market. Federal help, he knew, can be like a bear hugging a kitten.

But that touch was destined to be anything but light. An early hint of this came in Brailer's first year as ONC director, when *Modern Healthcare* magazine named him the most influential person in healthcare. (Bush came in fourth, just behind Hillary Clinton, which really ticked off the president.) Bush, of course, was well known for his backslapping jocularity, accompanied by a penchant for pinning nicknames on staff members and journalists. "Someone cut out the *Modern Healthcare* cover and put it on the president's desk when I met with him a few days later," said Brailer. "And he calls me 'Hollywood' to this day."

▶    ▶    ▶

While Bush correctly perceived a high level of bipartisan support for healthcare IT, there still were battles to be fought—this was Washington, after all, and the laws of political gravity had not been suspended. Moreover, Brailer was neither a creature of the Beltway nor someone who minced words, two characteristics that endeared him to the straight-talking president even as they irritated many White House and congressional staffers. "I think people got tired of me stepping on toes, overstepping my authority," he said. He knew he was making enemies, but he learned the lengths to which those enemies would go only when he saw the 2005 congressional budget proposal, which, rather than the $42 million he had requested, had a big fat zero in the box for ONC. "It was my lowest moment," he said. "I thought, 'This effort will die an ignominious death, and I'm going to be a laughingstock.'"

Going into a scheduled meeting with the president and his senior advisors a few days later, Brailer had been advised by White House allies not to bring up the budget; they hinted that Bush knew about the congressional fatwa and would not let it stand. The meeting began, and the group discussed about a half-dozen issues, but the budget, the elephant in the room, was left unaddressed. The meeting was drawing to a close, and Bush had not mentioned the money.

"I thanked the president and started to get up," Brailer recalled. "Then President Bush said, 'Are we done?' I looked around the room and probably turned deep red. I said, 'Well, sir, there *is* the question of my budget. You may know that Congress had the great wisdom to zero it out.'" At that point, Brailer swallowed hard, and added, "It's vital to the execution of your initiative."

The president turned to glare at his budget director, Josh Bolten, and said, "Josh, can we find $42 million in our $2.5 trillion budget?"

"I'm sure we can, sir," replied Bolten.

"And do I have the authority to do that?"

"Yes, in fact, you have the authority."

"So we're done, right?"

And with that, everyone stood and left the room. The Office of the National Coordinator for Health Information Technology, and with it the federal effort to wire the American healthcare system, remained alive.

▶   ▶   ▶

Of course, entire swaths of our economy—retail, airlines, banking, manufacturing—went digital without federal help, and one doesn't need to be a Tea Party member to worry that excessive government meddling could stifle technological innovation. Yet most thoughtful policy analysts acknowledge that healthcare technology has some unique features that create a legitimate case for a governmental role. The debate is over its scope and reach.

The first argument for government intervention is pragmatic—namely, that healthcare IT represents a market failure. Most people believe that government should step in when the market fails to produce a good or service that would make everyone's life better, and creating a national healthcare technology infrastructure, like the decisions made generations earlier to create interstate highway and national park systems, appeared to fall into this category.

The numbers support the diagnosis of a market failure. Before there was federal help, computerization of the American healthcare system was proceeding at a snail's pace. In 2008, two decades after the first electronic health records were installed, only 17 percent of doctors' offices had a basic EHR, as did only about one in ten hospitals.

Why the slow uptake? Both doctors and hospitals maintained that they would bear the cost of computerization (in both money and hassles), while others, mostly insurers, would benefit. As Clay Christensen, Jerry Grossman, and Jason Hwang observed in their 2009 book, *The Innovator's Prescription*, the job that an electronic health record is designed to do is systemic, but not necessarily communal. For independent physician practices (which care for nearly two out of three Americans) to invest in and adopt EHR systems that make it easier for *other* clinicians to care for their patients would be "an extraordinarily selfless act," they wrote. Swapping out a tried and tested paper prescription and record system for an expensive and complex EHR was simply not high on the physicians' Christmas shopping list.

Second, the government sometimes needs to act as a standard setter. This seemingly arcane matter of standards turns out to be central to the success of many industries. America's decision during the Lincoln administration to standardize the gauge of its railroad tracks at 4 feet 8½ inches created an efficient national railway system. In contrast, Australia still lacks a single standard railway gauge. Because of this, at some interchanges, passengers and freight have to be transferred from one train to another; there are even circumstances in which entire trains are picked up and transported on the backs of others.

Of course, the importance of standards is well appreciated in the technology world—it is why we can go to the hardware store and buy lightbulbs and electric cords and be confident that they will work when we get home. And the adoption of a single networking protocol, TCP/IP, was essential to the Internet's remarkable success. While the original TCP/IP model was developed by academic researchers and consultants working under Department of Defense contracts and the DoD was the first organization to mandate the use of TCP/IP (for its military computers), the universal adoption of TCP/IP involved voluntary agreements by the technology industry, and the protocol is currently managed by the Internet Architecture Board, a nongovernmental organization. Brailer, following this example, wanted the ONC to help set standards, but to do so with great restraint and humility, preserving key roles for patients, clinicians, professional societies, payers, hospitals, and manufacturers.

A third role that Brailer saw for the ONC was to promote something called interoperability, which relies on a type of standard setting but has a few unique twists. Interoperability is the reason that I can put my Bank of America card into a Citibank ATM and withdraw $100. If we want our computer systems to talk to one another, interoperability is what allows them to speak the same language.

Ensuring interoperability in the banking world is orders of magnitude easier than it is in healthcare. For my ATM card to perform its magic trick, there needs to be a way for BofA and Citibank to account for the transaction and appropriately debit the correct account, but the definition of "$100" is not in question. In contrast, for my computer system at UCSF Medical Center to communicate seamlessly with a system in Bakersfield (particularly if those systems are built by different companies), the fields have to line up (I might record my patient's prior heart attack in a box called "Past Medical History," but if I think the heart attack is relevant to the matter at hand, I might put it in a different box, called "History of Present Illness"), and so does the terminology (a low blood potassium level might be recorded as "low potassium," obviously, but also as "hypokalemia," "low K⁺," or even "↓K"). Technology vendors have little incentive to promote interoperability (it makes it easier to switch systems), and the same is often true for hospitals and doctors (it can make it easier for you to receive some of your care in one place and the rest in another). Yet having a seamless healthcare computer system would help everyone, which makes this, in policy-speak, a "public good."

Brailer set out to promote interoperability, by creating standards that would allow computer systems to exchange information (things like maintaining an active list of each patient's medical issues and referring to low potassium only in certain ways) and by facilitating the formation of regional entities called healthcare information exchanges. While national—even worldwide— interoperability is the ultimate goal, most people get their care within 30 miles of their home or business, so starting with local exchanges seemed like a reasonable plan.

Although $42 million wasn't a lot of money to accomplish these ambitious goals, it was enough to get things moving. When Brailer left the ONC in 2006 to return to the private sector, he never dreamed that within three years, the federal budget to promote the wiring of healthcare would climb from that $42 million he had fought so desperately to preserve.

By 71,000 percent.

▶    ▶    ▶

"You never want a serious crisis to go to waste," Rahm Emanuel, chief of staff to President-elect Obama, told the *Wall Street Journal* on November 19, 2008. "It's an opportunity to do things that you think you could not do before." The crisis that Emanuel was referring to, of course, was the global recession that had begun with the collapse of Lehman Brothers two months earlier.

The Obama administration knew that time was short; it needed to get money flowing through the veins of the American economy promptly or the damage might become irreparable. But if the money appeared to end up lining the pockets of the same Wall Street moneymen who were being blamed for the crisis, or if it failed to have the desired stimulatory effect, the political fallout would be devastating. The Obama team decided to spend the stimulus money on infrastructure, specifically on projects that were already on the launchpad. But how could the team explain this decision—and the complex underlying economic arguments—to a scared, impatient, and skeptical electorate?

The term *shovel ready* was coined in the late 1990s, when the Niagara-Mohawk Power Company in upstate New York used it in referring to abandoned industrial sites that were primed for development. The company even trademarked the phrase and bought the Internet domain shovelready.com. But the term remained obscure until December 7, 2008, when, in an appearance on NBC's *Meet the Press*, President-elect Obama used it to describe the types of projects to be funded under his stimulus plan. Repairing bridges and building highways—these were the kinds of things that people thought of when they heard about shovel-ready projects.

But David Blumenthal had another idea. In late 2008, Blumenthal, a Harvard health policy professor who would later become ONC director himself, was advising the Obama administration on its plans for healthcare technology. In a five-page white paper, he observed that "Doctors and hospitals are unsure they will realize any financial gains from electronic health records, and the systems are expensive: about $40,000 per physician, and roughly $5 million to $10 million for the typical, average-sized hospital." However, he continued, "federal funding—especially for financially weak or troubled providers—could help overcome these obstacles." While there had been some loose talk over the years about direct subsidies for healthcare computer purchases, the idea had not received any play among serious policy mavens, both because of philosophical objections and because it would require a pot of cash that seemed unimaginable.

Ezekiel Emanuel and Bob Kocher, the two physicians working on the Obama transition team's overall plans for healthcare, were immediately drawn to Blumenthal's proposal. The administration was committed to focusing on healthcare reform in its first 100 days in office, a commitment that did not waver despite the turmoil that had engulfed the economy. In addition to a push for universal coverage, a cornerstone of the healthcare plan was to shift the system from one dominated by fee-for-service reimbursement—which most experts believe promotes overuse of costly procedures (x-rays, surgeries, and the like) and hospitalizations—to one centered on "value." The chassis for this change was to be a new reimbursement model under which providers would be paid a fixed sum to care for groups of patients and held accountable for their performance on measures of quality, safety, and patient satisfaction.

But Emanuel and Kocher worried that any value-based system would rapidly become a target for the same type of attacks that had torpedoed the managed care/HMO movement in the mid-1990s, attacks centered on the dreaded "R word": rationing. Without good data, there would be no way to combat the inevitable caricatures of health reform, exemplified by Sarah Palin's 2009 "death panel" canard. Moreover, not all such broadsides would be political sloganeering—some would be legitimate. "There's a risk that somebody, some-where is going to do something really unethical and not treat a cancer patient with chemotherapy that could have cured him," said Kocher. The only way to make a shift from volume to value politically viable, the Obama team believed, was to start with a wired healthcare system—one that tracked patients, mea-sured outcomes, and detected and swiftly addressed instances in which people failed to receive the care they needed.

Moreover, Obama's policy experts worried that without good computer systems to follow their patients' outcomes and costs and remind them to deliver appropriate preventive treatments, doctors and hospitals would be unable to survive a switch in the payment model. Some critics have argued that health reform, in and of itself, would have created a vibrant market for computerization, thereby obviating the need for a government incentive to purchase the technology. Kocher doesn't buy it. "From a policy-making per-spective, we can't implement a payment model that most providers can't par-ticipate in, because it's disruptive to Americans if we knock their doctor out of business," he said.

And so the Obama transition team's logic went as follows: we need health-care reform to insure all Americans and to bend the cost curve; healthcare reform requires a digital infrastructure that does not currently exist; and the stimulus package is our once-in-a-lifetime chance to fund such an infra-structure. So they dove into the money pile and emerged with about $30 bil-lion—nearly 5 percent of the entire package—for a program called HITECH (short for Health Information Technology for Economic and Clinical Health).[2] "What was good was that these IT products were in existence, and so they could be bought within a year, and the goal of the stimulus was to stimulate the economy within a year," said Kocher. "And so it easily qualified as a shovel-ready project, even though it didn't need a shovel."

▶    ▶    ▶

And so it came to pass that, in the space of five years, an initiative born of a president's envy, nearly snuffed out in its infancy, and whose initial bud-get was $42 million now enjoyed a $30 billion war chest. While obtaining the

---

[2] Zeke Emanuel recalled approaching Sen. Max Baucus (D-Mont.), chairman of the Senate Finance Committee, at the same November 2008 *Wall Street Journal*-sponsored meeting at which his brother made his famous "crisis go to waste" comment. "I raised the idea of funding healthcare computeriza-tion with the stimulus money," Emanuel told me. "From the look on his face, it was clear that he'd never considered this before." Baucus's support would ultimately prove crucial to the passage of the HITECH bill.

cash represented the heaviest lifting, the ONC, the Obama administration, and Congress still had decisions to make about how to distribute the HITECH money.

By 2009, it was clear that the United Kingdom's Connecting for Health program—the one that had so enchanted President Bush when he heard about it from Tony Blair—had failed (the program would ultimately be deemed "a fiasco" and the bulk of the $16 billion investment written off). The rap was that it had been run like a military procurement program, by a leader, Richard Granger, whose confrontational "Just Do It" attitude placed him at loggerheads with British physicians and nearly everyone else.

Robert Wah, Brailer's first lieutenant at the ONC and now president of the American Medical Association, recalled Granger ridiculing the American effort during visits to Washington. "He'd come into the ONC office and say, 'I have billions, you have millions, ha, ha, ha.'" Brailer added, "Granger saw himself as being in the mold of the great shapers of British society. But it's just not the world for grand architects when you're dealing with providers who are trying to take care of sick people. It's a place for subtle, nuanced communication, expectation setting, and opportunistic advances."

Brailer is right. One of the great challenges in healthcare technology is that medicine is at once an enormous business and an exquisitely human endeavor; it requires the ruthless efficiency of the modern manufacturing plant and the gentle hand-holding of the parish priest; it is about science, but also about art; it is eminently quantifiable and yet stubbornly not. These themes will recur throughout this book, as they form the subtext of grand policy debates in the halls of Congress and clinical decisions made thousands of times each day at the bedsides of sick, anxious patients.

▶    ▶    ▶

In distributing the HITECH payments, which averaged about $44,000 per doctor and several million dollars to a midsized hospital, Kocher and his colleagues were aware of the risk of a top-down approach like the one that failed in the United Kingdom. But they couldn't endorse a no-strings-attached federal giveaway to hospitals and physicians. Kocher recalled the experience a decade earlier when WellPoint, a major insurer, had offered free computers to California doctors, hoping that they would use them to do their billing and documentation for WellPoint-insured patients. "The doctors didn't use them, and that lesson stuck with me—that free isn't cheap enough," Kocher said. "We needed to make sure that people were really using the systems."

When Congress approved the money for HITECH, it mandated an accompanying program known as Meaningful Use, a series of standards that hospitals and doctors—and their information systems—had to meet if they were to be eligible for the incentive payments. I'll have more to say about Meaningful Use later; for now, it's worth appreciating the controversy that this program has engendered. Some people see Meaningful Use as an appropriate government effort to push both vendors and users to adopt many key IT features, such as electronic prescribing and patient-focused communication tools. Others see it as the healthcare IT world's bête noire, Exhibit A in the case against aggressive government involvement in the technology field.

▶    ▶    ▶

In terms of its main goal, to rapidly transform healthcare into a digital industry, HITECH worked—adoption rates soared from the low teens in 2008 to about 70 percent in hospitals and doctors' offices by 2014. But Brailer, who fretted from the start about too expansive a government role, sees the events of the past few years as confirming his deepest fears about federal overreaching. Today he runs a large healthcare investment fund in San Francisco (this seems to be where federal policy makers with a technology bent end up, since Kocher now has a similar job in Palo Alto), which gives him a bird's-eye view of the health IT innovation ecosystem. He worries that HITECH locked in an existing set of clunky products and led the computer vendors to focus on meeting federal requirements rather than innovating.

I asked Brailer an unfair question: Given his well-known skepticism about too muscular a federal role, if he had still been ONC director in 2008, would he have turned down the $30 billion? No, he said with a chuckle, but he would have spent the money on standards, interoperability, a "Geek Squad" to help with training and implementation, and creating a cloud-based "medical Internet." "I never would have spent money on direct subsidies to providers," he added. Without them—and their obligatory accessory, the Meaningful Use regulations—"we would have a much more innovative IT sector because it would not be waiting on what the next rule is. . . . It would be people competing on their systems' new features and functions."

Brailer also believes that, once the payment model shifted toward value, the technology adoption rate would have come along just fine. And then, he said, "90 percent of the work that the ONC does would just melt away. In what other industry do we worry about how organizations put in their automation tools? Only in healthcare."

"We've built the Frankenstein I was most afraid of," he said, the sadness in his voice closely matching the tone I had heard from Matt Burton at the Mayo Clinic.

▶    ▶    ▶

Despite the disappointment of both Brailer and Burton, the history of technology offers room for hope. After all, Version 1.0 of any new technology is always far from perfect. Just think back to your first brick-sized cellphone, or your car's first GPS system, which sometimes commanded you to exit left off the Interstate via a nonexistent ramp. But the degree of disenchantment among clinicians—the "end users," in computer lingo—with today's electronic health records feels different. Some people believe that the answer is simply patience—that these things always get better with the passage of time.

But, as Paul Batalden, a prominent expert in quality improvement, famously said, "Every system is perfectly designed to get the results it gets." And this may well be a case in which we have to change the system—the system of recording patient information, of ordering tests and medications, of engaging patients in their own care, of educating doctors and nurses, of managing our technology within hospitals and clinics, of designing and building computers for healthcare, of paying for and regulating medical IT, and of instilling in humans the right amount of trust in, and skepticism of, technology—if we want better results. It all begins with a deeper understanding of where we are and how we got here.

# Part One

# The Note

# Chapter 3

# The iPatient

Some patients . . . recover their health simply through their
contentment with the goodness of the physician.

—Hippocrates, *Precepts*

You've probably played that parlor game in which you fantasize about what it
would be like to have a drink with one of the great figures in history. Perhaps
you'd choose Shakespeare, or Churchill, or Einstein. They all sound great to
me. But as a doctor and a student of health policy, I would sooner choose
Ignaz Semmelweis, the nineteenth-century Hungarian physician whose pioneering work on antisepsis led him to be committed to an asylum for heresy;
Sir William Osler, who articulated many of the key principles of medical diagnosis and treatment; or Avedis Donabedian, whose insights transformed our
understanding of healthcare quality.

Or a man named Arnold "Bud" Relman.

Relman, who died in 2014 at the age of 91, spent his early career at Boston
University, where he conducted pioneering research into the causes and
treatment of kidney disease. In 1968, he was recruited by the University of
Pennsylvania to become chairman of its department of medicine. A decade
later, he returned to Boston to become the editor of the *New England Journal
of Medicine*, the world's preeminent medical journal. He held this post for 14
years.

Relman was editor during a period of breathtaking scientific advances. Under his stewardship, the *NEJM* published the first reports of the disease that would later be called AIDS. A few years later, it published the first description of the discovery of HIV and, still later, the clinical trials that demonstrated the effectiveness of AZT in treating HIV infection. Relman's *NEJM* published seminal papers on new ways to treat and prevent coronary artery disease, research that led to halving the American death toll from heart attacks between 1980 and 2005. It also published major papers that proved the effectiveness of lumpectomy for breast cancer and the vaccine to prevent hepatitis B.

While this is extraordinary stuff, I'd want to chat with Relman mostly about his other passion: health policy. In a 2012 video commemorating the publication's two hundredth anniversary, he described why he loved being the *NEJM*'s editor. After a successful career as an academic physician and administrator, he said, "When I became editor it was as if I ascended in a balloon above a battlefield and, for the first time, I could see all the forces that were at work in the profession and outside the profession, see the scene as a whole."

And he used that perch to great advantage. "Early in my time at the *Journal*," he recalled, "I became aware of a change in the healthcare system, from a social service to an industry. Investors were entering the field of healthcare, hospitals were becoming businesses, all sorts of medical services were being commercialized. . . . The earning of money . . . was beginning to influence the practice of medicine." In addition to taking on what he called the "Medical-Industrial Complex," he tackled thorny issues concerning conflicts of interest, end-of-life care, and the snowballing costs of healthcare. Many of the national conversations that Relman started continue today.

I'd like to think that if Bud Relman had been *my* patient, I'd have gone out of my way to find the time to pull up a chair and pick his brain for insights about the state of medicine today and its evolution over the last century. At least, I hope so.

But when Relman was hospitalized in 2013 after falling down the stairs in his house and breaking his neck in several places, that wasn't what happened. After receiving months of treatment at Massachusetts General Hospital and the Harvard-affiliated Spaulding Rehabilitation Hospital, Relman complained bitterly that he had fought a losing battle with the electronic health record for the attention of his doctors and nurses. In a 2014 essay in *The New York Review of Books*, he wrote that at Spaulding, his care was overseen by an attending physician and his associate. "But neither physician seemed to be actually in charge of my care, or spent much time at my bedside beyond what was required for a cursory physical exam," Relman wrote.

Both physicians did, however, leave lengthy notes in Relman's computer record, "full of repetitive boilerplate language and lab data, but lacking in coherent descriptions of my medical progress, or my complaints and state of mind," Relman wrote. "Reading the physicians' notes . . . I found only a few brief descriptions of how I felt or looked, but there were copious reports of the data from tests and monitoring devices." Actual conversations with his physicians were "infrequent, brief, and hardly ever reported."

▶   ▶   ▶

I hear complaints like this so often from patients that it now seems noteworthy when someone feels that her physician *has* truly focused on her as a person. A colleague of mine, a successful physician-entrepreneur in his late sixties, recently told me about a visit to his primary care doctor after a long hiatus. "I had seen him a few years earlier, and I liked him," he said. "But this visit was entirely different. This time, he asks me a question, and as soon as I begin to answer, his head is down in his laptop. Tap-tap-tap-tap-tap. He looks up at me to ask another question. As soon as I speak, again it's tap-tap-tap-tap."

"What did you do?" I asked.

"I found another doctor."

The human craving for eye contact turns out to be hardwired in our consciousness. In a 2014 study, Cornell researchers found that adults were more likely to favor Trix cereal when its rabbit mascot on the box appeared to be looking at them, rather than looking away. Several studies have confirmed that eye contact is associated with higher levels of perceived empathy and connection. Northwestern University researchers videotaped 100 patient visits to primary care doctors and found that the doctors spent one-third of their time looking at their computer screens. When the doctor looked at the screen, the patient tended to look there as well. But when physicians looked patients in the eye, patients looked right back at them. "Eye contact is a really good surrogate for where attention is and the level of accord building in a relationship," said Enid Montague, one of the study's authors.

▶   ▶   ▶

In 2010, a seven-year-old girl, accompanied by her mother and her sister, went to see a pediatrician for a routine exam. The child later sent the doctor a crayon drawing depicting her visit. Many pediatricians have a corkboard in their office on which they post just such enchanting pictures. But I'm guessing that this one didn't make it onto the doctor's Wall of Fame.

How times have changed. In his famous 1891 painting *The Doctor*, Luke Fildes set out "to put on record the status of the doctor in our time." This evocative painting (shown on the next page) was inspired by the death of Fildes's own son 14 years earlier from tuberculosis. Sadly, Fildes's doctor could do little to save the boy from the ravages of the tubercle bacillus (effective treatment for the infection would not become available for another 75 years). Yet there is little doubt that the child in the painting, as well as his parents by the window, knew that the physician's sole focus was on his patient.

In contrast, how can the seven-year-old girl—and her mother—not conclude that this doctor cares more about the demands of his computer than about the child's health? If *The Doctor* captured the essence of being a physician in the twilight of the nineteenth century, is this crude and charming child's drawing destined to be an equally iconic representation of the doctor's world in the early years of the twenty-first?

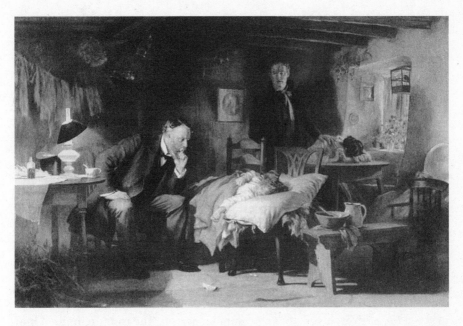

▶   ▶   ▶

Over the past decade, Abraham Verghese, an infectious disease specialist and bestselling author, has become increasingly concerned about how technology is cleaving the sacred bond between doctor and patient. "I joke, but I only half joke, that if you came to one of our hospitals missing a limb, nobody would believe you until they got a CAT scan, an MRI, and an orthopedic consult," the soft-spoken Verghese likes to say. In a 2011 TED talk, Verghese lamented that when we stop talking to and examining patients, dangerous things start to happen, including overlooking simple diagnoses that can be treated when they're caught early.

But we lose more than that. "We're losing a ritual that I believe is transformative, transcendent, and at the heart of the patient-physician relationship," said Verghese. "The ritual of one individual coming to another and telling him things that she would not tell her preacher or rabbi; and then, incredibly, on top of that, disrobing and allowing touch." The ritual, he concluded, also signals to the patient that "I will always be there; I will see you through this."

As computers muscled their way into the exam room in the early years of the twenty-first century, Verghese noticed that his trainees and colleagues gradually adopted a fundamentally new approach to the practice of medicine. In an influential 2008 article, he described what he called the "iPatient," an entity clothed in "binary garments." "Often, emergency room personnel have already scanned, tested, and diagnosed," Verghese wrote, "so that interns meet a fully formed iPatient long before seeing the real patient." While the real patient keeps the bed warm and ensures that his folder remains alive on the computer, "the iPatient's blood counts and emanations are tracked and trended like a Dow Jones Index, and pop-up flags remind caregivers to feed or bleed."

"The iPatient is getting wonderful care all across America," Verghese said in his TED talk, "but the real patient often wonders, *Where is everyone? When are they going to come by to explain things to me? Who is in charge?*"

▶    ▶    ▶

Sitting in Verghese's sun-drenched office on Stanford's idyllic Palo Alto campus, I asked what prompted him to write about the iPatient. He recalled arriving at Stanford in 2007 from his previous job in Texas and walking to the patient care floor, expecting to see the residents in the internal medicine training program he had been hired to direct. But, to his surprise, they weren't there. He discovered them cloistered in a windowless room, sitting shoulder to shoulder, each facing a glowing computer screen. The room reminded him of a vault. "It could have been in Alaska," he said. "I sensed some reluctance on the part of the residents to go out and see the patients. And I had a similar reluctance about being in that room. It just seemed so foreign."

I wondered if he blamed his residents for choosing to isolate themselves this way. His answer was characteristically charitable. To him, the residents, like the patients, were victims of the system. "This is no fault of theirs," he said. "It's that all the work, the work that's being assigned to them and the work that they now have to contract to others, consultants and the like—all of that work has to happen at the computer. It's not that they're choosing to sit there. They're forced to sit there. How else do they find out about their patients?"

How else indeed? What Verghese realized was that in the space of a few years, and without much discussion or forethought, the practice of medicine had been utterly transformed—from work whose backbone was the exchange of information occurring through personal, physical interactions with patients and colleagues, to work chiefly mediated by information technology. In a 2013 study, researchers at Johns Hopkins found that medical interns spent just 12 percent of their time talking to their patients, versus more than 40 percent of their time on the computers.

To understand this transformation and its impact, one must appreciate the long and colorful history—and the ultimate tyranny—of the doctor's note, and the medical record in which it lives.

# Chapter 4

## The Note

To advance professional improvement, a friendly and
unreserved intercourse should subsist between the gentlemen
of the faculty, with a free communication of whatever is
extraordinary or interesting in the course of their hospital
practice. And an account of every case or operation, which
is rare, curious, or instructive, should be drawn up by the
physician or surgeon.
> —Thomas Percival, nineteenth-century English physician
> and the father of modern medical ethics, 1803

If our computers could speak (yes, I know they can, sort of), they might be putting up a fuss about the previous chapter, particularly its implication that, by consuming every bit of the physician's attention, they bear sole responsibility for upending the doctor-patient relationship. After all, they'd say, isn't it true that other forces have been undermining this relationship for several generations? And that physicians have been complaining about the ceaseless need to feed the medical record for more than a century?

They'd be right. The physician-patient relationship has long been under siege from forces as diverse as the declining obeisance to experts (a phenomenon that can be traced more to Vietnam, Ralph Nader, and Google than to anything in healthcare), the influence of third-party payers, and malpractice lawsuits. In fact, two books chronicling the withering of the relationship—Edward Shorter's *Doctors and Their Patients: A Social History* and David Rothman's *Strangers at the Bedside*—were both published in 1991, when Sergey and Larry were freshmen in college and electronic health records were futuristic fantasies.

Clashes over the doctor's note have an even longer lineage. In fact, this deceptively simple and boring document has for generations served as an unlikely battlefield for issues as profound as power dynamics between physicians and nurses, the rights of patients, the ability of outsiders to monitor and influence clinical practice, even whether medicine is an art or a science.

While these are issues with very long bloodlines, there is no question but that the computer has upped the ante and focused the threat. To fully appreciate this, we need to reflect on the history of how doctors have related to patients through the ages, and how they have recorded their observations and organized their work.

▶    ▶    ▶

As with many things doctorly, the medical record dates back to the fifth century BCE in Greece. As described by medical historian Stanley Reiser, notes taken at the time of Hippocrates were stories, designed to chronicle the clinical course of a patient's illness through a crystalline portrait of his symptoms. For example, the case of a gentleman named Apollonius of Abdera is described this way:

> *There were exacerbations of the fever; the bowels passed*
> *practically nothing of the food taken; the urine was thin and*
> *scanty. No sleep. . . . About the fourteenth day from his taking*
> *to bed, after a rigor, he grew hot; wildly delirious, shouting,*
> *distress, much rambling, followed by calm; the coma came on*
> *at this time.*

The cases often ended with a starkly worded coda. In the case of Apollonius, it read: "Thirty-fourth day. Death."

To a modern physician, such notes—recorded in diary form and organized chronologically around the doctor's day rather than the clinical course of individual patients—are most remarkable for their absence of clutter. There are no physical examination findings, no laboratory or x-ray results. The physician makes no effort to proffer a diagnosis or explain the underlying science, and offers few ideas about therapies or hints at prognosis.

Doctors' notes did not undergo a fundamental change until the seventeenth century. Drawing on emerging classification schemes in botany and animal biology, physician Thomas Sydenham, often called the English Hippocrates, recognized that illnesses have certain reproducible patterns whose documentation would improve scientific understanding and might even point the way toward effective therapies. A patient with pleurisy, for example, is described as having "a violent pain and stitch shooting in one of his sides. . . . He is often provoked to cough which proves very painful to him." The system of identifying diseases by connecting them to clusters of symptoms remains the underpinning of diagnostic reasoning to this day.

But Sydenham and his contemporaries were limited in their ability to understand the cause of diseases such as pleurisy, or the underlying pathologic abnormalities that might explain swollen bellies, spiking fevers, or hacking coughs. That changed in 1761, when the technique of "clinicopathologic correlation"—linking patients' symptoms during life with their associated pathologies discovered at autopsy—was described by the great Italian anatomist Giovanni Morgagni. Morgagni's work shifted medical thinking from its medieval-sounding focus on imbalances in the four main "humors" (blood, phlegm, black bile, and yellow bile) toward its modern anatomic perspective: one that thought of each disease as having a "seat" in a certain part of the body, such as the bowel or the heart. This discovery would, about a century later, set the stage for the emergence of specialists, like gastroenterologists and cardiologists, who became experts in these body parts and their patterns of dysfunction. It also marked the start of the fragmentation of medicine from a generalist field to one dominated by specialists, raising a new need: how to coordinate the work of different clinicians, each focused on a particular body part or, later, on clusters of diseases like cancer or infections.

Of course, depending on an autopsy to figure out a patient's affliction is an unsatisfying, and not terribly productive, way of practicing medicine—like a chef waiting until her restaurant has failed to determine what was wrong with the food. Clinicians began to use their senses—touch, hearing, sight, even smell—to ferret out the causes of their patients' illnesses. They soon began recognizing patterns of findings that correlated with certain diseases: the panting and fruity-smelling breath of diabetic ketoacidosis; the exquisite "point tenderness" in the right lower abdomen in appendicitis; the dull thud when they tapped on the chest of a patient whose lungs were compressed by a lake of pleural fluid.

But this wasn't enough. Appreciating the limitations of patient stories and simple observation in unearthing the body's deep secrets, nineteenth-century physicians struggled to find ways to get under the hood—while the patient still lived. Some began to listen to heart and lung sounds by placing their ear on the patient's chest, but a French physician named René Laennec found this technique crude and more than a little awkward, particularly when examining a female patient. In 1816, the 35-year-old Laennec tightly rolled up a sheaf of paper and listened to a young woman's chest through it, thus creating a crude version of what would later become the stethoscope. Foreshadowing the reaction of many to today's new medical technologies, this diagnostic advance was not well received. In 1834, speaking of the stethoscope, the *Times of London* wrote,

> *That it will ever come into general use, notwithstanding its value, is extremely doubtful; because its beneficial application requires much time and gives a good bit of trouble both to the patient and the practitioner; because its hue and character are foreign and opposed to all our habits and associations.*

Some of this pushback, of course, is good old-fashioned resistance to change—a fundamental human characteristic that is hardly limited to doctors. But the early objections from within medicine also reflected physicians' views of themselves, particularly their desire to be seen as real professionals, to distance themselves from the barber-surgeons whose haphazard—and often dangerous—practices had sullied their field in days past. (Modern-day barbers' poles are said to be red-and-white-striped to recall the blood and bandages of medieval barber-surgeons.)

The findings from auscultation (the act of listening to the heart through the stethoscope) would eventually be accompanied by those drawn from other technologies: the otoscope (ears) and the ophthalmoscope (eyes) and, early in the next century, x-rays and blood tests. Each of these technologies produced new information ("the cardiac exam has no murmurs or extra heart sounds"; "the serum potassium is 3.4 mEq/L") that needed to be recorded and analyzed.

And so the physician's note, which had once been a chronological diary of patients' symptoms—the doctor's journal, in essence—morphed into a vessel brimming with observations. These observations were drawn from a multitude of sources: first from the patient's history; then from simple tools applied by the doctor, like the stethoscope; and later from increasingly sophisticated tools, like radiology and blood tests, performed by others when "ordered" to do so by the physician.

To Reiser, the discovery of the stethoscope had even broader implications. The rise of the stethoscope, and the triumph of auscultation that resulted, also marked the beginning of what the historian called "modern therapeutic distancing," as doctors' attention shifted from the words spoken by patients to the sounds produced by their organs. And thus began the transformation of the doctor-patient relationship.

Looking back, we can now see that the stethoscope was small potatoes: it separated Laennec from his patient by a mere 18 inches. Today's clinician can diagnose and treat patients based on reams of data collected through cameras and sensors. And while the people (and not all of them are doctors) analyzing these data may be in the next room, the advent of high-speed networks and wireless connectivity means that they may be across the street, or even across an ocean.

▶    ▶    ▶

As the number of available tools and the amount of salient information about patients mushroomed, physicians entered a world in which making a diagnosis or choosing a therapy could be based on science rather than intuition, plausibility, or tradition. For example, the technique of bloodletting had been accepted as effective for hundreds of years until, in 1835, the French physician Pierre Louis analyzed whether the procedure had any impact on patients' outcomes. His findings, using what he referred to as the "numerical method" (today we would call this a clinical trial, and the use of its results, evidence-based medicine), stood medicine on its head: bloodletting was absolutely worthless. Louis recognized the importance not only of his findings, but of his method as well. Bemoaning the slow pace at which medical research was progressing, he urged his fellow doctors to observe facts, then analyze them vigorously. "It is impossible to attain [medical progress] without classifying and counting [such facts]," he wrote, "and then therapeutics will advance not less steadily than other branches of science."

With that, the medical record, already straining under the weight of more and more data, was drafted for yet another mission: to provide the raw materials for clinical research. As this research began to identify effective treatments for certain well-defined diseases, the record also needed to take in physicians' assessments of their cases—a place where they could weave together the facts about their patients into a coherent hypothesis, accompanied by treatment plans.

Yet even as the medical record was being force-fed like a French goose, it was something else that turned it into a beast that could not be tamed—with either pen or keyboard: the push by outsiders to see, read, and analyze the note, each for his own purposes. This was what ultimately broke the backs of clinicians and set the stage for our current uneasy relationship with our electronic health records.

# Chapter 5

# Strangers at the Bedside

At first sight, the medical record seems a mere re-enactment
of time: tables listing past measurements; pages and
pages of notes of meetings and examinations. . . . Yet it
is a mistake . . . to conceptualize the record as a more or
less adequate representation of events. By being part and
parcel of the activity of transforming a patient's problem
into a manageable problem, by functioning as a structured
distributor and collector of work activities, the record is actively
involved in shaping the very events it "represents."
　　　—Marc Berg, Dutch physician and medical sociologist, 1996

The dawn of the twentieth century found the medical profession in a terrible
state. Medical education was a hodgepodge, most therapies had no scientific
basis or supporting evidence (notwithstanding Pierre Louis's insights), and
hucksters and charlatans were rampant. But, as often happens, out of this
chaos emerged great progress. William Osler, the preeminent academic physician of his day, pioneered the practice of bedside teaching and a new approach
to blending science with humanism. The 1910 Flexner Report, which called
for wholesale reform of medical training around scientific principles, led to
the closing of many shoddy for-profit medical schools, a shift in the locus of
training from these schools (which offered little clinical exposure) to teaching

hospitals, and aggressive licensing requirements for physicians. At the same time that institutions and principles were being fortified, so too was medical science, with the discovery of insulin for diabetes, ABO typing for blood transfusions, and modern anesthetic techniques.

The worlds of physicians and hospitals were revolutionized during this period, and the medical record both recorded and shaped the events. Inspired by innovations in business and industry, in 1907 the Mayo Clinic's Henry Plummer introduced the modern method of classifying patients with a single number and recording all of their clinical data in a single record. (Before Plummer, the "doctor's journal" style of medical records made it virtually impossible to follow the course of an individual patient over time.) In 1918, the newly formed American College of Surgeons launched a "hospital standardization" program that required hospitals to keep comprehensive records on every patient, including all treatments and outcomes. These records were subject to periodic audits, and surgeons wishing to join the College needed to submit detailed notes on 100 patients, an early step toward what would later become board certification. The radical idea was that such records could be used to measure quality and improve it.

One Boston surgeon, Ernest Codman, promoted an even more revolutionary tack. Codman was an active bird hunter who had learned to gauge his own skill by measuring his ratio of kills to spent shells. With this in mind, in 1910 he began advocating for a so-called End Results Hospital, in which patient outcomes would be carefully tracked and reported. Codman believed that this would allow patients to make informed choices about where to receive surgical care, and would stimulate hospitals and doctors to improve the care they delivered.

Fifty-seven years after Codman's death, The Joint Commission—the major accreditor of U.S. hospitals today—named its top quality award after him. In Codman's day, though, his ideas infuriated the members of Boston's medical establishment, who felt that the quality of *their* care was self-evident. And this was not a mere gentlemanly professional dispute. Not only was he drummed off the staff of Massachusetts General Hospital, but in 1914, one surgical colleague, Dr. Edward Martin, wrote a letter to Codman, saying, "The very enemies who lurk in second story windows with muffled rifles are waiting your passing."

While the idea of using the medical record to measure the quality of care was important (and, as Codman learned painfully, threatening to many doctors), for generations there was very little skin in that particular game. Nearly a century would pass before Codman's dream of public reporting of outcomes by both physicians and hospitals became a reality, and payment for both groups came to turn on these measurements.

▶   ▶   ▶

As important as quality measurers like Codman and the College of Surgeons were, two other players had even more decisive roles in reshaping the medical record.

The first was malpractice attorneys. The earliest malpractice cases in the United States were filed in the first quarter of the nineteenth century. There was soon an explosion of such cases, driven by the emergence of a phenomenon known as marketplace professionalism—a peculiarly American notion that professions, while partly capable of self-policing (through peer review, board certification, and the like), ultimately need to be held accountable by the legal system, just like other businesses. While this seems hard to imagine today, many established doctors welcomed malpractice suits in the belief that they would selectively target the countless charlatans in practice at the time. "Even the most egregious Quacks escape punishment as things now stand," wrote one Yale physician in 1827.

The medical record, of course, became the central icon in the business of malpractice. From the time of Pierre Louis's bloodletting studies, data drawn from such records determined the "standard of care" by which malpractice cases were judged. Moreover, since malpractice verdicts turned on evidence that the physician's care deviated from established practice, doctors needed to be sure that, if things went sideways clinically, their notes justified their actions. This is not idle paranoia: in my experience as an expert witness in a few dozen malpractice cases, I've seen several verdicts pivot on a handful of words in the chart. In one, a neurologist was drawn into a case in which a patient died from another physician's pain prescription overdose. The neurologist wrote, in a throwaway line that had nothing to do with his overall assessment, "agree with pain management, as written." By documenting his endorsement of the fatal prescription, the words "as written" cost him tens of thousands of dollars in the final settlement.

▶   ▶   ▶

As much as the need to document (and often practice) defensively drove a change in the medical note, the impact of the malpractice system paled next to that of third-party payers.

The country doctor of the nineteenth century enjoyed a dyadic relationship with his patient. He was generally a small businessman in a solo practice, paid by the patient (in money or, in some rural communities, in crops, livestock, or in-kind labor). It was a one-on-one relationship based entirely on trust. The emergence of third-party payment, especially by the federal government after the 1965 passage of the legislation that created Medicare, changed everything.

Today, when I take care of a patient in the hospital, my fees are governed by a strict set of guidelines that range from arcane to ridiculous (the same would be true for office visits). After I see a patient, the patient's insurer (Medicare, Aetna, or any of a dozen others, each with slightly different but equally annoying rules) decides how much to pay the hospital, and me, based entirely on my note. It might pay $100 for a "high-level" visit to a hospitalized patient, $70 for a "medium," and $45 for a "low." Since a busy doctor might have 2,500 visits in a year, we're talking about real money.

While the idea of reimbursement based on patient complexity is reasonable, in practice it creates a number of troubling side effects that play out in the chart. Because the level is based partly on "medical complexity" (basically, the patient's degree of illness and the difficulty of the decision making), there is a powerful incentive to enumerate all the clinical problems in the note, even those that are tangential to the matter at hand. The incentives also drive doctors to use certain buzzwords that are associated with higher billing rates. For example, Medicare might pay a hospital about $5,000 for a stay with a primary diagnosis of "pneumonia," but closer to $10,000 for "pneumonia with major complications." This is what makes the effort to find and record such complications economically meaningful.

There's more to the game. The payments also factor in the completeness of the patient's social history (occupation; cigarette use and alcohol consumption), the number of items in the "review of systems" ("no fever, shortness of breath, chest pain, sweating, abdominal pain, or diarrhea" counts as six; the magic number is generally ten for a high-level visit), and the number of body parts examined. ("Lungs are clear without crackles or wheezes; heart has a regular rhythm and rate without murmurs, rubs, or gallops" counts as two. Here, the goal is nine, but extremities count as only one—no extra credit for listing the arms and legs separately.) This would be fine if all this mumbo-jumbo made a difference in the care of the patient, but it rarely does.

It certainly does, however, make a difference in the way we write our notes, and I have a natural experiment to prove it. In contrast to the way internists like me are paid, surgeons are generally paid a "global rate," meaning a fixed sum for a given type of surgery, like a cardiac bypass or a hip replacement. While surgeons' notes must prove that they visited the patient on the days after an operation, the actual content of the note doesn't influence their payment. It shouldn't surprise you, then, that notes written by internists read like novellas (ones in which we're paid by the word), while a colleague of mine jokes that a typical post-op surgical note reads something like "Feeling well and doing swell."

▶    ▶    ▶

A few years ago, a geriatrician named Eugenia Siegler reviewed nearly two centuries' worth of medical notes at New York Hospital, the Cornell-affiliated teaching hospital on Manhattan's Upper East Side. In a 2010 article, Siegler vividly illustrated how the explosion in data and the billing pressures have transmuted the note from patient story into bureaucratic monstrosity. Her article began by asking a question: Which of these two notes, both involving patients suffering from paralysis, do you prefer? Choice 1 is this:

> *The first symptoms always affect the extremities of the limbs and the lower limbs particularly. When the whole body becomes affected, the order of progression is more or less constant: (1) toe and foot muscles, then the hamstrings and glutei, and finally the anterior and adductor muscles of the thigh; (2) finger and hand, arm, and then shoulder muscles; (3) trunk muscles; (4) respiratory muscles, tongue, pharynx, oesophagus, etc. The paralysis then becomes generalised but more severe in the distal parts of the extremities. The progression can be more or less rapid. It was eight days in one and fifteen days in another case which I believe can be classified as acute. More often it is scarcely two or three days and sometimes only a few hours.*

The second choice is this:

> *vs stbl, ō comp.; no Δ resp. 02 sats ok; xam un-Δ'd—see note 11/12; fam. visit.; no nursing issues; labs = no incr. aldolase,*

*CK's; note: this enctr. took 65' & inv. a hi deg. of complex. in
dec. making.*[3]

The first note was clearly written by one human about another, but the second seems as if it were written by an automaton to please a robotic actuary. In today's world, not only is all this documentation factored into payments for the doctor and the hospital, but increasingly, quality measures—which are now beginning to influence payments and rankings on "Top 100" lists—are also swayed by the words used in an electronic health record.[4]

Certain measures, such as whether the physician documented that she counseled the patient to stop smoking, are drawn directly from the medical record. The role of the note in measures like mortality or hospital readmission rates (in other words, how patients fared ["outcome measures"] rather than what we did ["process measures"]) is subtler and involves a bit of math. But it is equally important in influencing our documentation.

For outcome measures, a technique called case-mix adjustment is used to account for how sick the patient is. Think of it as being like the degree of difficulty of an Olympic dive. Without such adjustments, hospitals or doctors caring for sicker patients would always look worse, even if they provided superb care. Based on a patient's level of illness (divined from the record), a computerized algorithm determines the patient's "expected" chances of a bad outcome, such as a postoperative infection or death. An "observed-to-expected" ratio of 1.0 means that the outcome—let's say the mortality rate—was precisely what was estimated, a ratio of 2.0 means that twice as many patients died as expected, and a ratio of 0.5 means that half as many died. This is a scientifically reasonable way of handling the thorny problem of risk adjustment, but it does create an awkward incentive to make patients appear as sick as possible in the record.

The bottom line is that in today's world, a note that documents a high degree of complexity creates all sorts of business advantages for hospitals and doctors—through its effect on billing level, the "degree of difficulty" of the case, and eligibility for "top doctors" and "top hospitals" lists. We'll return to all of this later, when we consider how computerization, which many people

---

[3] The first note is from the mid-nineteenth century, and the second from modern times. The latter roughly translates into: "Vital signs stable, no complications overnight; no change in respirations—oxygen saturation is normal; exam is unchanged, see my prior note of November 12; family visit occurred; no nursing issues; laboratory studies show no increase in aldolase or CK [enzymes released when muscles are damaged]. Note that this encounter took 65 minutes and involved a high degree of complexity in decision making."

[4] It has been estimated that there are more than 1,000 U.S. hospitals that are on one "Top 100" list or another, and virtually all of them use these designations in their marketing.

had hoped would be a life preserver for the physician drowning in paperwork, has become an anchor.

▶   ▶   ▶

By the time the 1980s rolled around, observers had come to recognize that the medical record had turned into a Christmas tree that was sagging under the weight of its many ornaments: a narrative account of the patient's symptoms; physical examination findings; laboratory and radiology test results; notes (including assessments and plans) from physicians, nurses, nutritionists, and physical therapists; doctors' orders for tests and therapies; responses to treatments; and more. And the number of outside parties with a keen interest in the content of the record had also become enormous, now including government agencies, insurers, researchers, and quality measurers.

Note that this is as much a problem of perspective as it is of bulk: a doctor's note written with an eye toward winning a future malpractice case or generating the highest payment or complexity rating will inevitably slant the facts in certain directions, even if it remains in fair territory on the playing field of truthfulness. Such a note will be vastly different from one whose goal is to remind oneself of a patient's medical problems from one visit to the next or to communicate with colleagues about a patient's clinical issues. And a record that will be seen by the patient herself will also be painted with very different brushstrokes from one that is destined to be viewed only by insiders (we'll return to this issue later, when we discuss the movement to offer patients such access). Medical historian Stanley Reiser captured the impossibility of all of this when he called the medical record a "contradictory hybrid: a confidential and public document."

▶   ▶   ▶

Nineteenth-century notes were completely lacking in structure; they consisted almost entirely of narrative description. But around 1900, with the growth in the volume of information that needed to be recorded and the burgeoning scrutiny by outsiders, hospitals began insisting on the use of standardized forms, with special tables for recording physical examination findings, laboratory studies, nurses' notes, the quality of patients' sleep, even the result of enemas. In 1911, Siegler found in her research, New York Hospital specified the type of ink to be used in writing the note.

Accustomed to unfettered autonomy, physicians pushed back against these constraints, staging little rebellions by writing notes across the columns, sometimes spilling onto the backs of pages, and even doodling. Of course, physicians' responses to standardization were predictable, as was the pushback from other parties whose work was stymied by the doctors' random, sometimes illegible, jottings. In 1921, Johns Hopkins statistician Raymond Pearl noted the challenges in trying to apply to physicians the kinds of methods that worked perfectly well in other areas of science and business. Such attempts, he wrote, "will at once be scornfully or even derisively received by some," who will argue that they will inhibit their individuality. Pearl agreed that they would. "It will inordinately cramp such portions of their individuality as finds its expression in carelessness, inaccuracy, forgetfulness, and inattentive observation."

▶    ▶    ▶

Of course, physicians' concerns about standardization were not simply about the freedom to write in blue ink. With the growth of the science and complexity of medicine and the increasing interest of outsiders in their work, physicians sensed that their beloved profession—particularly the sanctity of their relationships with patients—was beginning to slip away.

Some have argued that medicine experienced a golden age in the first few decades of the twentieth century, a narrow window during which physicians, for the first time, had a few effective therapies to offer their patients, while still enjoying a doctor-patient relationship that was blissfully unencumbered. Physicians, already masters at questioning patients and performing the physical examination, now enjoyed access to new technologies such as the stethoscope, the reflex hammer, and rudimentary x-ray and laboratory studies. Yet technology had not yet consumed medical practice, the pace was leisurely, payment was straightforward, and the patient remained the central focus of the physician's attention. The spirit of the day was captured in a famous 1925 lecture given by Professor Francis Peabody to the Harvard medical student body:

> *The good physician knows his patients through and through, and his knowledge is bought dearly. Time, sympathy, and understanding must be lavishly dispensed, but the reward is to be found in that personal bond which forms the greatest satisfaction of the practice of medicine. One of the essential qualities of the clinician is interest in humanity, for the secret of the care of the patient is in caring for the patient.*

Over the next 40 years, the discoveries and development of antibiotics, chemotherapy, ICUs, heart surgery, and CT scans made an immense difference in the lives of both doctors and patients. Yet these miracles also planted more seedlings of discontent, as tests and therapies grew ever more complicated and various medical specialties emerged to manage the complexity. The growth of specialization meant that the lifelong relationship between a grateful and unquestioning patient and a kindly doctor was now only one of *many* doctor-patient relationships. Today, the average elderly patient in the United States sees seven physicians (two generalists and five specialists) in four different practices each year. While each new doctor adds expertise, from the patient's vantage point, the end result is often cacophony.

By the 1960s, the medical record was charged with incorporating still more stuff—new test results, treatments, and consultative opinions—and weaving them into a seamless whole that could be viewed by everyone, exactly when they needed to see it. If good medical care was now like a symphony, the medical record was called upon to be its score. And the music had evolved from the rhythmic predictability of Bach to the atonality of Schoenberg.

▶   ▶   ▶

The paper chart created another insurmountable problem when it came to the need for coordination of a patient's care: key information could live in only one place at a time. With the advent of computers, the idea of having digital data available whenever and—years later, after the arrival of networked computers—wherever it was needed became viable. To see why this prospect was so exceptionally attractive to so many interested parties, let's take a moment to consider the nature of the problem that needed to be addressed.

The provision of healthcare is remarkably information-intensive. A large healthcare system processes about 10 million computerized transactions each day, twice the number of transactions that takes place every day on the NASDAQ. And the average four-night stay at a large teaching hospital like mine is accompanied by close to 400 orders (for medications, tests, diet, even whether patients are allowed to walk to the bathroom), each an opportunity for error.

But high volume is just the beginning. Consider the task of tracking a single patient's current diseases, medical history, medications, allergies, test results, risk factors, and personal preferences (such as for cardiopulmonary resuscitation). Tricky? Sure, but now do it over months or years, and then add in the fact that the patient may be seen by many different providers, scattered across a region. To make payment decisions, the insurer needs access to some of this information, as does the source of the insurance, which in the United States is often the patient's employer. But, because of privacy concerns, both should receive only essential information; to tell them of the patient's HIV status, or his psychiatric or sexual history, would be highly inappropriate, damaging, and quite possibly illegal.

Now up the ante. Assume that the patient is in a car accident and is taken to an emergency department in a distant state, where he is stabilized and admitted to the hospital. Ideally, the doctors and nurses would be able to see his clinical history, preferably in a format that highlighted the information they needed without overwhelming them with extraneous data. Orders must be processed instantaneously (none of the "orders are processed on the next business day" so familiar from commercial transactions). During the patient's hospital stay, not only would there be seamless linkages among all the new observations (the neurosurgeon can easily view the ER notes; the resident can quickly find the patient's vital signs and laboratory studies), but also the various components would blend together effortlessly.

When the medium is paper, of course, all this is a fantasy. Computerization offered the hope of turning the dream of an always available, perfectly organized medical record into a reality. While the problem of providing everyone with easy access to key patient information has not yet been completely solved, digitizing the record has fixed much of the geography problem. This fact—that multiple people can see a patient's record at the same time, not tethered to the location of a paper chart—has led to exciting changes, but also to some disconcerting, and unanticipated, consequences.

▶   ▶   ▶

It is often said that geography is destiny, and this certainly was true when it came to the medical record. By about 1920, it was no longer acceptable for notes to live in bound journals stored, as they had previously been, in the medical library or the physician's study. The concept of "the chart" emerged, at first as a sheaf of papers housed in a large three-ring binder. In the case of hospitalized patients, it made sense for these charts to be stored on the patient's floor, in an area generally known as the nurses' station. As the central repository for the lone copy of the patient's health record, the nurses' station immediately turned into a congregational space for doctors and nurses, a medical water cooler that drew clinicians together to do their work and discuss their patients (and, on medical television shows, to spark those steamy doctor-nurse romances).

If you needed to see a patient's physician, there was a good chance that you'd find him in the doctors' room, next to the nurses' station, working on the chart.

The degree to which the existence of a single copy of a record determined the clinical work flow and the accompanying social interactions became obvious only after it went away, as Abraham Verghese learned when he discovered all his residents in their dungeon at Stanford. As we'll see in the next chapter, the first hints of what this might look like emerged when another type of record, the x-ray, went digital.

▶   ▶   ▶

Recording information about patients, ranging from their symptoms to their lab results, is a mere prelude to the real work at hand: trying to make an accurate diagnosis, from which both therapy and prognosis are drawn. In the 1960s, an iconoclastic physician named Larry Weed realized that physicians faced a problem not simply of handling ever-increasing mountains of information, but also of managing enormous complexity. Weed's background as a laboratory scientist—a field in which hypotheses are generated, variables are isolated, and observations are recorded—convinced him of the value, indeed the necessity, of approaching the patient's record more systematically.

Not long ago, I stumbled upon a video of Weed giving Grand Rounds at Emory University in 1971. It's fun to watch for many reasons: the packed audience composed largely of white men in white jackets with narrow ties, the grainy black-and-white images a nostalgic reminder of Life Before High Def.

But the real treat is seeing the 47-year-old Weed, angular and frenetic, by turns humorous and annoyed, his hands slicing through the air to punctuate his key messages or to point accusingly at the audience for their sins of sloppy charting and the mental slovenliness it illustrates. Using no notes or slides, he began his lecture by flipping through a typical medical chart, thick as an urban phone book. It was filled with "garbage," he bristled. The note required a structure, Weed insisted, one centered on the patient's clinical problems.

This was revolutionary stuff at the time, and Weed was ready for resistance from doctors who argued that their random jottings were clinical brushstrokes as they practiced "the art of medicine." Weed said,

> Art is not a scribble in the middle of the night. . . . We debase
> the word art itself when we call what we've been doing art. . . .
> As Stravinsky says, art is nothing more than placing limits and
> working against them rigorously . . . and if we refuse to place
> them . . . you do not have art, you have chaos, and to a large
> extent that's what we've had.

Weed dubbed his method of organizing the physician's narrative the SOAP note, for Subjective, Objective, Assessment, and Plan. The idea was to lead off with the patient's history (Subjective), then present the Objective data (physical examination and results of blood tests, radiographs, and other studies), and finally end with an Assessment and Plan for each of the patient's problems. Some of these problems would be established diagnoses ("congestive heart failure due to mitral valve regurgitation"), while others would be symptoms or signs yet to be explained ("abdominal pain" or "enlarged spleen"). Each problem would be further characterized as active or inactive; active ones would be accompanied by a diagnostic and therapeutic plan, and subsequent notes would track these problems over time until they were resolved.

Weed called his overall structure the Problem-Oriented Medical Record, and it remains the cornerstone of our system for organizing our notes. It is, in its own way, as revolutionary as Morgagni's discovery of the anatomic seat of illnesses two centuries earlier. Soon, it would also become the foundation of efforts to build a computerized diagnostician.

▶   ▶   ▶

In the 1970s, experts began to tout the computer as the savior for the note's many flaws and contradictions: the need to record voluminous quantities of dynamic information; the need for many different parties to access this information, often simultaneously; the need to capture and promote accurate analyses of the patient's problems; the need to record treatment plans and ensure that they were enacted safely; the need to link to an ever growing body of scientific literature to promote evidence-based medicine and measure the quality of care. While each of these problems might have been straightforward for an electronic health record to address in isolation, the multifaceted demands made even these "easy" problems devilishly difficult to solve electronically. This is partly because, in attempting to solve all of them, the electronic records that emerged weren't very good at solving *any* of them.

In virtually every other industry, the need to solve similarly knotty problems rapidly led to widespread computerization. Only in healthcare, it seemed—our most complex and information-laden industry—were these forces insufficient to create a business case for going digital. There was, however, one large swath of the medical universe that did go digital without federal incentives, with a minimum of fuss and bother, and about a decade before the rest of healthcare did.

# Chapter 6

# Radiology Rounds

Every place is given its character by certain patterns of events
that keep on happening there. . . . The more living patterns
there are in a place—a room, a building or a town—the more
it comes to life as an entirety."
                    —Christopher Alexander, *The Timeless Way of Building*

When I was a medical student in the 1980s, the beating heart of the Hospital of
the University of Pennsylvania was not the hospital's mahogany-lined executive suite, nor the dazzling operating room of L. Henry Edmunds, Jr., HUP's
most famed cardiac surgeon. No, it was in the decidedly unglamorous, dimly
lit Chest Reading Room, where all the x-rays were hung on a moving contraption called an alternator that resembled the one on which the clothes hang
at your local dry cleaner. Controlled by a seated radiologist operating a foot
pedal, the machine would cycle through panel after panel until it arrived at
your films. The radiologist took his foot off the pedal, the machine ground to
a halt, and the dark x-ray sheets were brought to life by intense backlighting.

Saying that HUP's epicenter was the Chest Reading Room is a bit unspecific.[5] It really was in the seat of the late Wallace Miller, Sr., a crusty but endearing professor of radiology and one of the best teachers I've ever known.

---

[5] While all radiologists learn to interpret a variety of studies (plain x-rays, CT scans, ultrasounds), in
large medical centers, radiologists live in specialized departments, organized either by body parts
("the chest room," "the neuro room") or by technology ("the ultrasound room").

Undoubtedly, there are similarly gifted teachers of radiology in many academic hospitals today, but most of their pedagogy is directed at their progeny: future radiologists. Sadly, today's students in fields outside radiology miss out on the kind of contact that I had with Dr. Miller; many of my internal medicine trainees barely know where UCSF's radiology department is. Because radiology was the first medical specialty to computerize, what has happened to it—at once shocking and, in retrospect, entirely predictable—is our canary in the digital coal mine, its experience offering important lessons for patients, clinicians, and healthcare systems.

▶    ▶    ▶

At Penn in the 1980s, everybody—and I mean everybody, from the lowliest student to the loftiest transplant surgeon—brought films to "The Wal" to decipher. For students like me, time spent with him was at once exhilarating and terrifying. "What's this opacity?" he asked me once, the memory burned into my hippocampus by that cognitive curing process known as overwhelming anxiety. "A . . . a pneumonia?" I stammered. "Mooiaaa," retorted The Oracle, an unforgettable signature sound that was uttered as Miller smartly turned his head away in mock disgust. I loved it. We all did.

A few years ago at my own hospital, the ward team on which I was the attending physician admitted eight new patients. After hearing each patient's story from my interns and students, I suggested that we head as a group to the radiology department on the third floor to review the key films. I might as well have asked my crew to hop on one foot and cluck like chickens. They humored me, but it was clear that these young physicians and trainees saw this as an odd, sweetly nostalgic request from an attending whose clinical instincts were honed in the Reagan era. What else did I have up my sleeve, they must have wondered. Leeches?

They were right, in a way. During my formative years, teams could no more skip the visit to the radiology department than they could forgo listening to the patient's heart and lungs. In those days, after the interns and students presented the clinical histories of the new patients to their attending, the trek to the radiology department always came next. Between 8 and 10 every morning, the medical and surgical teams passed through the radiology department like a fleet of Ford Escorts rolling through a car wash. Most of their time was spent in the chest reading room looking at plain x-rays of the thorax, since radiographs of the abdomen and brain were still grainy daguerreotypes, magnetic resonance—a phenomenon that would soon power the miraculous MRI scanner—was a technique you learned in your college organic chemistry class, and a PET scan was the x-ray the veterinarian performed on your dog.

This review of films was collegial, educational, and fascinating. It also gave us focus and direction. "This is a 52-year-old woman with lupus, shortness of breath, and fever. What do you think, Wally?" we asked. "Well, might just be the atelectasis [collapsed airways] of lupus lung, but it looks a bit hypovascular on the right side. Is she at risk for a PE?" he'd say, referring to the possibility of a pulmonary embolism, a blood clot to the lungs. This back-and-forth inevitably helped the clinicians develop a thoughtful plan or come to a correct diagnosis.

We went to the radiology department for all these wonderful interactions, the intellectual give-and-take that is the lifeblood of any profession. But even if we had no interest in schmoozing with the radiologists, we *had* to go there if we wanted to see our films.

Remember films?

▶    ▶    ▶

In 1888, George Eastman revolutionized photography when he produced a relatively inexpensive camera known as the Kodak (its slogan was: "You press the button—we do the rest"). Eastman's innovation was to capture the image on a celluloid strip called film, which quickly rendered obsolete the messy wet photographic plate process that had been the industry standard. Seven years later, Wilhelm Röntgen, a prominent physics professor at Germany's University of Würzburg, was studying the effects of cathode rays and stumbled upon the discovery that the rays could travel through certain solid materials (wood and rubber, for example, but not lead) and produce an image. He asked his wife to place her hand on a glass photographic plate while he trained his new "x-rays" (he called them this because he didn't understand their composition) on it for 15 minutes. The resulting image marked the birth of radiology and secured Röntgen's place in history, but it scared the hell out of his wife. As Röntgen's biographer wrote, "She could hardly believe the bony hand was her own and shuddered at the thought that she was seeing her own skeleton. To Frau Röntgen, as to many others later, this experience gave a vague premonition of death."

It also gave birth to a field that would transform medicine. Yet there was much work still to be done. Early radiology images were captured on heavy, stiff glass cassettes. In the 1920s, these were supplanted by x-ray film, flexible pieces of translucent cellulose nitrate. Forty years later, the flammable cellulose nitrate films were replaced by polyester blended sheets coated with a photographic emulsion made from a mix of gelatin (extracted, ironically, from cadaver bones) and light-sensitive silver halide crystals. These bulky, floppy translucent sheets remained the staple of radiology departments everywhere until the turn of the twenty-first century, when the field went digital.

David Avrin, a radiology professor at UCSF, remembers the day he knew that the film era was coming to an end. For most of Avrin's career, the dominant study had been that old workhorse, the plain chest x-ray, which produces only two pieces of film: one viewing the chest head-on (the PA view, for "posterior-anterior"), and one looking at it from the side (the "lateral"). Things became more complicated with the arrival of the early CT scanners of the 1980s, but with an output of around a dozen images per study, life was still manageable.

But after the advent of multidetector CT scanning in the late 1990s, a single examination of the abdomen might produce hundreds of images, with each "slice" showing a portion of the belly only one or two millimeters thick. The idea of printing out these images on sheets of film (an odd thing to do in the first place, since the CT scan, unlike a regular x-ray, is digital from the get-go) at a cost of $4 or so per sheet became prohibitive. Hanging the films produced by a single CT study might cover the walls of a high school gymnasium.

In the late 1990s, Avrin was asked to give a second opinion on a CT study performed at another hospital. The accompanying written report indicated that the outside radiologist had spied a worrisome abnormality. The films arrived in a 2 × 1.5 foot jacket weighing almost 10 pounds. "I looked at over 200 different images, and I couldn't find the abnormality. And then I realized that, to save money, they had just sent me the even-numbered slices; they didn't print the odd-numbered ones. The lesion was on an odd-numbered slice, so I couldn't see it. At that moment, I realized that film was toast."

▶    ▶    ▶

In addition to the sheer volume of images and the inefficiency of printing them, there were several other forces that drove the rapid transition from film-based to computerized radiology (known as PACS, for Picture Archiving and Communication System). The first was the plummeting cost of digital storage. In 1956, the earliest computer hard drive contained fifty 24-inch disks and had a total storage capacity of 5 megabytes. Today, of course, you can buy a flash drive with 6,500 times the storage (32 gigabytes) for about $15 and slip it into your pocket. This turned PACS into a cost-effective alternative to running a space- and labor-intensive film library.

Second, after a period in which radiology vendors vied for the primacy of their own standard (think Sony versus Betamax), by the late 1990s a protocol known as DICOM had come to be universally accepted. This allowed various types of studies (plain x-rays, CT scans, ultrasounds) to be viewed on the same monitor—a tangible example of standards paving the way for interoperability.

Finally, radiologists tend to be tech-savvy (Avrin has a PhD in electrical engineering in addition to his MD, making him only a little atypical), and hospitals are used to buying multimillion-dollar gizmos, chock-full of technology, for their radiology departments. The combination of these factors meant that, while it took a massive infusion of federal dollars to prompt the rest of the healthcare system to computerize, radiology went digital at breakneck speed, and without fuss.

Well, maybe a little fuss. Patrick Luetmer, a neuroradiologist and information technology leader at the Mayo Clinic, told me about the Clinic's transition from film to PACS. Mayo is famous for its executive checkups, in which a corporate titan steps onto a very expensive medical assembly line that culminates in two or three days of testing and consultations by Mayo specialists. For it all to work, the visit has to be as tightly choreographed as a Balanchine ballet. The patient might see an internist first thing on Morning 1, then walk to radiology for a CT scan, then to a cardiologist or a surgeon. In the days before computers, Mayo's tradition was that the patient's chart and x-rays accompanied him on every visit so that each specialist had all the information he needed. The films were placed in a big folder (along with a hastily-produced, typed interpretation of the film by the radiologist), and an elaborate system of runners, along with those famous pneumatic tubes, moved both papers and films to their proper destinations.

After PACS was launched, ditching the expensive, labor-intensive process of carting around the huge x-ray folders seemed like a no-brainer. After all, the clinicians could now see the images and read the radiologists' reports on their computers. Yet Mayo's tradition-revering specialists balked, which meant that the radiology department was forced to continue ferrying the film folders around just to mollify them. They "did not want to let go of the safety net that film represented," recalled Luetmer.

Like a spouse scheming to see if her partner is raiding the refrigerator at night, the radiologists sneakily put a little piece of cellophane tape across the open end of the film folder. By checking whether the tape was intact when the folder was finally returned to the radiology department after its sojourn (sometimes the folder had visited the offices of half a dozen different specialists), they could see whether *anybody* had looked at a film or a written report. About 90 percent of the time, Luetmer recalled, the cellophane was intact—meaning that the specialists were exclusively using the electronic images. After about a year, Mayo finally abandoned the films, the folders, and the transport system.

▶    ▶    ▶

Just as your record player and LPs are now long gone (or, if you're like me, stored—who knows why—in boxes in the basement), in your local hospital today, the films, the analog x-ray machines, and even those charming film-conveyor belts have left the building. In 2000, only 8 percent of U.S. hospitals had some version of PACS; by 2008, more than three out of four did. Interestingly, this adoption curve is nearly identical to that of electronic medical records and computerized prescribing. The difference is that the latter occurred a decade later, and only after billions of federal dollars of fiscal fertilizer were sprinkled around.

While the main catalyst for PACS was economic, the quality of the images and the ability to manipulate them were also important. Unlike regular films, CT scans need to be viewed at various contrast levels: one setting is best to look at bones, another to look at lungs, and still another to look at soft tissue like muscle. PACS allowed radiologists to toggle through these views, in the same way that Instagram lets you play with your photos. You can also use a nifty magnifying glass to zoom in on a part of the image. An unexpected benefit was "stacking": rather than looking at 100 images arrayed in a 10 × 10 grid on a one-dimensional page, the images could be digitally stacked, one on top of another, allowing the radiologist to scroll through them swiftly by rolling a mouse ball. Moreover, computerization let the radiologist look at the images from home, enabling senior experts to weigh in on subtle findings that trainees might flub. And while the images were fuzzy at first, today they're as crisp as high-definition television.

Perhaps most important, PACS obviated the need for maddening searches for prior x-rays. Twenty years ago, when a chest x-ray revealed a lung nodule, the first commandment on the radiologist's report was to "obtain old films." The rationale: if the nodule had been unchanged for many years, it could safely be ignored—such stability simply wasn't consistent with a diagnosis of cancer. But searching for old films was often an exercise in frustration: they were lost, or locked up, or at another institution, or in a filing cabinet in the thoracic surgeon's garage, behind the golf clubs. When my colleagues and I came up empty-handed, which was more often than not, the patient frequently paid the price in the form of an unnecessary biopsy. But PACS made finding old films a breeze (assuming that they were done at the same hospital or had been scanned into the system). They're usually just a click away.

▶    ▶    ▶

While PACS was widely anticipated and generally accepted by radiologists, some prescient observers worried that computerization might lead to unbidden effects on the field. In 1999, Stephen Baker, chair of the Department of Radiology at New Jersey Medical School, fretted that PACS might turn radiologists into "disembodied functionaries, more akin to servicing technicians than professional colleagues." Paul Chang, professor of radiology at the University of Chicago and an early leader in digital radiology, describes the day his father, a retired radiologist, took him to task. "Before PACS, we were the doctor's doctor," his father berated him. "Medicine and surgery rounds started in radiology. . . . Every morning the clinicians and the radiologists collaborated." His father's less-than-endearing nickname for his famous son: "The Man Who Ruined Radiology."

▶    ▶    ▶

The advantages of PACS are so vast that few would want to turn back the clock. Yet the effects on those of us who order x-rays and the radiologists who read them have been profound, and they're not all positive. The fact that we can now review our images without trekking down to radiology means that we rarely do make the trip—which is why my young colleagues on rounds looked at me as if I had grown a second head when I asked them to go there.

But the impact is not just on the clinicians who order the films. After my team humored me by accompanying me to the radiology department, I conducted a little sociology experiment. Standing outside my hospital's chest reading room,[6] I delivered a brief speech:

> Watch what happens when we enter. Does anybody turn
> around and welcome us, ask, "How can I help you?" and seem
> genuinely enthusiastic? When they go over the x-ray, do they
> delve a layer deeper than what they said in the formal report?
> Do they make any teaching points? Does the radiologist sug-
> gest courses of action or ask provocative questions?

I did this because I am deeply concerned that mine is the last generation to have learned the habit of going to the radiology department. Nostalgic for my interactions with Wally Miller and his like, it saddens me that our current trainees will never know how much they can learn from a great radiology teacher, and how much their patients' care can be improved by actually talking to a real live radiologist. Yet I know that even if I bring my young horses to water, whether they visit the radiology department after I am no longer their wrangler will be determined by the quality of their experience. Ergo my ad hoc sociology experiment.

After my speech, we entered the chest reading room. We were greeted by a wall of radiologists' backs, their faces trained like lasers on the computer screens in front of them. Not a single head—located atop the shoulders of about eight different radiologists—turned to greet us. (I fantasized that the entire department had been in a bus accident, their necks immobilized in stiff cervical collars.) After a couple of awkward minutes of crescendo throat clearing, one of the radiologists grudgingly swiveled around to face my team and me. "Oh, do you need something?" he asked. ("No, we got lost on the way to the morgue," I nearly blurted, but I thought better of it.) "Sure; can you help us look at a few films?" He did, kind of, but he offered his help stiffly, in a whisper animated mostly by passive aggression.

---

[6] At the time, the least user-friendly room in our radiology department. Today, under different leadership, it is far better.

Then, just when I thought it couldn't get any worse, it did. "What do you think of this area?" I asked, pointing to a confusing patch of whiteness on one patient's chest CT scan. "Did you look at the official report?" he hissed. (In other words, are you an illiterate moron? Or perhaps you don't know how to turn on the computer.) The unspoken message was clear: *Get out of my space; I'm busy*. Now, I understand that he might well be busy, and that it has to be annoying having clinicians interrupt you every few minutes to go over images, particularly after you've just reviewed them with a different set of specialists and dictated a report. But that is the radiologist's job. Or at least it used to be.

Allison Tillack, a young radiologist and a medical anthropologist whose PhD thesis involved observing the world of radiologists for a year at a prominent academic hospital, has explored how the computerization of radiology has transformed the worlds of radiologists and those who use their services. "The ability of PACS to alter the accessibility and tempo of medical imaging has resulted in visits to the reading room being viewed now by non-radiology clinicians as a 'waste of time' and by radiologists as an 'interruption,'" she wrote.

While I was well aware of the changing perceptions of radiology by nonradiologists, until I met Tillack, I had not appreciated the degree to which the field of radiology is itself in a PACS-fueled funk. After all, the field remains extremely popular among medical students, as many perceive it as offering the perfect blend of "great lifestyle" (that is, banker's hours and limited overnight call) and high income, which averaged $340,000 in 2013. In fact, it's often said that today's medical students are attracted to the "ROAD specialties": *R*adiology, *O*phthalmology, *A*nesthesiology, and *D*ermatology, all of which are lucrative and none of which involves a lot of contact with those pesky sick people. In her research, Tillack found that the vast majority of radiologists and radiology residents identified the lack of direct patient contact as one of the main attractions of the field.

Given all these pluses,[7] many frontline clinicians think of radiologists as having "won the game." Yet I should have gotten a hint of the field's handwringing in 2005, when I saw the results of a survey of physicians regarding their satisfaction with their chosen specialty. The happiest doctors were radiation oncologists (the folks who deliver radiation therapy to cancer patients), who do satisfying work, earn a good income, and have predictable hours. The least happy were cardiac surgeons, who train forever and, in recent years, have

---

[7] At least for them; I personally enjoy seeing patients. So do some radiologists, particularly those in patient-facing specialties of the field, like interventional radiology.

seen much of their business eroded by stents and other nonsurgical approaches to heart disease.

Radiologists show up a bit below the mean on the satisfaction scale—just behind the perennially overwhelmed and undercompensated primary care doctors. When I show this slide to physician audiences, I often quip, "I guess this means that the radiologists didn't understand the question." This always gets a good laugh.

But I've come to realize that the dissatisfaction and anxiety are real. In a 2012 paper, Tillack and a colleague described "the loneliness of the long distance radiologist." One radiologist told them, "Before, I knew the face, name, wife's name, and kids' names of all the clinicians, but now I don't know who you are if you joined the medical staff after we got PACS. . . . Before, when a clinician showed up, I could ask them and find out what's really going on with the patient."

I hear similar stories from every radiologist I meet. Patrick Luetmer, the Mayo Clinic neuroradiologist, described what happened when his MRI suite was remodeled. The suite was originally configured with two MRI "donuts" (the huge magnets that are responsible for the image) on either side of a central workstation in which Luetmer sat. There, he could monitor the scans as they were being performed, and talk to both the patients and the radiology assistants. Clinicians sometimes wandered down to look at the scans with him.

A few years ago, as part of a big efficiency push, Mayo decided that a third MRI machine was a better use of that central area than the radiologist's air traffic control desk. Luetmer's workstation was moved to an office a few hundred feet away, where he could follow the scans on his computer monitor and communicate with the techs via a special text messaging system. "One day I tried to see if I could go the whole day without speaking to anyone. And that's what happened—I didn't speak to a single person. It was incredibly isolating."

▶   ▶   ▶

The radiologists were lonely, sure, but their situation involves something far deeper. Hari Tsoukas, an expert in organizational studies at the University of Cyprus, highlights the distinction between "information" and "knowledge." Information, he wrote, "consists of objectified, decontextualized, time-less, impersonal, value-free representations," whereas knowledge is "context-dependent, personalized, time-bound, and infused with values." Adds Tillack, "Hunches, hypotheses, frustrations with patients or their families, second-guessing, judging of colleagues, and similar activities that mark how uncertainty is negotiated on a daily basis in medical practice are rarely reflected in the medical record . . . this knowledge can only circulate in private or semi-private contexts—by its very definition, this knowledge cannot be made a matter of public record." By purging the informal conversations during which such information was exchanged, the emergence of PACS left radiologists information-rich (*Think of all those pixels! And old films just a click away!!*), but knowledge-poor.

There's something more. Organizational expert Jody Hoffer Gittell, a professor at Brandeis University, studies "relational coordination," the process by which workers communicate with and relate to each other. Relational coordination, she has found, is crucial in environments characterized by task interdependence, uncertainty, and time constraints. As a PhD student at MIT, she studied the airline industry, particularly the field known as Flight Ops, the folks who manage to get a plane into a gate and turn it around for the next departure.

Gittell noticed that Southwest Airlines did something that other carriers considered inefficient: it assigned a single ops agent to coordinate one flight departure at a time. That person was communicating with all the players, sometimes face to face, or by phone, or by walkie-talkie. In contrast, the ops agents at American and the other major carriers were managing 10 to 12 flights at a time; much of their work consisted of checking off completed tasks on a computer screen. "Check, okay, bags are on, fuel's on, okay, load is balanced, flight can leave," is how Gittell saw the American agents working. At first, this seemed far more efficient than the Southwest procedure.

But the more she observed the process, the more her viewpoint changed. As she watched the Southwest agents essentially pulling together a virtual team every time they turned a flight around, she came to see this as a type of "collective sense-making" that helped defuse potential conflicts between the inflight crew and the ground crew. "There were a lot of power issues around the handoff," she said, "but they were handled because there was someone who had everyone's respect and could quarterback the flight departure."

"There's computerization, of course," she added, "but the Southwest agents weren't relying on it in place of the human interaction." And she found that Southwest's performance—in terms of quality and efficiency—was better than that of the other airlines. The "inefficiency" of maintaining these personal relationships paid off.

▶   ▶   ▶

Radiologists' alienation runs deeper than the lack of collegial exchange and the inability to find out what's really going on with the patients. It's also about power, status, and expertise. The fact that the traditional film lived only in the radiology reading room gave radiologists a monopoly over their entire eco-system. PACS, observes Tillack, created a new normal in which "the 'right' to see [the image] is no longer mediated by radiologists, as it was in the reading room," and has thus "eroded radiologists' claims for authoritative knowledge over the interpretation of medical images."

Once the radiology department no longer housed the films, the impact was immediate and dramatic. Without any changes in policy or very much forethought, the mid-1990s transition to filmless operations at the Baltimore VA hospital led to an 82 percent decrease in in-person consultation rates for general radiology studies. Today, many clinicians—particularly specialists like neurologists, pulmonologists, and surgeons—look at images themselves and act on their own interpretations; many don't even bother to read the radiologist's formal report (which usually takes several hours, sometimes even a day, to reach the chart) unless they have unanswered questions or judge the study to be particularly challenging.

▶   ▶   ▶

If you're not feeling sorry for radiologists yet, try this: part of the rationale for PACS was to increase efficiency, but that virtue has also become a curse, as radiologists increasingly feel like Lucy and Ethel on the assembly line of the chocolate factory. Among teleradiologists (radiologists reading x-rays from a distant site, often covering emergency departments at night while the hospital's own radiologists are sleeping), there's a well-known adage that captures the relentless objectification of their modern predicament: "Great case. Next case." As with so many other aspects of our modern digital lives, PACS sped up the clock, and did so without mercy.

That clock is constantly ticking. "Instead of waiting for films to be acquired, printed, sorted, and hung, radiologists now are always playing catch-up, looking at more 'stuff' in less time," observed Tillack. That miraculous access to old films also creates an obligation for the radiologist to actually review them.

And it's not just the old films that need to be examined; PACS makes vast amounts of information available with every study. In the early days of CT, the output of a scan might have been about 12 "slices," each one representing a ¼-inch section through the thorax or abdomen, akin to a thick slice of deli-cut salami. But today's ultra-fast CT scanners can produce images of more than 50 slices *per inch* of the human body, more like ultra-thin cuts of prosciutto. And PACS, with its massive memory bank and blazingly fast transmission speeds, can easily display every slice, which means that the radiologist has to scroll through hundreds of images in order to read a single CT study. This combination of more information in each scan, more old studies to compare, and more time pressure is unremitting.

The clock is ticking for other reasons as well. Since the image is available to the ordering clinician the moment it is created, radiologists feel obliged to perform their review quickly lest their reading seem like old news, like an afternoon newspaper in the Age of Twitter. Piling on, after recognizing the efficiency of PACS, insurance companies and Medicare slashed the reimbursement for each interpretation, pushing radiologists to read more films in less time in order to maintain their incomes. Said one radiologist, "With PACS, work is busier now. We have 70 percent more cases to read than 10 years ago. . . . At the end of the day . . . I'm fried."

▶    ▶    ▶

On top of this, there are even greater threats to radiologists' livelihoods and happiness. One of them flows from the growing pressure on healthcare systems to slash their costs. Currently, virtually every x-ray performed at a U.S. hospital is sent for a formal reading by a radiologist, who is paid a fee by an insurance company.[8] In today's cost-cutting environment, it's probably only a matter of time before some healthcare systems permit their frontline specialists to officially read certain films, reserving radiologist "overreads" for those images that the clinicians have questions about or the ones with super-high malpractice risk if they are misread. Radiologists can be counted on to fight such a move by frantically waving the banner of quality, but they will need to demonstrate that the value of having them review every film is worth the considerable expense.

Moreover, a major theme of Obama-era health reform is a shift from our historical fee-for-service, piecework payment model to one that dispenses a single payment to a hospital and doctors to manage all the care for a group of patients ("accountable care organizations," ACOs for short) or a given episode of disease ("bundled payments"). Under such systems, the risk for the cost of care shifts from the insurer to the providers, and it's up to the latter to decide how to divvy up the cash. Ron Arenson, chairman of the department of radiology at UCSF, sees this as the greatest threat to his field. "If the world moves to bundled payments, we won't do well," he said. "We're not very high in the pecking order."

---

[8] The exception is that many x-rays performed in private physicians' offices are not read by radiologists.

Some nonradiologists, particularly ER doctors working nights and week-ends, have little sympathy for their colleagues' new predicament. In fact, they have begun to wonder why radiologists *should* be compensated for next-day readings when they've already looked at the images themselves, acted on their interpretations, and assumed the risk of being sued if anything goes wrong. In a 2011 editorial entitled "The Life Cycle of a Parasitic Specialist," ER physician William Mallon took off the gloves.

> *[On Monday morning] these parasites will commence to feed on the financial juices of the lowly unfortunate emergency physicians, who had to work the entire weekend without radiologic support or backup. . . . The radiologist arrives well rested, café latte in hand, and promptly installs himself in a dark room to re-read and bill for all the films the emergency physicians read over the weekend. . . . Never has a specialty done so little for so many and been paid so much.*

Ouch.

▶    ▶    ▶

Another challenge to radiology made possible by the death of film has come in the form of teleradiology. Once x-rays went digital, it was no longer crucial for radiologists to be in the same building as the patient or the treating clinicians. As a result, many multihospital systems consolidated their reading rooms, particularly on weekends and nights, with centralized radiologists supporting multiple sites. Predictably, once the technical challenges of connectivity were solved, teleradiology companies emerged to fill this need. As is often the case with contented "legacy" providers (in healthcare and other industries), tradi-tional radiologists were only too happy to have their colleagues read their films during off-hours. Who wouldn't be?

The playing field soon expanded across national borders, as radiologists in Zurich, Israel, and Singapore began to read nighttime x-rays for American hospitals. (This movement was fostered by the time zone differences, since these "nighthawk" radiologists could read after-hours films during their local daytimes.) Hundreds of hospitals now use nighthawks, and everybody seems happy about it, including the domestic radiologists, who are sleeping soundly while the overnight images are read half a world away.

But one wonders whether this is the start of so-called disruptive innovation, the concept made famous by Harvard's Clay Christensen. Disruption often begins with a fat and happy incumbent content to preserve its existing enviable position in a market. In industries ranging from commercial aviation to steel manufacturing, an upstart comes in and grabs an unattractive part of the market (in this case, nights and weekends). But once a low-cost company has squeezed through a crack to capture a slice of a previously locked franchise, it is rarely content to stay put. With the average U.S. radiologist earning about $350,000 per year and the average Indian radiologist earning less than one-tenth of that, one wonders whether the same World-Is-Flat forces that have revolutionized other industries but mostly bypassed healthcare will be unleashed.

This is where radiologists' loss of trust and collegiality with other clinicians may exact its heaviest toll. "Some people see teleradiology as a big threat, but I don't," UCSF's Arenson told me. "I think that relationships with radiologists are important." I do too, which is why I believe he may have his head in the sand: if physicians don't get much out of visiting the radiology department or have even forgotten where it is located, we have little reason to fight to keep it in our buildings. Or, for that matter, our country.

Like all legacy providers faced with a technological or global workforce threat, radiologists can be counted on to argue that quality would take a huge hit if we outsourced their work to less expensive providers, domestic or foreign. The degree to which the field has accepted nighttime readings from non-U.S. radiologists will, of course, undermine this argument. It's hard to make the claim that a Bangalore-based teleradiologist is sufficiently competent to read an image for your hospital at 3 a.m., but not at 3 p.m.

▶   ▶   ▶

Finally, there is the ultimate threat: replacement by the machine. Of course, this issue is marbled throughout healthcare as we enter the digital age. To date, most claims that "this technology will replace doctors" (in areas ranging from diagnostic reasoning to robotic surgery) have proven to be hype (an issue we'll explore in detail later when we talk about IBM's Watson and medical diagnosis). However, in fields that are primarily about visual pattern recognition, the promise (or, if you're a radiologist, the threat) is much more real. Studies have shown that computers can detect significant numbers of breast cancers and pulmonary emboli missed by radiologists, although nobody has yet taken the bold step of having the computers completely supplant the humans, partly because there are armadas of malpractice attorneys waiting to pounce, and partly because, at least for now, the combination of human and machine seems to perform better than either alone.

But over the long haul, I wouldn't bet on the humans here, particularly since one of the hottest areas in artificial intelligence research is "deep learning"—research that has created computers that are reasonably skilled at "reading," "hearing," and, yes, "seeing." The same kind of software that now allows Facebook to guess that a certain collection of pixels is a picture of *you*, or that alerts the casino's security guards to keep an eye on *that guy*, is likely to eventually crack the code in radiology, and in similar areas such as dermatology and pathology.

▶    ▶    ▶

Slowly, radiologists are waking up to their peril. Rather than isolating themselves from clinical care, some are now relocating their reading stations in clinical areas, such as the ER and the ICU, to be in the line of sight of their clinician colleagues. Others are resurrecting interdisciplinary conferences and training their staff in customer service. Technological solutions that allow radiologists and frontline clinicians to communicate through PACS and the electronic health record are springing up (through programs that create a mash-up of a Skype-like communication tool and a John Madden–style telestrator). Said Paul Chang, the University of Chicago radiologist whose advocacy of PACS so upset his father, "We have to go beyond isolating ourselves and concentrating on messages in a bottle, where we just write a report and are done with it, but instead fostering collaboration."

Since radiology represents such a large segment of healthcare expenditures (and also a source of harm through the risk of radiation), some healthcare systems are even putting radiologists in the position of being gatekeepers to their own technology. It's a role they might not have accepted in the past, but, faced with an existential threat, many now welcome it. Said David Levin, a radiologist at Thomas Jefferson University, "We have to act more like consulting physicians . . . to look at the appropriateness of the requests for advanced imaging studies . . . rather than just going ahead and doing the study."

▶    ▶    ▶

Radiology's experience over the past 15 years offers a crystal ball for the rest of the healthcare system. The speed with which computerization unleashed a series of forces that completely transformed an established field would be all too familiar to travel agents, journalists, and others who have been run over by the digital bulldozer, but it has shocked many healthcare observers, even astute ones. Will the computerization of the rest of medicine similarly upend the lives of other kinds of doctors, as well as their patients? The early returns are in, and the answer is yes.

# Chapter 7

# Go Live

In all science, error precedes the truth, and it is better it
should go first than last.
                    —Horace Walpole, Fourth Earl of Orford (1717–1797)

The YouTube video opens to show a balding middle-aged man sitting on a
stool, strumming a guitar. In a gentle, twangy croon, the man, Robert Schwab,
chief quality officer for Texas Health Presbyterian Hospital in Denton, Texas,
sings "The Ballad of Go-Live," a week-by-week chronicle of what happened
when his hospital turned on its electronic health record system in 2012. He set
his lyrics to the melody of the Simon and Garfunkel folk ballad "Homeward
Bound."

> I'm sitting at the nurses' station, my ticket filed in desperation.
> Waiting for the help desk guy, to give me something I can try . . .
> to get a patient list so I, can finish rounds before I die.
> On Go Live night, it feels like death. On Go Live night . . .

Somehow, he makes it through Week 1, and the song continues [the tune is
now the song's chorus]:

> One . . . at least I logged on.
> One . . . I've got to slog on.

*One . . . I've discharged someone.*
*[Mournfully] But I don't know who.*

▶    ▶    ▶

The unanticipated consequences of electronic health records begin at the beginning, with a ritual known as "Go Live," when an entire organization flips a switch and converts from one way of doing work to another.

Of course, problematic implementations of large computer systems aren't limited to healthcare organizations: efforts to install massive new systems have failed famously in the FBI, the U.S. air traffic control system, the Internal Revenue Service, and, most recently, with the disastrous launch of the Healthcare.gov site in 2013. But the HITECH dollars have resulted in tens of thousands of Go Lives—in doctors' offices and hospitals—in the space of a few years, making this perhaps the largest widely distributed nationwide computer installation in American history, an El Niño of electronic despair and anxiety.

▶    ▶    ▶

My own hospital, UCSF Medical Center, went live with an EHR built by Epic Systems of Verona, Wisconsin, on June 2, 2012, at 2:25 a.m. All in all, it went reasonably well, thanks to a vast amount of planning and a superb IT team and support staff. And part of our advantage was that it wasn't our first experience with turning on the digital switch. We, like many other healthcare organizations, had started our EHR journey with one system and later changed to another.

A swap like this is not like deciding that you don't like the color of the wallpaper that looked so lovely in the store—the cost of pulling one system out and installing another can run upward of $100 million for a large hospital. Our prior system had been built by a Vermont company, IDX, that was purchased by General Electric in 2006. When GE acquired the struggling vendor, we all breathed a sigh of relief: surely the world's greatest technology firm would not only salvage our system, but improve it. After all, the company brings good things to life.

But year after year, the system failed to deliver much beyond frozen screens and user-unfriendly, even dangerous interfaces. An interesting thing happens when you are a customer of a company like GE; I liken it to the way I feel about modern art. When I visit, but then am underwhelmed by, a highly touted exhibition of stark white canvases or stacks of empty seltzer bottles, I assume that the problem must be with me—I just don't *get* it. So it was with our GE system:

we assumed that if we were unsatisfied with the system, it *must be us*. Turns out it wasn't. GE's system is poorly rated by an independent rating agency and is stumbling badly in the hospital EHR business. (John Halamka, chief information officer at Boston's Beth Israel Deaconess Medical Center, calls GE's EHR offerings "Imagination at Work.") We ultimately decided to jettison the system in 2009.

Over the last several years, Epic has nearly cornered the market among large hospital systems, particularly academic medical centers (I'll have more to say about the company later in the book). Virtually every large hospital that has switched from one system to another in recent memory has chosen Epic's. It has become today's healthcare version of what IBM was in the 1980s, when the saying went, "Nobody ever lost their job going with IBM." Epic is the safe choice.

Make that *safer*. In 2013, *Healthcare IT News* reported that the Epic installation at the 600-bed Maine Medical Center in Portland, Maine, had seemingly gone off without a hitch in late 2012. But by mid-2013, the hospital reported a $13.4 million operating loss over the prior six months, largely attributed to the hospital's failure to send bills off to insurers for many of its services. When he was interviewed just before Go Live, Maine Med chief information officer Barry Blumenfeld told the magazine, "The change is a wrenching one. . . . Everyone has to do things differently than they did before." Six months later, Blumenfeld was looking for a new job.

▶    ▶    ▶

The first indication that an EHR Go Live was not tiddlywinks came in 2002, when Cedars-Sinai Medical Center in Los Angeles launched its brand-new system and the doctors nearly went on strike.

For many in healthcare, the Cedars fiasco served notice that a Go Live was unlikely to be as easy as it had seemed during the vendor demo or—since Cedars had built its own system—during early-morning discussions over bagels and coffee. Cedars' experience was particularly scary because everyone knew that the hospital hadn't done things on the cheap. After all, Cedars-Sinai, which sits at the intersection of Gracie Allen Drive and George Burns Road, is where the Hollywood glitterati go when they're sick.

But money can't buy everything, and in this case it failed to produce a usable system. Physicians grumbled about overabundant alerts, inflexible work flows, and massive inefficiency. One doctor told the *Los Angeles Times* that, while it previously took him five seconds to prescribe vancomycin, a commonly used intravenous antibiotic, it now took him more than two minutes. "If I have to add five to ten minutes to each patient," he complained, "that adds hours to my day." Some administrators thought that these grievances were exaggerated; one actually took to secretly clocking colleagues with a stopwatch.

Cedars executives insisted that they'd kept the rank-and-file physicians in the loop as the system was being developed, but the doctors disagreed. "They poorly designed the system, poorly sold it, and then jammed it down our throats and had the audacity to say everybody loves it and that it's a great system," said one surgeon. Although no fatalities were identified during the Go Live, patient safety problems were plentiful, including that of a baby who received a short-acting anesthetic for his circumcision—a day before the procedure.

Soon after Go Live, the monthly meeting of the medical staff—usually a sleepy, clubby affair—was transformed into a near-riot, including threats to impeach the chief of staff. The medical center got the message and agreed to ditch the system within a month of going live. The cost, in 2002 dollars: $34 million. "The important lesson of the Cedars-Sinai case is that electronic health record implementation is risky," David Brailer told the *Washington Post*. "Up to 30 percent fail."

▶    ▶    ▶

The trauma of a Go Live isn't limited to large medical centers. In fact, hospitals' deep pockets and ability to hire specialized experts arguably make their implementations easier than those in doctors' offices. Since two-thirds of American physician-patient encounters take place in offices with four doctors or fewer, the computerization of small practices is a very big deal.

In 2004, Richard Baron, the lead physician for a four-person practice in Philadelphia, decided to go paperless. Baron had been spending part of his time helping to lead a Medicaid HMO plan, where he was able to easily answer questions like, "Let me see which of Dr. Smith's female patients between ages 50 and 65 had a mammogram in the past two years," a riddle that Baron himself was unable to solve in his own paper-based practice. He knew that he could manage his patients better if he went digital.

But there was something else motivating this risky move, which very few of his primary care colleagues dared make at the time. Having just turned 50, he was having a bit of a midlife crisis, and was hungry for a professional challenge to keep himself excited and engaged. "I thought to myself, it's either the red sports car, a mistress, or an electronic health record," he told me. "The

EHR seemed safer." A one-time change in the accounting methods used by his malpractice insurance company had generated a windfall of about $100,000, enough to soften the financial blow of installing a new IT system. Without that fluke, he would not have been able to afford the transition. "This was really painful, really scary, really expensive, and if there is a national imperative to get people to computerize, you'd better put some money on the table," he said, in support of the federal HITECH payments.

Baron still remembers his Go Live (on July 14, 2004—fittingly, Bastille Day) as if it were yesterday. "The office staff came to work that day, and none of them knew how to do their job," he said. For Baron and his colleagues, the first several months "felt like feeding an infant. You're just putting massive amounts of data into it because it starts off empty, and you're kind of hoping it will be quiet," he said. "A number of times, we wanted to throw the thing against a wall." During that year, "We were all mad at each other. We were a dysfunctional group, and everybody in the office hated me," he said. "It nearly broke up the practice."

The details of daily practice created the biggest problems: medication refill requests, phone calls, lab slips, reports from outside doctors. Everything needed to be entered into the EHR, and everything required a work flow that differed markedly from the one they'd been using for 15 years. "Although the vendor urged us to think through and document the new work flows in advance," he and his colleagues wrote in a 2005 article describing their experience, "we found ourselves making innumerable decisions about how we would use the system before we really understood how it worked." This meant a huge amount of real-time improvisation, which Baron, now CEO of the American Board of Internal Medicine, likens to redesigning an airplane while in flight.

▶    ▶    ▶

Despite the trauma, most organizations make it through Go Live seared but alive, and one of the reasons that Epic has come to dominate the EHR field, at least for large hospitals, is that its approach to implementation, while awfully expensive, is also tried and true. Yet even an Epic installation is so intense that an organization and its clinicians would be forgiven for believing that they're home free once they have survived it.

But, like rafters who have successfully traversed a Class IV patch of white water, it's a good idea to take a deep breath and then settle in for more choppiness ahead.

# Chapter 8

# Unanticipated Consequences

We have the capacity to transform health with one thunderous click of a mouse after another.

—U.S. Secretary of Health and Human Services
Michael Leavitt, in 2005

Emergency department physicians spent 44 percent of their time entering data into electronic medical records, clicking up to 4,000 times during a 10-hour shift.

—*Becker's Health IT & CIO Review* magazine,
October 11, 2013

In a brilliantly tart essay published in the *Journal of the American Medical Association* in 2006, an internist named Robert Hirschtick described what happened when his hospital, Chicago's Northwestern Memorial, went digital. As physicians learned to use the new timesaving features of their electronic health records, he wrote, "Their notes have been rendered incapable of conveying usable information by their bloated and obfuscated nature."

He pinned part of the blame on the computerized templates, which created such syntactical gems as "Hospital Day 1: The patient complains that The patient has been transferred here from St. Eligius at her request."

But Hirschtick reserved his sharpest barbs for the computer's "copy and paste" feature, which allows doctors to turn yesterday's note into a template for today's. In an ideal world, he wrote, with each update of the medical record, old information and diagnostic impressions would be deleted and new ones added. In reality, however, "There is no deletion, only addition." The unfortunate result: progress notes become progressively longer and begin to verge on nonsense. "The admitting diagnostic impression, long since discarded, is dutifully noted day after day," Hirschtick wrote. "Last month's echocardiogram report takes up permanent residence in the daily results section. Complicated patients are on 'post-op day 2' for weeks." One is left scratching one's head over how utilization review—the department charged with ensuring that patients need to remain in the hospital each day—could possibly interpret such statements.

Ross Koppel, a University of Pennsylvania sociologist who has been studying problems with EHRs for more than a decade, describes one case in which a patient was documented as having the same blood pressure, taken from his foot, every day for a month. The problem was that the foot had been amputated at the start of that month.

The combination of all the checkboxes, templates, and copy and paste has led to notes that are so loaded with bilge—much of it of questionable utility and some of it of questionable veracity, as you'll see—that, while the billers may be overjoyed, clinicians cannot do their work. One physician told me about caring for a desperately ill patient in an ICU. Each day's note was brimming with nonsense, most of it cloned from the prior day's note. Lacking MS Word's "Compare Documents" function, he came up with his own ingenious way of figuring out what had happened to the patient in the prior 24 hours: he printed out the current day's note and the prior day's note (each over a dozen pages long), and held one over the other against a bright window in the ICU. This method allowed him to pinpoint the couple of paragraphs in the lengthy document that had changed overnight. It was his only way of seeing what was going on.

▶    ▶    ▶

Let's take a look at some of the major problems that physicians have encountered with their EHRs. As you join me on this House of Horrors tour, it is important to remember that there are other, more positive views on these early days of wired healthcare. In fact, many doctors and patients have forged a cranky truce with their systems, and it is nearly unheard of for a clinician or hospital that has made the switch to digital to return to pen and paper. There is no question in my own mind that my hospital is better and safer since we computerized. Still, as you will see, there is much to improve, and the status quo is infuriating and often dangerous.

## PHYSICIAN UNHAPPINESS

In 2014, Arizona General Hospital ran a recruiting ad for physicians. The ad touted the hospital's ER, advanced radiology suite, and state-of-the-art operating rooms—the kinds of things that doctors like to see in a modern hospital. But only one section of the ad was in bold and capital letters; there could be little doubt that Arizona General believed that this was its ace selling point. It read: **NO EMR.**[9]

How could it be that in this day and age, a hospital would see the absence of computerization as a plus? In 2013, Steve Stack, board chair of the American Medical Association and a true believer in healthcare technology, explained the reasons: "EHRs have been and largely remain clunky, confusing, and complex. Though an 18-month-old child can operate an iPhone, physicians with seven to ten years of postcollegiate education are brought to their knees by their electronic health records."

That same year, investigators at the RAND Corporation reported the results of an in-depth study of 30 physician practices designed to assess the effects of healthcare reform on doctors' professional satisfaction. The researchers did not set out to examine physicians' reactions to their EHRs; in fact, their initial plans called for a survey containing not a single question about computers.

Before administering the surveys, the investigators sat down with groups of doctors to be sure they weren't missing something. "We had one question in the interview guide that asked, 'Tell us about your EHR,'" said Mark Friedberg, who led the study for RAND. "And people would go on for 10 or 15 minutes about that question. It was one of those surprises that is very obvious in retrospect but, at the time, wasn't obvious to us." The RAND team scrambled to rework the survey, and the results confirmed what they had been hearing: rather than delighting their users, as Apple and Google do regularly, the EHR was a towering source of physician dissatisfaction.

---

[9] The term *electronic medical record* (EMR) originally referred to a simple electronic chart, while the term *electronic health record* (EHR) implied additional functions, including connections to other clinicians and, often, a patient portal. Today, the two terms are often used interchangeably. In this book, I've favored the slightly broader term, EHR.

It wasn't that the doctors romanticized the days of pen and paper. "Everybody acknowledged the legibility and safety issues inherent in handwriting, the craziness of having to schlep charts from one place to another, the danger of taking care of patients you didn't know from home without having the record available," Friedberg told me. Because of this, the physicians approved of EHRs in concept and saw great potential for the future ("Our study does not suggest that physicians are Luddites, technophobes, or dinosaurs," Friedberg wrote in a blog). However, "poor usability, time-consuming data entry, interference with face-to-face patient care, inefficient and less fulfilling work content, inability to exchange health information, and degradation of clinical documentation" were all wellsprings of deep discontent.

Friedberg was surprised not just by the degree of angst, but also by how the physicians explained their new predicament. When physicians have trouble with technology, Friedberg said, there is frequently an undercurrent of shame and self-blame. Many of their rants against EHRs, he said, began with, "It must just be me, I'm a bad typist," or, "I know the younger people don't have this problem, but I do." This isn't surprising, he said. "These are highly competitive, highly educated people who really don't like the idea of being behind the curve at all. Except, you hear this from everybody, so they're evidently not talking about it with each other."

The survey results weren't all bad news for electronic health record boosters: 61 percent of physicians felt their EHR improved the quality of care they delivered to patients. But only one in three felt it had improved their job satisfaction, and one in five said they would go back to paper if they could. Tellingly, the more advanced the EHR (for example, systems that offered reminders, alerts, and messaging capability), the greater the unhappiness.

Many physicians pointed to data entry as the greatest source of heartburn. A separate 2013 survey reported that, since going digital, 85 percent of office-based doctors felt they were now spending more time on documentation, and two-thirds of them were seeing fewer patients. The RAND team saw physicians trying all kinds of solutions, including electronic dictation software. The results were decidedly mixed. "We have Dragon [dictation software]," one primary care doctor said, "which you have to be careful of, because I just [dictated] 'Patient's prostate is bothering him' and it turned out 'Patient's prostitute is bothering him.'"

Friedberg did a bit of head-scratching about why the EHRs made the doctors so grumpy. Sure, the systems were maddening, but there seemed to be something more at work. And then it dawned on him that many physicians today feel as if they're being attacked from multiple directions—pay cuts from insurers, new Medicare regulations, nasty Yelp reviews, malpractice suits. In the past, Friedberg said, "They'd say, 'I can always go into the exam room or the OR and tune all of that out.' But now the EHR is there. It has invaded their sacred space."

▶   ▶   ▶

One of the most fascinating solutions to the physician-as-data-entry-clerk problem has been the emergence of scribes, often premedical students or paramedics who are hired by physicians to perform documentation in real time. Studies have shown that the use of scribes—who are most commonly employed in primary care and ER settings—increases both patient and physician satisfaction, and, for many practices, their costs are covered by increased physician productivity. A January 2014 article in the *New York Times* brought scribes to national attention. The article was written by Katie Hafner, who happens to be my wife.

That article has an interesting backstory. I had been hearing about scribes from Christine Sinsky, a primary care physician in Dubuque, Iowa, who studies "joy in practice" among primary care physicians. (The CliffsNotes version of her findings: there isn't much.) In the 23 physician practices that Sinsky observed, she found that scribes were one of a small number of innovations that reliably led to happier doctors and a better-functioning clinic. I told Katie that she should consider writing about this remarkable turn of events. "In every other industry, they bring in computers and start laying people off," I told her when I suggested the story. "Only in healthcare do we bring in computers, and then hire extra people to use them."

▶   ▶   ▶

Scribes may help create the note, but there is no relief in sight for physicians who are being crushed under the weight of the electronic information they now receive about their patients. There is a parallel here to the complaints from the radiologists, who are now overwhelmed by having to wade through impossible amounts of data from old films that they never used to see. Friedberg observed:

> *Let's say you're a primary care doctor. The way certain*
> *EHR products are configured, every time your patient sees*
> *a specialist, or goes to the hospital, or gets a result on any*

*test—even one you didn't order—you get an e-mail, and*
*they're not necessarily prioritized in any way. . . . The doctors*
*are terrified of all this information coming in. Before EHRs,*
*this information just wasn't being transmitted. But now that*
*everything's connected and it's unfiltered, you are now the*
*weakest link in the information chain, and that's a really*
*uncomfortable place to be."*

## THE LACK OF USER-CENTERED DESIGN

Roni Zeiger, who previously was Google's top physician and now runs a Web-based start-up that hosts communities of patients, attributes the remarkable level of clinician dissatisfaction to bad design. I asked Zeiger why health IT companies didn't pay more attention to the user's experience. "When you're building for experts, you don't think much about the user interface," he said. "The Wall Street guy using a spreadsheet will be fine as long as it works, no matter the design. But the mom using a photo-sharing program—it's got to be easy and intuitive. When health IT started, there was no consumer market. And medicine is an unusually expert-centric and somewhat arrogant field, so we were slow to embrace user-centered design."

Although he spends most of his time designing software, Zeiger still sees patients once a week at an urgent care clinic near his Silicon Valley office. And he's frustrated by what he sees. "Now is one of the worst times in history to be practicing medicine," he said. "We're the first generation that has to use these tools, and they suck. Some of the kinks are technical, and those are understandable. But the ones that are really problematic are the ones that owe to this lack of design thinking."

I asked him about Epic, the industry leader and the computer system he uses in his practice. He admires the company. "They are very smart, and they've built a great business. But they didn't really focus on what the customer—the doctor or the patient—needed to do the work."

This wasn't entirely the fault of the vendors, he added. While clinicians probably weren't asked what they wanted in a computer system, he said, "Had they been, they might not have been able to give an answer. Was it Epic's responsibility to teach their customers what they really wanted? Steve Jobs would say yes, but that's a lot to ask of a company."

He's right, of course. As Richard Baron discovered when his office practice went digital, it's awfully difficult for someone who has never practiced in a wired environment to appreciate that the technology might not just create a better way of doing the same work, but truly transform the nature of the work. This issue extends well beyond IT. Henry Ford is reputed to have said, "If I had asked people what they wanted, they would have said faster horses."

## RELATIONSHIPS

Steve Polevoi is the director of quality for the Emergency Department at UCSF Medical Center. In the predigital days, he told me, the ER nurses and doctors lived and breathed teamwork, constantly chatting as they went about their work. This was partly because the nurse would be the first to see the patient, and, if she had concerns, she would tell the doctor. Then the doctor would see the patient and, if he needed to order a test or have an IV started, he'd tell the nurse. Now everything gets reported and ordered in the EHR, and it's on to the next task.

Even worse, each "side" retreats to its own corner of the department to do its computer work. Walk around the ER and you'll see them: doctors and nurses, just inches away from each other, staring at their computers without exchanging a word. A 2014 study bore this out: implementation of the EHR was associated with a significant decrease in the quality of communication between doctors and nurses. James Stoller, chair of the Cleveland Clinic's Education Institute, has dubbed this phenomenon "electronic siloing." It's a version of what the radiologists experienced when their world went digital, and what Abraham Verghese saw when he found the wards at Stanford devoid of doctors.

All of these concerns became tragically concrete on September 28, 2014, when Thomas Duncan became the first patient in the United States to be diagnosed with Ebola. Three days earlier, Duncan, age 42, had come to the emergency room of Texas Health Presbyterian Medical Center in Dallas and was found to have a high fever and other symptoms consistent with, though certainly not diagnostic of, Ebola. A triage nurse obtained the history that Duncan had recently been in Liberia, the outbreak's epicenter, and recorded it in a note in the electronic health record. Unfortunately, the doctor who then saw Duncan remained unaware of the travel history and sent the patient home. In the days that followed, the patient exposed dozens of people to the virus.

Duncan returned to the hospital, desperately ill, on September 28 and was admitted. He died of Ebola 10 days after his admission. It's unclear whether the delayed diagnosis made a difference in his outcome, or whether it contributed to the spread of the virus to two nurses who cared for him.

On October 1, the hospital issued a statement, blaming its EHR (Epic) for the error because of "separate physician and nursing workflows." A day later, the hospital retracted this statement, saying there was nothing wrong with the computer system—the Liberian travel history was in the nurse's note and was completely accessible to the physician. It's just that the doctor didn't look at it, and the nurse didn't tap the physician on the shoulder and say, "Hey, the guy in Bed 4 has a temp of 103 and is just back from Liberia."

While the hospital was absolutely wrong to try to pin the problem on Epic, the computer *was* partly at fault, in a much more subtle way. In the modern emergency room, there's just not as much shoulder tapping as there used to be.

▶    ▶    ▶

Other industries have witnessed this phenomenon, too. Alan Jacobsen, a Boeing psychologist and human factors expert, recalls many flights that he took sitting in the jump seat of a DC-9, an old workhorse of a jet with virtually no automation. The pilot and copilot were engaged in constant conversation— much of it over navigation, since the copilot was poring over a paper map and there were an awful lot of decisions that required negotiation and judgment.

Today, when Jacobsen observes flight crews on modern, hyperautomated jetliners, he sees far less interaction. I asked him why this is a problem. After all, the computers are producing more accurate, less ambiguous information than the maps ever could, so wasn't there simply less to talk about? He replied, "One of the advantages of that interaction is that, if you encounter a nonnormal situation, there is a preexisting relationship. You don't have to devote as many resources to getting the team members on the same page." In medicine, where much of what we do is manage "nonnormal situations," the degree to which the EHR chips away at teamwork is a new, and largely unaddressed, hazard.

## THE FACELESS NOTE

Christine Sinsky, the Dubuque primary care doctor, told me about a patient of hers who had been seen in a local ER. She received this note summarizing the patient's history:

> *The patient presents with palpitations. The onset was just
> prior to arrival. The course/duration of symptoms is resolved.*

*Character of symptoms skipping beats. The degree at present*
*is none. The exacerbating factors is none. Risk factors consist*
*of none. Prior episodes: none. Therapy today: none. Associ-*
*ated symptoms: near syncope.*

If you can't really figure out what happened to this patient (yes, we know his heart was thumping and he nearly passed out), join the club. By dint of the use of checkboxes and pick lists, all hints of this patient's story have been stripped away, leaving a note that has been lobotomized—made more bland and far less interesting and useful.

John Birkmeyer, a prominent Dartmouth surgeon and researcher, recalled, in the days before EHRs, reading the notes from his clinic visits the night before taking patients into surgery. "I might have eight cases—this kind of hernia, that kind of hernia—I'd look at my notes, and I'd know who the patient was," he told me. "There was something about what I said in the notes—like, "His hernia is most bothersome with exertion, particularly when he plays tennis"—that I could attach to that patient and remember nuances about the person and the procedure." He continued:

*And then enters Epic, and I see the kinds of conditions that*
*are tailor-made for the system. I do the same procedures over*
*and over again, and so it's click right [for the side of the her-*
*nia] or left; autopopulate this; click him or her . . . and sud-*
*denly every one of my notes looks the same. Now when I show*
*up for surgery, it's useless to have read my notes beforehand*
*because every patient also looks exactly the same. It's like I*
*never saw them before. I can't even picture their faces.*

This checkbox mentality has even turned Larry Weed's beloved Problem-Oriented Medical Record—in which the patients' issues are articulated, assessed, and addressed—into a desiccated wasteland, devoid of thought or narrative arc. Part of the catch is that, while it is useful to enumerate problems one at a time, the real art of medical diagnosis comes in seeing the connections *between* problems—realizing that the patient's fever, heart murmur, and stroke, when woven together, add up to a diagnosis of bacterial endocarditis, an infection of a heart valve. Moreover, in addition to the clinical diagnosis, we need to consider each case in its context: that the patient is scared, her mother died of cancer at an early age, she can't afford her medications, and she has a teenager at home who's struggling with Asperger's. How, exactly, does one tell *that* story by robotically checking a bunch of electronic boxes?

All of this worked better when we did our documentation on paper, perhaps because we weren't so exhausted from all the thunderous clicks that we still had the time and energy to actually think about the case and the context. In 2012, I wrote that the electronic medical record needed one more field, which I called the über-assessment field. A mouse-over would reveal its instructions:

> *In this field, please tell the many people who are coming to see your patient—nurses, nutritionists, social workers, consultants, your attending—what the hell is going on. What are the major issues you're trying to address and the questions you're struggling to answer? Describe the patient's trajectory—is he or she getting better or worse? If worse (or not better), what are you doing to figure things out, and when might you rethink the diagnosis or your therapeutic approach and try something new? Please **do not** use this space to restate the narrow, one-problem-at-a-time-oriented approach you have so competently articulated in other parts of this record. We know that the patient has hypokalemia and that your plan is to replace the potassium. Use this section to be more synthetic, more novelistic, more imaginative, more expansive. Tell a story.*

## AN EPIDEMIC OF KWASHIORKOR

In January 2014, the U.S. Office of the Inspector General released the results of audits on two Catholic community hospitals, one in Des Moines, Iowa, and the other in Santa Fe, New Mexico. The OIG found that the hospitals had collectively overcharged Medicare $236,000 for cases billed as kwashiorkor, the rare belly-bloating form of profound malnutrition seen largely among children in famine-ravaged regions of sub-Saharan Africa. Shockingly, Medicare had paid out more than $700 million in hospital bills in 2010 and 2011 for cases that listed kwashiorkor as one of the diagnoses. The Des Moines and Santa Fe audits showed that (to no one's surprise) in none of the 217 "kwashiorkor" cases did patients actually have the dread disease, which rarely, if ever, occurs in developed countries.

How did this sham epidemic come about? Earlier, I described the way that physician and hospital billing generally work, with Medicare and private insurers paying based on the complexity of the diagnosis, along with the number of patient history facts (such as cough, belly pain, and blurry vision) and organs examined (heart, lungs, eyes, and the like) tallied on the page. It's a silly way to pay for healthcare and it's in the process of changing, but for now, it is what it is, and everybody knows the rules. EHR vendors, in marketing their products to hospitals (particularly to the finance folks, who ultimately need to sign the massive check), need to be sure that the systems are primed to maximize such reimbursement.

One of the touted selling points for EHRs prior to the $30 billion federal incentive program was the potential to save money: a 2005 RAND study estimated that wiring the United States healthcare system would save approximately $81 billion annually. But once EHRs were installed, Medicare found that hospitals with electronic systems often *increased* their billing by documenting more of the required tidbits, which then supported more lucrative diagnosis codes. In the days of pen and paper, hospitals were constantly "educating" their doctors: *remember to document the family history; remember to document at least nine organ systems on your physical exam; remember to call it "pneumosepsis" and not just "pneumonia."* But, because they could not review the paper chart until after the patient had been discharged, this education often had limited effect.

The EHR changed all that. Now, hospitals could install software to identify patients who appeared to have, let's say, malnutrition and a low blood protein level. The system, in turn, could then prompt the doctors or the coders to tag such cases as "kwashiorkor," and do so in real time. In their mea culpa letters to Medicare (which included refund checks for the overbilled amounts), both the Iowa and New Mexico hospitals blamed "computer errors." Well, sort of.

In addition to the "upcoding" of diagnoses like kwashiorkor, hospitals and doctors have also taken advantage of the other tools in EHRs to maximize their billing, in most cases quite legally. In what is considered a core function of EHR systems, one can no longer click past the family history or the "review of systems" without filling it in, and templated physical examinations allow a physician to populate a complete examination (*the lungs are clear to auscultation; the heart is regular without murmurs, rubs, and gallops; the abdomen is soft, nontender, and there is no hepatosplenomegaly*) with a single click. I hope you're appreciating the rich irony here: hospitals and doctors are using the Medicare subsidy (Medicare is the federal agency that doles out the HITECH dollars) to buy computer systems that allow them to bill Medicare more effectively.

Much of this reimbursement-maximizing activity probably represents accurate documentation of what really happened in the exam room; the EHRs have simply given physicians and hospitals an upper hand in this ludicrous but high-stakes cat-and-mouse game. "We're continuing to see the use of cut-and-paste in healthcare organizations because clinicians find it is one of the only ways they can manage the documentation process," said Michelle Dougherty, senior director of research and development at the American Health Information Management Association.

But, as the inspector general suspects, some of the notes have crossed the line from nonfiction to fiction. In a March 2014 post on the popular *KevinMD* blog, a premedical student working as an ER scribe (and writing anonymously, though believably) ticked off the many and varied effects of scribes: increased efficiency, higher patient satisfaction, increased profits. Then he listed a more disturbing one: "Increased fraud."

In the Epic system, clicking a little button documenting that the physician counseled the patient about quitting cigarettes generates an extra twenty or so dollars in payments from the insurance company. According to the scribe, physicians frequently tell him to click the button even when they have not performed any such counseling. When the scribe objects, "The physician responds, 'You probably just weren't paying attention.'" The scribe also told of the use of templates that documented head-to-toe physical examinations that, in some cases, never happened. "I know they did not counsel the patient. I know they did not ask for social history. I know they did not listen to the patient's heart rhythm or breath sounds."

"These are small, tiny transgressions," wrote the scribe. "But small things add up, and in the end, the burden of all this comes back onto the patient. More importantly, if thousands of small lies are okay and never brought to light, how many bigger lies are out there?"

While I understand the desire to just click the template (some physicians justify this as a victimless crime; many also feel that, if the patient isn't complaining of shortness of breath or cough, then the lungs probably *are* clear), this is still fraud, and it's wrong. That said, the root cause of all of it is the absurdity of the billing system. Perhaps this will be what causes Medicare and other insurers to replace the current system with one that moves us away from the need to document clinically irrelevant trivia in order to justify our time—ideally, in my view, with one in which physicians are paid a salary with incentives based on quality and patient satisfaction.

## DISTRACTIONS

Not only is the need to fill out all the fields and check the boxes annoying, but it is also distracting. In a 2013 study, Michigan State researchers assigned 300 volunteers to a complicated computer task, one that required the subjects to mentally keep track of their place in a sequence of events. The researchers then interrupted the volunteers with a quick additional task. When the interruption lasted for about 3 seconds, the rate of errors doubled. When it lasted for 4.4 seconds, the rate tripled. "What this means is that our health and safety is, on some level, contingent on whether the people looking after it have been interrupted," lead researcher Erik Altmann told the *Atlantic*.

This issue of distractions is, of course, well appreciated in aviation. In fact, one of the sacred rules of the field is known as the "Sterile Cockpit," which prohibits distractions, including conversations about matters other than flight safety, when the plane is flying at an altitude below 10,000 feet—generally during takeoff and landing.

Bob Myers, Boeing's chief flight deck engineer, told me how aviation safety engineers have held the line on distractions. "Airlines are always saying to the pilots, 'Can't you just document what time you took off, how much gas you had when you started and ended, did you have any passenger complaints?' We have been successful in defending our stance that pilots shouldn't do that stuff below 10,000 feet, and the FAA has supported this." I told Myers about the remarkable amount of documentation that physicians have to do, much of it in the middle of caring for sick patients. He was horrified. "That's the difference—when you're in the OR, or in with the patient, you're below 10,000 feet, and you shouldn't be doing that stuff."

Yet we do. Christine Sinsky can't help but wonder how much she misses while multitasking. She once nearly overlooked a patient's pulmonary embolism, as well as his underlying cancer, because she was trying to get her "electronic bearings," her own hard drive spinning from the demands of the electronic interface. "Remember to double click the first time you do a dictation, but only single click and then drag the bar when adding an addendum; otherwise you will erase your earlier dictation," she said in describing the tyranny of her EHR. "Twenty-one clicks and five screen changes are required to complete the billing invoice. Don't forget to add a 'P' for primary in front of one of the diagnoses, and don't include more than four diagnoses."

Moreover, in today's healthcare, distractions "below 10,000 feet" come in electronic forms other than the EHR. In a case published in a patient safety journal I edit, a resident was instructed by her attending physician to discontinue a patient's blood-thinning medication in anticipation of an upcoming invasive procedure. In this hospital, like many others, the electronic record can now be accessed from a tablet or smartphone, as well as a regular computer. The resident began to enter the "discontinue Coumadin" order into her phone when up popped a new text message—she was invited to a party that weekend! By the time she answered the text, the team had moved on to the next patient, and the resident forgot to stop the anticoagulant. The patient suffered an episode of bleeding around the heart that could have been fatal. As with so many aspects of our lives, the fact that our professional and personal worlds now coexist on our devices creates its own dangers.

## THE "PAPERLESS OFFICE"

On a warm summer morning in Dubuque, Iowa, I had a chance to watch Christine Sinsky as she cared for a half-dozen patients in her primary care practice. Thank goodness there are still doctors who want to do this difficult, undercompensated, and largely thankless work. The experience was at once inspiring and maddening.

Sinsky entered the small exam room in her Dubuque multispecialty office building. She is tall and slender, looking like the marathon runner that she is. One of her nurses accompanied her, serving as a scribe of sorts while also carrying out a number of other key activities. The nurse had already gathered some history before Sinsky entered the room to see her first patient, an elderly man with white hair and a pot belly; every Christmas, he plays a department store Santa. He was wearing a Harley-Davidson T-shirt that said "Motorcycles: Ride Free, Live Free." On the wall of the small room was a series of colorful posters, one showing the four food groups and another instructing people to wash their hands. A third showed a child's drawing of a bunch of flowers with the caption, "Don't regret growing old. It is a privilege denied to many."

Sinsky sat knee-to-knee with her patient. Her laptop was open on her desk, but she was working hard to maintain eye contact. After gathering some of

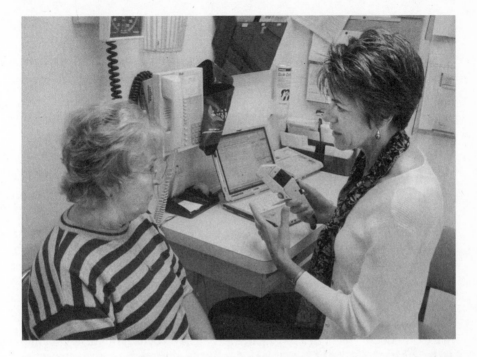

the history, she activated her computer's dictation system. Before she started, though, she turned to the patient. "I'm going to tell computer what we know so far," she said, and she began dictating into the laptop.

As both a primary care doctor and a consultant on practice redesign, Sinsky has done everything she can to make her office work effectively. She believes deeply in the collaborative care model, and she and her nurse work as a team to care for the patient and to produce the note. Unfortunately, the technology doesn't help here—both the EHR she uses and the regulations she operates under are obstacles to collaborative documentation; the work flow is built around the doctor doing nearly everything. Even when Sinsky simply wants the nurse to open a portion of the electronic chart so that Sinsky doesn't have to waste 90 seconds and 10 clicks getting to the right place, her organization's interpretation of the Meaningful Use rules prohibits this (though in the paper world, it was fine for someone else to open the chart to the appropriate page for the doctor).[10]

---

[10] Nothing in the federal regulations actually prohibits collaborative documentation. But compliance officers at Sinsky's clinic, like others elsewhere, have interpreted the rules conservatively, creating internal policies that further hamstring clinical practice. Here, they fear that a doctor will sign a chart with a rule violation created by a nurse's or clerk's action. The safest posture if you're a compliance officer is to make the doctor do everything.

Sinsky once pined for a paperless office and believed, naively, that she would have one once her practice computerized. Yet there is an extraordinary amount of paper floating around her clinic. Because the computer system doesn't allow Sinsky to navigate the patient's record in an intuitive way—namely, to listen and then record some patient history, then to flip to an old progress note and an x-ray or lab result, then to write an order for a new medication, and then to record a bit more history—her staff spends hours the day before every clinic session printing out most of the electronic record. It's the only way she can see what she needs to see. "I print out thousands of pages a day—well over a ream of paper—in preparing things for two doctors," Sinsky's nurse, Deb Althaus, told me.

In Sinsky's practice, which employs a system made by a company named McKesson, each physician spends, on average, seven minutes a day "refreshing" locked computer screens, ten minutes signing in repetitively, and thirteen minutes completing rote attestations (for example, of dictations done in prior sessions). Creating an electronic invoice takes a minute for each patient, with 21 clicks, eight scrolls up and down, and five screen changes. With a primary care doctor seeing 20 to 30 patients in a day, you can do the depressing math. Sinsky estimates that at least half her day is now spent on such clerical activities.

## ERROR-PRONE INTERFACES, AND THE SYSTEM'S RESPONSE

Ross Koppel, the Penn sociologist, has spent the past decade observing IT systems. While he believes the potential for benefit is large, he has observed a galaxy of glitches: lab results buried in screens filled with irrelevant data; endless scrolling required to find information that should be contiguous; dropdown menus missing essential options or offering irrational ones; identical icons (say, an image of a pen) representing several different actions. In a 2012 article, Koppel added, "Sign-ons and sign-offs vary by sub-menu within the same system (i.e., 'end,' 'finish,' 'submit,' 'quit,' 'done,' 'next') and can all do very different things, some with dire consequences for patients." Even more worrisome, he noted, "Physicians who voice such observations are labeled technophobic, resistant, and uncooperative."

The latter point is important. Christine Sinsky told me about an alert built into her hospital's IT system, which was made by Cerner (note that it's a completely different system from the one she uses in her clinic, which poses another problem, since relatively little information flows between the two).

The alert is designed to remind physicians to give a blood thinner to hospitalized patients at risk for deep-venous thrombosis (DVT, blood clots in the legs that can break off to cause a life-threatening pulmonary embolism). So far, so good—this is an important preventive activity, and we docs, humans that we are, periodically forget such things.

The problem is that the computer presents this reminder even when the patient is already on a blood thinner or has a preexisting clotting disorder. I didn't fret too much when she described this glitch to me. While it would be ideal if the computer realized that a patient who is already anticoagulated (information that the system already "knows") shouldn't receive another blood thinner, surely, I thought, you can easily silence the alert, perhaps by clicking a simple "patient is already anticoagulated" box.

But you can't. In fact, the only way to quash the insistent alert is to go through a six-step process that culminates in the physician's *actually ordering the second blood thinner*—which, if it were administered and the patient bled, would represent malpractice—and then (if the physician remembers to do so) going back into the orders module to electronically cancel the second drug.

Seriously.

Sinsky brought up this problem with her hospital system's chief medical information officer. She is one of the most reasonable people I know, and her note to the CMIO was respectful and well articulated. Yet the response was belittling and unhelpful: "The Advisor [the name of the alert system] is now up across Trinity [her healthcare system] and working well. What specifically is not working for you?"

Nearly a year later, the problem persisted.

"I used to complete many 'near miss' forms or call up hospital IT personnel out of a desire to make the system safer for patients," she said. "I eventually realized that such efforts not only were futile, but were harming me politically. The user is almost always blamed and risks overt or covert retaliation."

I heard several stories like this: clinicians who tried to notify their hospitals and clinics about poorly designed, even dangerous, interfaces, but who found themselves rebuffed or even ostracized. Gordon Schiff had a similar experience soon after he took a faculty position at Boston's Brigham & Women's Hospital, one of Harvard's crown jewels. For more than a decade, the hospital has used a home-built system (it recently switched to Epic because of the growing costs of maintaining its own system). Schiff is a primary care physician and a patient safety expert; he has even studied safety issues in information technology. He found Brigham's homegrown EHR adequate, but periodically he'd identify a problem. "When I had a question, I'd pick up the phone and say, 'Look, this screen doesn't make sense. How do I order this?' or 'Where do you find that?'"

He phoned the help desk two or three times a week, yet little changed. Finally, after a few months of this, he received a call from the IT supervisor. "He told me that I was harassing the help desk, bothering them. I sincerely thought I was helping them."

Schiff spent his early years at Cook County Hospital in Chicago, and has a long history of political activism. But the buttoned-down Brigham is a world away from the freewheeling, We're-Doing-God's-Work zeal of Cook County. "I was very bruised," he said. "At Cook, I would have started a petition or passed a resolution of the medical staff. Here, I just hid my tail between my legs." And, of course, the system went unfixed.

## HOLD HARMLESS AND NONDISCLOSURE CLAUSES

Building and installing a healthcare IT system is so complicated that nobody can reasonably expect perfection straight out of the box. Precisely because of this, it's vital that both vendors and local IT departments welcome feedback and respond to it appropriately. As Schiff and Sinsky's experiences illustrate, this is often not the case, for myriad reasons. It could be that the local department is overwhelmed or lacks the skills to manage the issues. Or that concerns raised by clinicians represent personal preferences or a failure to read the manual or take the training seriously. Or perhaps a CIO convinced an organization to spend hundreds of millions of dollars for a given system and is less than enthusiastic about learning of its shortcomings. Or maybe it just isn't clear who is responsible for the fix: the local IT department or the software company that sold and installed the system.

The obstacles that stand in the way of information sharing are one of a list of health IT concerns voiced by Ross Koppel, the University of Pennsylvania sociologist. Over the past 15 years, Koppel has brought an ethnographer's eye to observing physicians and nurses as they use their electronic health records, emerging as health IT's most vocal—and credible—critic. Unlike some of the more fringe figures in the field, he is a well-respected academic and far from a Luddite.

Koppel told me that he had not intended to take on the role of gadfly. In principle, he is an advocate of health technology; he feels that a return to paper would be "insane." But he wants "good health IT," and what he has seen over the years has provoked him to take a hard line. He is terribly bothered by the kind of local roadblocks experienced by Sinsky and Schiff. But he reserves his harshest words for the technology vendors. "If I had seen the vendors being more responsive to the needs of clinicians, rather than saying, 'I'm sorry, that will be in the next upgrade,' I don't think any of my passion would have been aroused. I would have said, 'Leave them alone.'"

In a controversial 2009 article in the *Journal of the American Medical Association*, Koppel exposed a dark underbelly of the health IT industry. He and coauthor David Kreda claimed that "Healthcare IT vendors enjoy a contractual and legal structure that renders them virtually liability free—'hold harmless' is the term of art—even when their proprietary products may be implicated in adverse events involving patients."

The legal principle is known as "learned intermediaries"—in this case medical experts, who, the theory goes, are in the best position to make an informed medical judgment regarding the best care to render based on their deep knowledge of both the patient and medical practice. The vendors' case seems like a version of the "guns don't kill people, people kill people" argument: errors reflect poor implementation practices or screwups by users. This is certainly true at times, but, as you've seen, there are scores of errors that are all but inevitable given clunky software, including poor user interfaces. It seems right that the vendors would at least share responsibility if patients were harmed in such circumstances.

On top of this, Koppel and Kreda described contracts that prohibit users from discussing a product's flaws in open forums, or even sharing screen shots.[11] I asked Koppel how the nondisclosure agreements work in some of these contracts.

> Nondisclosure says that you can't say or display anything that speaks badly about their software. You, Bob, can turn to the doctor next to you and say, 'Hey, Sam, look at this fucked-up screen.' You can write into a vendor's listserv and say, 'Boy, I can't find my labs.' But if you took a screen shot and sent that to a medical society or even wrote an e-mail to the members of your society, you could be sued for millions.

---

[11] Epic denies having ever had gag clauses in its contracts. Athenahealth, another EHR vendor, actually carries malpractice insurance; its CEO, Jonathan Bush, told me that "we *do* practice medicine." In 2013, a vendor association supported by the Office of the National Coordinator for Health Information Technology (ONC) issued a "Code of Conduct" that commits vendors to "not contractually limit our customers from discussing patient safety issues in appropriate venues." The definition of such venues is vague—I was required to obtain Epic's permission to share the screen shots you'll see in the coming chapters as I describe a medical error that relates, at least in part, to its EHR.

In this, we see a tension that is unique to the electronic health record. If EHRs were purely business applications, chronicling transactions between corporations, then the enforced nonsharing of their flaws might seem natural, comporting with industry standards. After all, there is intellectual property to protect and competitors to keep at bay.

But EHRs are *not* simply business applications—they have become the tools that we use to take care of our patients. Seen in that light, we'd want as much sharing as possible about those things that work and, especially, about those that don't. This too represents an industry norm—when the industry is healthcare, where we routinely present cases of harm in conferences and even write them up in our journals in order to learn and improve. In my view, it is high time that we reconciled these conflicting worldviews and threw our weight behind the transparency we need to keep patients safe.

# Part Two

# Decisions and Data

# Chapter 9

# Can Computers Replace
the Physician's Brain?

Any doctor who could be replaced by a computer should be.
—Warner Slack, Harvard informatics expert

One of my favorite (albeit disorienting) days in researching this book occurred on April 29, 2014, when I interviewed two brilliant, immensely successful 59-year-old Indian Americans, one after the other. The first, physician-author Abraham Verghese, emphasized the essential role of the doctor in both diagnosis and counseling. A few minutes with the charming and persuasive Verghese is enough to convince anyone that the practice of medicine is an utterly human enterprise.

I left Verghese at his Stanford office and drove two miles to the opulent headquarters of Vinod Khosla, a cofounder of Sun Microsystems who is now a prominent venture capitalist. Since 2012, Khosla has been predicting that most of what physicians currently do can, will, and should be done by computers. "By 2025," he has written, "more data-driven, automated healthcare will displace up to 80 percent of physicians' diagnostic and prescription work."[12]

Though Khosla's comments have irked many a physician, I'm not willing to dismiss him as a kooky provocateur or a utopian techno-evangelist. First of

---

[12] Khosla later softened his prediction slightly, writing in 2014, "This is not to say that 80 percent of physicians will be replaced, but rather 80 percent of what they currently do might be replaced, leading to new possibilities and functions for the physicians."

all, his investment track record has made him a Silicon Valley rock star. More important, as recently as a decade ago, some very smart and savvy computer engineers and economists believed that another seemingly intractable problem, building a driverless car, was beyond the reach of modern technology. Just consider the challenges: a kid running into the street after a soccer ball; a texting teenager swerving in the middle lane; a traffic light on the fritz.

And the left turn. "Executing a left turn across oncoming traffic," two highly respected economists, MIT's Frank Levy and Harvard's Richard Murnane, wrote in 2004, "involves so many factors that it is hard to imagine the set of rules that can replicate a driver's behavior." Yet six years later, Google's unveiling of its driverless car demonstrated that this "insoluble problem" had been solved. As of April 2014, the Google car had clocked nearly 700,000 miles and been involved in two accidents. One reportedly occurred after a human took over the wheel, and the other when the Google car was rear-ended by, one presumes, another human driver. The driverless car might well be safer than one controlled by a fallible *Homo sapiens*.

If the driverless car weren't enough of a challenge to human superiority, who could have watched IBM's Watson supercomputer defeat the *Jeopardy* Hall of Famers in 2011 and not fretted about the future of physicians, or any highly skilled workers, for that matter? "Just as factory jobs were eliminated in the twentieth century by new assembly-line robots," wrote all-time (human) *Jeopardy* champion Ken Jennings soon after the lopsided match ended, "Brad [Rutter, the other defeated champ] and I were the first knowledge-industry workers put out of work by the new generation of 'thinking' machines. 'Quiz show contestant' may be the first job made redundant by Watson, but I'm sure it won't be the last."

Soon after the well-publicized trouncing, IBM announced that one of its first "use cases" for Watson would be medicine. Sean Hogan, vice president for IBM Healthcare, told me that "healthcare jumped out as an area whose complexity and nuances would be receptive to what Watson was representing."

▶   ▶   ▶

Andy McAfee, coauthor with Erik Brynjolfsson of the terrific book *The Second Machine Age*, agrees with Khosla that computers will ultimately take over much of what physicians do, including diagnosis. "I can't see how that *doesn't* happen," McAfee, a self-described "technology optimist," told me when we met for lunch near his MIT office. McAfee and Brynjolfsson argue that the confluence of staggering growth in computing power, zetabytes of fully networked information available on the Web, and the "combinatorial power" of innovation mean that areas that seemed like dead ends, such as artificial intelligence in medicine, are now within reach. They liken the speed with which old digital barriers are falling to Hemingway's observation about how a person goes broke: "gradually, then suddenly."

In speaking with both McAfee and Khosla, I felt a strange obligation to stick up for my teams: humans and the subset of humans called doctors. I told McAfee that while I was in awe of the driverless car and IBM's victories in chess (over world champion Garry Kasparov in 1997) and *Jeopardy*, he just didn't understand how *hard* medicine is. Answering questions posed by Alex Trebek like, "While Maltese borrows many words from Italian, it developed from a dialect of this Semitic language" (the correct response is "What is Arabic?"—Watson answered it, and 65 of the 74 other questions it rang in for, correctly) is tricky, sure, but, at the end of the day, one is simply culling a series of databases to find a fact—a single right answer.

Medical diagnosis isn't like that. For one thing, uncertainty is endemic, so that the "correct" answer is often a surprisingly probabilistic notion. For another, many diagnoses reveal themselves over time. The patient may present with, say, a headache, but not a worrisome one, and so the primary treatment is reassurance, Tylenol, and time. If the headache worsens over the next two weeks—particularly if it is now accompanied by additional symptoms such as weakness or nausea—that's an entirely different story.

McAfee listened sympathetically—he's obviously heard scores of versions of the *You just don't understand; my work is different* argument—and then said, "I imagine there are a bunch of really smart geeks at IBM taking notes as guys like you describe this situation. In their heads, they're asking, 'How do I model that?'"

Undaunted, I tried another tack on Khosla when we met in his office in Menlo Park. "Vinod," I said, "in medicine we have something we call the 'eyeball test.' That means I can see two patients whose numbers look the same"—things like temperature, heart rate, and blood counts—"and my training allows me to say, 'That guy is sick [I pointed to an imaginary person across the imposing conference table] and the other is okay.'" And good doctors are usually right, I told him, as we possess a kind of sixth sense that we acquire from our training, our role models, and a thousand cases of trial and error.

Before Khosla could dismiss this as the usual whining from a dinosaur on the edge of extinction, I tossed him an example from his own world. "I'll bet you have CEOs of start-ups constantly coming through this office pitching their companies," I said. "I can imagine two companies that look the same on paper: both CEOs have Stanford MBAs; the proposals have similar financials. Your skill is to be able to point to one and say, 'Winner' and to the other, 'Loser,' and I'm guessing you're right more often than not. You're using information that isn't measurable. Right?"

Nice try. He didn't budge. "The question is, 'Is it not measurable or is it not being measured?'" he responded. "And, when does your instinct work and when does it mislead? I think if you did a rigorous study, you'd find that your 'eyeball test' is far less effective than you think."

▶   ▶   ▶

The Man Versus Machine argument is well-trod terrain, and it is usually put to rest with an "and," not an "or." In many fields, the best results seem to occur when computers and people work together, taking advantage of our complementary strengths. In healthcare, the arguments are particularly interesting and charged because of the height of the stakes, the complexity of the human condition, and medicine's unique demands to blend the technical, scientific matters of diagnosis and treatment with deeply moral and philosophical questions that are not really in play when the challenge is finding a hotel room, picking a stock, or making a left turn.

There is a rich 50-year history of efforts to build artificial intelligence (AI) systems in healthcare, and it's not a particularly uplifting story. Even technophiles admit that the quest to replace doctors with computers—or even the more modest ambition of providing them with useful guidance at the point of care—has been overhyped and unproductive. But times have changed. The growing prevalence of electronic health records offers grist for the AI and big-data mills, grist that wasn't available when the records were on paper. And in this, the Age of Watson, we have new techniques, like natural language processing and machine learning, at our disposal. Perhaps this is *our* "gradually, then suddenly" moment.

▶   ▶   ▶

The public worships dynamic, innovative surgeons like Michael DeBakey; passionate, insightful researchers like Jonas Salk; and telegenic show horses like Mehmet Oz. But we seldom hear about those doctors whom other physicians tend to hold in the highest esteem: the great medical diagnosticians. These sages, like the legendary Johns Hopkins professors William Osler and A. McGehee Harvey, had the uncanny ability to deduce the truth from what others found to be a jumble of symptoms, signs, and lab results. In fact, Sir Arthur Conan Doyle, a physician by training, modeled Sherlock Holmes on one of his old professors, Joseph Bell, a renowned diagnostician at Edinburgh's medical school.

For most doctors, diagnosis forms the essence of their practice (and of their professional souls), which may help explain why we find it so painful to believe that this particular skill could be replaced by silicon wafers. The late Yale surgeon Sherwin Nuland called the elusive diagnosis "The Riddle" and, in his masterful book *How We Die*, wrote of it with near-religious reverence:

> *I capitalize it so there will be no mistaking its dominance over every other consideration. The satisfaction of solving The Riddle is its own reward, and the fuel that drives the clinical engines of medicine's most highly trained specialists. It is every doctor's measure of his own abilities; it is the most important ingredient in his professional self-image.*

In the 1970s, a Tufts kidney specialist named Jerome Kassirer (who later became editor of the *New England Journal of Medicine*) decided to try to unlock the cognitive secrets of the great diagnosticians. If he succeeded, the rewards could be great. The insights, problem-solving strategies, and reasoning patterns of these medical geniuses might be teachable to other physicians, perhaps even programmed into computers.

Kassirer focused first on the differential diagnosis, the method that doctors have long used to inventory and sort through their patients' problems. The differential diagnosis is to a physician what the building of hypotheses is to a basic scientist: the core work of the professional mind. Let's say a female patient complains of right lower abdominal pain and fever. We automatically begin to generate "a differential," including appendicitis, pelvic inflammatory disease, kidney infection, and a host of less common disorders—some of them quite serious. Our job is to weigh the facts at hand in an effort to ultimately "rule in" one diagnosis on the list and "rule out" the others. Sometimes, the information we gather from the history and physical examination is sufficient. More often, particularly when patients are truly ill, we require additional laboratory or radiographic studies to push one of the diagnoses over the "rule in" line.

There is considerable skill, and no small amount of art, involved in this process. For one thing, we need to figure out whether the patient's symptoms are part of a single disease or are manifestations of two or more distinct illnesses. The principle known as Occam's Razor bids us to try to find a unifying diagnosis for all of a patient's symptoms. But as soon as medical students memorize this so-called Law of Clinical Parsimony, we whipsaw them with Hickam's Dictum, which counters, irreverently, that "patients can have as many diseases as they damn well please."

Setting the "rule in" threshold is yet another challenge, since it's wholly dependent on the context. For diseases with relatively benign treatments and prognoses—let's say, stomach discomfort with no alarming features—I might make the diagnosis of "nonulcer dyspepsia" if I'm 75 percent certain that this is what's going on. Why? Dyspepsia is a not-too-serious illness, the other illnesses that might present with the same symptoms aren't likely to be acutely life-threatening either, and dyspepsia has a safe, inexpensive, and fairly effective treatment. All of this makes a 75 percent threshold high enough for me to try an acid-blocker and see what happens.

Now let's turn to a patient who presents with acute shortness of breath and pleuritic chest pain. In this patient, I'm considering the diagnosis of pulmonary embolism (a blood clot to the lungs), a more serious disorder whose treatment (blood thinners) is riskier. Now, I'd want to be at least 95 percent sure before attaching that diagnostic label. And I won't rule in a diagnosis of cancer—with its psychological freight, prognostic implications, and toxic treatments—unless I'm close to 100 percent certain, even if it takes a surgical biopsy to achieve this level of confidence.

Kassirer and his colleagues observed the diagnostic reasoning of scores of clinicians. They found that the good ones employed robust strategies to answer these knotty questions, even if they couldn't always articulate what they were doing and why. The researchers ultimately came to appreciate that the physicians were engaging in a process called "iterative hypothesis testing" to transform the differential diagnosis (or, more accurately, diagnoses, since sick patients often have a variety of abnormalities to be explained) into something actionable. After hearing the initial portion of a case, the doctors began drawing possible scenarios to explain it, modifying their opinions as they went along and more information became available.

For example, when a physician confronts a case that begins with, "This 57-year-old man has three days of chest pain, shortness of breath, and light-headedness," she responds by thinking, "The worst thing this could be is a heart attack or a pulmonary embolism. I need to ask if the chest pain bores through to the back, which would make me worry about aortic dissection [a rip in the aorta]. I'll also inquire about typical cardiac symptoms, such as sweating and nausea, and see if the pain is squeezing or radiates to the left arm or jaw. But even if it doesn't, I'll certainly get an EKG to rule out a heart attack or pericarditis [inflammation of the sac that surrounds the heart]. If he also reports a fever or a cough, I might begin to suspect pneumonia or pleurisy. The chest x-ray should help sort that out."

Every answer the patient gives, and each positive or negative finding on the physical examination (*yes, there is a heart murmur; no, the liver is not enlarged*) triggers an automatic, almost intuitive recalibration of the most likely alternatives. When I see a master clinician at work—my favorite is my UCSF colleague Gurpreet Dhaliwal, who was profiled in a 2012 *New York Times* article—I know that these synapses are firing as he asks a patient a series of questions that may seem unrelated to the patient's presenting complaint but are directed toward "narrowing the differential."

It turns out that there's an even more impressive piece of cognitive magic going on. The master clinician embraces certain pieces of data (the patient's trip to rural Thailand last year) while discarding others (an episode of belly pain and bloating three weeks ago). This is the part of diagnostic reasoning that beginners find most vexing, since they lack the foundational knowledge to understand why their teacher focused so intently on one nugget of information and all but ignored others that, to the novice, seemed equally crucial. How do the great diagnosticians make such choices?

We now recognize this as a relatively intuitive version of Bayes' theorem. Developed by the eighteenth-century British theologian-turned-mathematician Thomas Bayes, this theorem (often ignored by students because it is taught to them with the dryness of a Passover matzo) is the linchpin of clinical reasoning. In essence, Bayes' theorem says that any medical test must be interpreted from two perspectives. The first: How accurate is the test—that is, how often does it give right or wrong answers? The second: How likely is it that this patient has the disease the test is looking for?

These deceptively simple questions explain why, in the early days of the AIDS epidemic (when HIV testing was far less accurate than it is today), it was silly to test heterosexual couples applying for a marriage license, since the vast majority of positive tests in this very low-risk group would be wrong. Similarly, they show why it is foolish to screen healthy 36-year-old executives with a cardiac treadmill test or a heart scan, since positive results will mostly be false positives, serving only to scare the bejesus out of the patients and run up bills for unnecessary follow-up tests. Conversely, in a 68-year-old smoker with diabetes and high cholesterol who develops squeezing chest pain while jogging, there is a 95 percent chance that those pains are from coronary artery disease. In this case, a negative treadmill test only lowers this probability to about 80 percent, so the clinician who reassures the patient that his negative test means that his heart is fine—"take some antacids; it's OK to keep jogging"—is making a terrible, and potentially fatal, mistake.

As if this weren't complicated enough for the poor IBM engineer gearing up to retool Watson from answering questions about "Potent Potables" to diagnosing sick patients, there's more. While the EHR at least offers a fighting chance for computerized diagnosis (older medical AI programs, built in the pen-and-paper era, required busy physicians to write their notes and then reenter all the key data), parsing an electronic medical record is far from straightforward. Natural language processing is getting much better, but it still has real problems with negation ("the patient has *no* history of chest pain or cough") and with family history ("there is a history of arthritis in the patient's sister, but his mother is well"), to name just a couple of issues. Certain terms have multiple meanings: when written by a psychiatrist, the term *depression* is likely to refer to a mood disorder, while when it appears in a cardiologist's note ("there was no evidence of ST-depression") it probably refers to a dip in the EKG tracing that is often a clue to coronary disease. Ditto abbreviations: Does the patient with "MS" have multiple sclerosis or mitral stenosis, a sticky heart valve? Finally, the computer can't read a patient's tone of voice or the anxious look on her face, although engineers are working on this. These clues—like one patient saying, "I have chest pain," and another, "I HAVE CHEST PAIN!!!"—can make all the difference in the world diagnostically.

Perhaps the trickiest problem of all is that—at least today—the very collection of the facts needed to feed an AI system is itself a cognitively complex process. Let's return to the example of aortic dissection, a rip in the aorta that is often fatal if it is not treated promptly. If the initial history raises the slightest concern about dissection, I'm going to ask questions about whether the pain bores through to the back and check carefully for the quiet murmur of aortic insufficiency as well as for asymmetric blood pressure readings in the two arms, all clues to dissection. If I don't harbor a suspicion of this scary (and unusual) disease, I'm not going to look for these things—they're not part of a routine exam.

Decades ago, MIT's Peter Szolovits, an AI expert who worked with Kassirer and his colleagues in the early days, gave up thinking about diagnosis as a simple matter of question answering. This was mostly because he came to appreciate the importance of timing—a nonissue in *Jeopardy* but a pivotal one in medicine. "A heart attack that happened five years ago has different implications from one that happened five minutes ago," he explained, and a computer can't "know" this unless it is programmed to do so. (It turns out that such issues of foundational knowledge are fundamental in AI—computers have no way of "knowing" some of the basic assumptions that allow us to get through our days, things like *water is wet, love is good,* and *death is permanent.*)

Moreover, much of medical reasoning relies on feedback loops: observing how events unfold and using *that* information to refine the diagnostic possibilities. We think a patient has bacterial pneumonia, and so we treat the "pneumonia" with antibiotics, but the patient's fever doesn't break after three days. So now we consider the possibility of tuberculosis or lupus. This is the cognitive work of the practicing clinician—focused a bit less on "What is the diagnosis?" and more on "How do I best manage this situation?"—and an AI program that doesn't account for this will be of limited value.

▶   ▶   ▶

Now that you appreciate the nature of the problem, it's easy (in retrospect, at least) to see why the choice by early healthcare computer experts to focus on diagnosis was risky, perhaps even wrongheaded. It's like tackling Saturday's crossword puzzle in the *New York Times* before first mastering the one in *USA Today*. Larry Fagan, an early Stanford computing pioneer, told me, "We were not naive about the complexity. It's just that it was the most exciting question."

Diagnosis is not just exciting, it's at the heart of safe medical care. Diagnostic errors are common, and they can be fatal. A number of autopsy studies conducted over the past 40 years have shown that major diagnoses were overlooked in nearly one in five patients. With the advent of CT scans and MRIs, the number has gone down a bit, but it still hovers around one in ten. Diagnostic errors contribute to 40,000 to 80,000 deaths per year in the United States. And reviews of malpractice cases have demonstrated that diagnostic errors are the most common source of mistakes leading to successful lawsuits.

Medical IT experts jumped into the fray in the 1970s, designing a series of computer programs that they believed could help physicians be better diagnosticians, or perhaps even replace them entirely. That decade's literature was replete with enthusiastic articles about how microprocessors, programmed to think like experts, would soon replace the brains of harried doctors. The attitude was captured by one early computing pioneer in a 1971 paean to his computer: "It is immune from fatigue and carelessness; and it works day and night, weekends and holidays, without coffee breaks, overtime, fringe benefits or human courtesy."

By the mid-1980s, disappointment had set in. The tools that had seemed so promising a decade earlier were, by and large, unable to manage the complexity of clinical medicine, and they garnered few clinician advocates and miniscule commercial adoption. The medical AI movement skidded to a halt, marking the start of a 20-year period that insiders still refer to as the "AI winter." Ted Shortliffe, one of the field's longstanding leaders, has said that the early experience with programs like INTERNIST, DXplain, and MYCIN reminded him of a cartoon that showed an obviously distressed patient who had just been interviewed by a physician. Evidently the poor man had come from an archery field, because protruding from his back was a two-foot-long arrow. The doctor had turned to his office computer and, after examining the screen, proclaimed, "Rapid pulse, sweating, shallow breathing. . . . According to the computer, you've got gallstones."

Vinod Khosla is prepared for this. He knows that even today's generation of medical AI programs will produce some crazy output, akin to when Watson famously mistook Toronto for an American city during its *Jeopardy* triumph. (It was worse in rehearsal, when Watson referred to civil rights leader Malcolm X as "Malcolm Ten.") Khosla points out that the enormous cellphones of the late 1980s would seem equally ridiculous when placed alongside our iPhone 6.0s. He calls today's medical AI programs "Version 0," and cautions that people should "expect these early systems and tools to be the butt of jokes from many a writer and physician."

▶   ▶   ▶

In retrospect, one of the problems with the early AI programs was that they tried to think like clinicians, creating thousands of little rules ("when the urine dipstick tests positive for blood, it is probably a kidney or bladder problem, but if the microscopic exam shows no red blood cells, it might be myoglobinuria, so check a CK level") and articulating all of them in a series of if/then statements. This rapidly proved to be untenable. For one thing, as you saw with Occam's Razor and Hickam's Dictum, our rules sometimes conflict with each other, requiring a human tiebreaker.

Moreover, clinical medicine is a tree with tens of thousands of diagnostic branches, and "rules-based programming" rapidly runs into trouble as it tries to climb that particular tree. AI experts came to realize that the only hope for tackling a field as complex as medicine was to switch paradigms. And that's precisely what happened: the breakthroughs that paved the way for IBM's chess and *Jeopardy* victories were less about teaching the computer how these games are played and more about feeding millions of facts and situations into it, and then programming it to identify the ones associated with success. By this logic, Watson really never learned to "play" *Jeopardy*. Instead, it used its bottomless memory, natural language analytic abilities, and prodigious processing power to identify patterns of words and concepts that in prior games were judged to be either correct or wrong. Armed with this knowledge, the engineers then "tuned" the algorithms with an eye toward winning future games.

These cases illustrate a perennial debate in AI, one that pits two camps against each other: the "neats" and the "scruffies." The neats seek solutions that are elegant and provable; they try to model the way experts think and work, and then code that into AI tools. The scruffies are the pragmatists, the hackers, the crazy ones; they believe that problems should be attacked through whatever means work, and that modeling the behavior of experts or the scientific truth of a situation isn't all that important. IBM's breakthrough was to figure out that a combination of neat and scruffy—programming in some of the core rules of the game, but then folding in the fruits of machine learning and natural language processing—could solve truly complicated problems. When he was asked about the difference between human thinking and Watson's method, Eric Brown, who runs IBM's Watson Technologies group, gave a careful answer (note the shout-out to the humans, the bit players who made it all possible):

> *A lot of the way that Watson works is motivated by the way that humans analyze problems and go about trying to find solutions, especially when it comes to dealing with complex problems where there are a number of intermediate steps to get you to the final answer. So it certainly is inspired by that process. . . . But a lot of it is different from the ways humans work; it tends to leverage the powers and advantages of a computer system, and its ability to rapidly analyze huge amounts of data and text that humans just can't keep track of.*

However Watson works, we find ourselves today in a world with new tools, new mental models, and a new sense of optimism that computers can do pretty much anything. But have we finally reached the age when computers can master the art of clinical reasoning? Let's take a closer look at Watson, and at a tiny competitor that has taken a different approach.

# Chapter 10

# David and Goliath

There is a science in what we do, yes, but also habit, intuition, and sometimes plain old guessing.

—Atul Gawande, *Complications: A Surgeon's Notes on an Imperfect Science*

When IBM announced that Watson's first post-*Jeopardy* focus would be healthcare, the media immediately ran with the Man Versus Machine meme, dubbing the computer "Dr. Watson." "Meet Dr. Watson: *Jeopardy* Winning Supercomputer Heads into Healthcare," proclaimed one headline. "Paging Dr. Watson: IBM's Medical Advisor for the Future," read another.

IBMers immediately steered clear of the "Dr. Watson" narrative, with its implied cockiness and gauntlet throwing. Paul Grundy, IBM's global director of healthcare transformation, told me: "Certainly none of us on the clinical side ever talked about this being Dr. Watson. That's not what it does." Added Michael Weiner, who runs IBM's healthcare strategies: "Sure, we said, 'Look, a machine beat a man at a quiz show,' but I don't think that's the power of this conversation. I think the power is what man and machine can accomplish together in the healthcare space. I think that is what's going to knock everybody's socks off."

Having heard versions of this from five different IBM physicians and engineers—all using similar language—I can only assume that "It's not Dr.

Watson!" appears at the top of the company's *Watson Talking Points* memo. Why? I'm guessing that the reasons are part historical, part business, part legal, and part technical.

Historical: the company is well aware of the history of overpromising and underdelivering in medical AI and doesn't want to play into another cycle of hype. Business: IBM will be selling to organizations filled with and, in some cases, run by doctors, and getting into a shooting match with your client is generally a bad sales strategy. Legal: if Watson is merely a tool, an aid to physicians, it may succeed in steering clear of liability when something goes wrong (a version of the "hold harmless" issue). Technical: it appears that the Watson folks generally do appreciate the complexity of medical diagnosis. Even if IBM's ultimate goal is to replace doctors, for now, the engineers need doctors to teach them how to do that. In fact, at the Cleveland Clinic, Watson is being put through its paces in a way that simulates going to medical school. "Watson learns," said Grundy. "It needs to interact with doctors, to be part of an ecosystem in which they're involved."

▶    ▶    ▶

While Watson has received much of the press, well before the *Jeopardy* challenge, a scrappy London start-up, motivated by the near-death of a child, was already trying to solve the problem of AI-based diagnosis. The name of the child, and the software, is Isabel.

It wasn't in Jason Maude's life plan to get into the computerized diagnostic business, or the healthcare business at all, for that matter. In 1999, he was a successful London financier—the head of equity research for the global firm AXA Investment Managers—when his three-year-old daughter, Isabel, came down with chicken pox. She received the usual treatments, but her condition kept deteriorating. Isabel's physicians told Maude that such changes were still consistent with the original diagnosis of chicken pox. But they were wrong. The doctors had missed a second diagnosis: necrotizing fasciitis, a life-threatening flesh-eating infection. Isabel ended up requiring emergency surgery, suffered the shutdown of multiple organs, and had a long and stormy stay in a London ICU. Fortunately, she lived and is doing reasonably well at age 19, although she still requires ongoing reconstructive surgeries.

When I met with him in London in the spring of 2014, Maude told me that there were three things that convinced him to try to build a new kind of diagnostic software. First, during Isabel's hospitalization, he was amazed that the doctors weren't using computers to prompt them to consider all possible diagnoses. Second, "medicine is beautifully written down. There are very few industries that have textbooks, journals, and all this data on the Internet." And third, "from my background in finance, I knew about some clever searching software."

I asked Maude whether he was aware of the AI winter—the junkyard of failed computerized diagnostic programs built in the 1970s and 1980s—when he decided to build a medical AI program. He was, but he tried using one of the existing programs and thought, "Well, it's pretty rubbish." "I think I'm sort of naturally bloody-minded," he said, using the British slang for cantankerous. "I thought, 'I'm just going to make Isabel better.'" Joining the long line of people who have underappreciated the complexity of this problem, he predicted that his quest would take "maybe three to five years." Fifteen years later, he's still at it.

Although Isabel can now grab pieces of history from the notes in the EHR (the physician still needs to confirm that they are the correct ones), in the early days, it required doctors to enter the cardinal symptoms and signs, things like "crampy abdominal pain" and "persistent fevers." Everybody told Maude that doctors wouldn't take the time to enter these details. He knew his tool had to be efficient, but he also saw this argument as a red herring. "When a physician tells me, 'I don't have time,'" he said, "I think it's because you don't think it's important. People use Google, and they've got to enter things into the search box."

This issue lies at the heart of an important conundrum in medicine—not so much about information technology or AI, but about how we measure and reward quality. Over the past decade, there has been a movement to jettison our traditional system of paying for *things* (visits, surgeries, x-rays, and the like) in favor of paying for *performance*. With that has come a profusion of quality measures—which, as you've learned, is partly what is driving physicians crazy with their EHRs, as their systems are forcing them to record these measures, not just for billing, but to be sure they get top grades on public scorecards and maximize any performance-based bonuses.

While the goals of the quality measurement movement are noble, there is another big problem: it is much easier to measure "Did you give the correct medicine for asthma?" or "Did you document that you counseled the emphysema patient to stop smoking?" than "Did you make the correct diagnosis?" Because of this, not only are hospitals and training programs deemphasizing diagnosis, but the business case for building and purchasing products like Isabel remains weak. After all, a hospital can look stellar on most publicly reported quality measures even if it has a miserable batting average in diagnostic accuracy, which is neither measured nor reported.

The absence of a business incentive to improve diagnosis is only part of the problem. There is also a cultural resistance among physicians. "Their parents tell them from an early age what wonderful children they are," said a frustrated Maude. "You're so clever because you're always getting A's. And if the core skill of being a physician is diagnosis and you think you're very good at it, there is a reluctance to look for tools to help. It has to happen in my head, they think; otherwise, I'm a failure."

Maude is hopeful about the new generation of physicians, who are more likely to acknowledge their limitations, and for whom the use of electronic tools is second nature. I believe he's right. When I was a resident in the 1980s, more than once I found myself stumped about a diagnosis or treatment, but I was too embarrassed to admit that to my patient. At times I even told little lies—"Excuse me, my pager just went off"—before I left the room to look something up.

Thankfully, this façade is beginning to crumble. Mark Smith, the former CEO of the California HealthCare Foundation and a leading health policy expert, was a resident with me at UCSF in the 1980s and held a similar attitude at the time. Today, when one of his AIDS patients at San Francisco General Hospital asks a question he doesn't know the answer to, he pulls over a computer screen, does a quick Google search, and he and the patient read the answer together. "This is contrary to everything I was taught about the importance of instilling confidence by showing patients that you know these things," Smith told me. But for tough questions, like "What fraction of patients with hepatitis C go on to develop liver cancer?," "I'm now much more comfortable saying, 'You know, that is a number I don't keep in my head. And I don't have to—let's look it up!'"

I believe this change in attitude will make newer physicians much more receptive to Isabel-type tools than prior generations. And that's a great thing.

▶    ▶    ▶

If ever there was a David and Goliath story, this is it. I asked Maude whether he worried about Watson, with its billion-dollar budget and 2,000-person staff. He pointed to the care with which his team has developed its algorithms, and the fact that they have always positioned Isabel as a relatively simple, practical tool.

While there is a bit of fancy machine learning going on, Isabel's algorithms are mostly manually constructed by a small staff, aided by substantial clinician input and fueled largely by classic descriptions of disease presentations in textbooks and key articles. "I often think we've got something that's really clever, but people don't believe in it," said Maude of his product. "But IBM comes out with all the stuff about Watson, and everyone believes in it, even though there is nothing there. There's nothing that is actually working." IBM's strategy, he said, is to "just throw loads of stuff at it and the machine will magically sort it out." Maude sees that as a flawed approach. "Ninety percent of the reason why Isabel works so well is that it's been handcrafted," he said. "I don't know whether the computer can say, 'Well, let's forget the dry cough, since I think it's from some other cause.' You end up with mountains of data, and then what? You get lost because you're drowning in data."

▶    ▶    ▶

How good is Isabel? In the summer of 2014, my 20-year-old daughter, Zoë, developed an illness characterized at first by numbness and tingling in her right arm. I was at a loss to explain this, but there were no other worrisome symptoms, so I recommended that she watch it for a day or two. Two days later, she developed a high fever and muscle aches. At that point, I thought it was likely to be a viral infection (though I couldn't quite explain the arm symptoms), and so did the physician at a Harvard-affiliated ER, where Zoë was seen.

A few weeks later, after the diagnosis had become clear, I tried out Isabel to see how it would have handled the situation. Here's what I needed to enter:

*Age: Young adult (17–29)*
*Gender: Female*
*Not pregnant* [I hope]
*Travel history: North America*
*Clinical features: Fever, muscle aches, numbness hand* [There is no option
for "numbness arm"]

I clicked *Get Checklist*, and Isabel produced a list of 10 diseases with the best fit, including Lyme disease (an infection that can affect nerves and muscles), antiphospholipid antibody syndrome (an immune disease that causes abnormal clotting), polymyositis (an inflammatory disease of muscles), and microscopic polyangiitis (an inflammatory disease of blood vessels). One of the 10, compartment syndrome, was accompanied by a little red flag, since it is a "Don't Miss" disease. Isabel is right: in compartment syndrome, there is something compressing the nerves in the arm, which must be freed up surgically before permanent nerve damage sets in.

Looking at the 10 diagnoses, I thought, "That's not a bad list," but I was surprised by the omission of two other diseases—frankly, the ones I worried about most. One was multiple sclerosis, which often shows up in young women accompanied by unusual neurological syndromes. When I clicked "Show All," I saw it was there, just not in the top 10 (it was number 33, probably because fever is unusual in MS, although infections can sometimes cause quiescent cases of MS to flare up). The other was epidural abscess, an infection adjacent to the vertebrae that presses on nerves as they exit the spinal cord. It, too, was on the list, at number 31, but it would have shown up if I had clicked the *Don't Miss* button (the diseases associated with the red flags)—it was there, just below compartment syndrome. But why did epidural abscess come in so low on the overall list of diagnoses? I'm guessing that it was because the disease is unusual, and because it would be odd to have no back pain associated with the infection (she had no such pain). In fact, when I added *back pain* to the list of clinical features as a test, epidural abscess leapfrogged to number 2, just after Lyme disease. I was impressed.

Zoë was treated with fluids and Tylenol, and—as Peter Szolovits observed— the key to the diagnosis was in the way things evolved. A few days later, she developed a severe sore throat. When I added "sore throat" to the list of clinical features, infectious mononucleosis, which had been number 16 on the initial list, jumped to number 2, again just after Lyme disease (see figure on next page). In real life, she returned to the doctor, and blood tests confirmed the diagnosis of mono.

"Isabel is not meant to replace your clinical judgment," reads the lawyerly disclaimer at the bottom of the page. No, it's not, but it is clearly a helpful adjunct to a busy clinician's reasoning process. And, for any illness on the list, a single click takes one to a series of Web-based educational resources.

At the end of the 2012 *New York Times* profile of Gurpreet Dhaliwal, Dhaliwal mentioned that he periodically used Isabel in his work and cited an outbreak of hantavirus at Yosemite National Park at the time. In several of the early patients, the diagnosis had been missed. "It's a febrile illness that looks like the flu," he said in the *Times* story. "It's so rare, the last time you might have seen it was your medical school classroom." Using a tool like Isabel might have caught some of the cases early, perhaps preventing some of the deaths, he added. "You might think you're in familiar territory, but the computer is here to remind you there are other things."

Maude remains firmly convinced that a skilled professional is needed to input the relevant clinical features (a task that involves substantial filtering and judgment) and interpret the output. I think that, at least for the foreseeable future, he's right about that, too.

▶    ▶    ▶

While the tiny Isabel staff soldiers on, the immense Watson team has chosen, at least at first, to focus on a problem that's easier than diagnosis: therapy. Working with clinicians at several prestigious institutions, including the Cleveland Clinic and Memorial Sloan Kettering Cancer Center, Watson engineers are trying to learn which information—clinical, radiologic, or genetic—the system needs if it is to determine the best treatments. The goal, then, is to provide recommendations and supporting evidence for the practicing oncologist. In a collaboration with the New York Genome Center, the Watson team is attempting to identify the culprit mutations in patients with a highly aggressive form of brain cancer, marrying this information with a rapid search of the world's literature to find promising therapies—therapies that might never have been tried for this particular cancer before. Will this work? Who knows, but the notion surely is electrifying.

If you're like me, you may be struck by the Watson team's reliance on the human expert to provide the "right answer," at least during the program's construction. The AI technique is known as supervised learning, which means that the engineers are tweaking the dials on all of their algorithms in order to find the best answer. "Right now, we have no better way of knowing what the right answer is than asking doctors," explains MIT's Szolovits.

To Vinod Khosla, this highlights a key point. The computer doesn't necessarily have to figure everything out for itself. It can make an equally important contribution by bringing the knowledge of experts "to scale," to use one of Silicon Valley's favorite terms. Khosla agrees that by his 2025 date, even programs like Watson will probably not match the diagnostic accuracy of Gurpreet Dhaliwal or the therapeutic sophistication of Sloan Kettering's best specialists. But, he points out, unless you receive your medical care in Lake Wobegon, half the doctors you see will be below average. And, in certain parts of the world, a smartphone may be the only diagnostician available. In these cases, handing over some of the diagnostic reins to "Dr. A" (Khosla's shorthand for "Dr. Algorithm") will represent significant progress.

Additionally, there is a saying in health policy that to tackle the problem of healthcare costs effectively, we'll need a system in which "everyone is practicing at the top of their license." This means that the highly trained (and highly compensated) specialist does only those things that she is uniquely good at. Things that can be done by a generalist physician (with the right support) should be. Ditto things that could be done by a well-trained nurse instead of a physician, or by a patient or family member rather than a clinician.

In light of this, if Watson is going to replace any physicians, it will likely be at the low end of complexity—for routine problems that today are handled by a primary care doctor but, given the right tool, could be managed by a nurse at your average Minute Clinic. Alternatively, we may also learn that a Watson-like tool can help at the *highest* end of care, where super specialists see many cases of unusual diseases and the name of the game is keeping up with the literature. "If you do a single thing—and especially if there is a lot of money in that single thing—you should put a 'Welcome, Robots!' doormat outside your office," wrote technology expert Farhad Manjoo in *Slate*. "They're coming for you."

Physicians can be counted on to fight this, arguing that their relationship with patients is central to healing, even if nonphysicians or technology tools can safely assume some of the tasks. Mark Smith appreciates the argument, but reminds me, "Doctors think they are more important in their patients' lives than their patients do."

I asked Smith about the competing positions taken by Khosla and Verghese. "I tend to be a little more on the Khosla side," he said, "though I understand and sympathize with Verghese's angst. He's just going to have to get over it."

▶    ▶    ▶

As we've seen, most of the energy in health IT over the past decade has gone not to artificial intelligence (we're just emerging from the AI winter), but to the more tractable issues of collecting and representing data, moving them around, and providing basic decision support. The latter has been one of the most fruitful avenues—studies have shown that well-timed and well-delivered decision aids, such as reminders to deliver preventive care or to treat a given problem with a certain medication, can markedly increase the rate of appropriate treatments. This is not a trivial matter, since if they're not well constructed or carefully integrated into the work flow, even these seemingly simple forms of decision support can risk unintended consequences, as illustrated by Christine Sinsky's dangerous DVT treatment prompt I told you about in Chapter 8. Moreover, when physicians are bombarded with decision aids in the form of pop-up screens, there is a risk of alert fatigue.

Does this mean that Watson's creators have abandoned their quest to master the art of diagnosis? Hardly. But for now, IBM recognizes that its best position is as an ally and adjunct to doctors, rather than as a competitor. For the next few years, the emphasis is likely to be on "little AI": decision support for bite-sized problems, treatment advice for defined clinical scenarios, and help with all of those "simple transforms" that so rankled Matt Burton, the Mayo Clinic surgeon turned informaticist.

Interestingly, this bite-sized approach may ultimately prove to be the best path to the more ambitious goal of the fully digital doctor. While the Google car might technically be ready for a road near you, there's no shortage of hurdles to surmount, including existing laws that insist on human drivers and the absence of driverless car insurance. But, observed technology journalist Alexis Madrigal in 2014, while it may be many years before our highways are packed with driverless cars, most of us will encounter autonomous driving "in little autopilot moments when we cede temporary control to a computer" as we move from the familiar wonder of cruise control to new features that nudge us back into our lane when we wander or help us parallel park in a tight space. "This is how the future creeps into the present," said Madrigal. "While it might seem like your main computing device transformed from a Dell desktop into a smartphone overnight, there were thousands of little steps along the way that led to the moment when you realized the world had changed beyond recognition."

# Chapter 11

## Big Data

What would life be without arithmetic, but a scene of horrors?
—Rev. Sidney Smith, 1835

On a sultry afternoon in the summer of 2014, I visited the Washington, DC office of Karen DeSalvo, the new director of the Office of the National Coordinator for Health Information Technology (ONC). DeSalvo, an internist and the former commissioner of health for New Orleans, had a full agenda as she tried to reposition the ONC for the post–Daddy Warbucks era (the last of the 30 billion HITECH dollars were doled out in late 2014), as well as navigate the swirling controversies over Meaningful Use, interoperability, usability, and more. After we discussed these weighty topics, she pivoted the conversation; she wanted to talk about underwear. Intelligent underwear. "Sensing underwear," she said jauntily, "that's my favorite thing. I was driving yesterday, thinking of all the uses for sensing underwear!"

I was a little taken aback. First of all, sitting in a large, sterile government office on the seventh floor of the Hubert Humphrey Building on Independence Avenue, within a stone's throw of the Capitol dome, the topic was a bit more tabloid than I was expecting. Moreover, I'm not sure that I *want* my underwear sending off signals.

As DeSalvo sees it, smart underwear has its place. "If I had a parent with diabetes in a nursing home," she explained, "there are things I'd want to know, things that might be helpful." These things include hydration, body temperature, and heart rate. One can envision other uses for sensing underwear, including monitoring a recovering alcoholic for a relapse and checking to see whether a forgetful patient has taken his medications.

The improbable story of intelligent underwear began with a June 2010 article titled "Thick-Film Textile-Based Amperometric Sensors and Biosensors" and published in *Analyst*, the official journal of Britain's Royal Society of Chemistry. This article did not, at first glance, appear to be one that would titillate audiences around the world, nor one that would send the healthcare IT Hype-O-Meter into the red zone. Yet the findings were remarkable. After purchasing underwear from local department stores, a team of bioengineers from UC San Diego used advanced textile screen-printing techniques to fuse carbon-based electrodes into the elastic waistband. In the article, they presented their findings: the electrodes, which held up under moderate tests of bending and stretching (and apparently can survive both bleach and your Maytag's various cycles), reliably measured concentrations of certain body chemicals present in sweat that correlate with levels of blood alcohol and stress.

The UCSD researchers weren't aiming for the *National Enquirer*, but their paper created a media buzz regarding other potential uses for "wearables." Exercise pants that give you a heads-up if you're working out your right- and left-sided muscles asymmetrically. Headgear that can follow your sleep patterns, and even send a text message to your office staff alerting them that you might be grumpy after a fitful night. Socks that can monitor a diabetic's capillary flow, issuing a warning when they've detected an elevated risk for a foot ulcer caused by poor circulation.

And the flow of electrons need not be unidirectional. Companies are working on sensors that not only identify problems like high stress levels or low blood pressure, but also deliver appropriate treatments, perhaps through the skin. Even the underwear can go both ways: a product called "Fundawear" allows a person to signal another person's underwear to vibrate (in several different strategic locations) via an iPhone app. This immediately jumps to number one on the list of reasons not to lose your phone.

▶   ▶   ▶

Creating sensors to measure a wide range of biological phenomena, like your stress level or the physiologic effects of certain drugs, was once a daunting engineering problem. But over the past five years, these challenges have been overcome through the development of gizmos ranging from the tiny accelerometers in your Fitbit or Jawbone to nanosensors that can be safely ingested. And, of course, the outputs of all these miraculous devices can now connect to our smartphones and to the Internet. This means that the so-called Quantified Self movement is shifting from a technical problem (how to capture the data) into an analytics question (how to make sense of the data). And this is where the hope butts up against the hype.

▶    ▶    ▶

The consulting firm Gartner defines big data as "high volume, high velocity, and/or high variety information assets that require new forms of processing to enable enhanced decision making, insight discovery, and process optimization." The concept has been well known in the consumer space for years, in ways that are sometimes obvious to shoppers (as in Amazon's book recommendations) and sometimes less so (as in the Facebook advertisements for Pampers that begin popping up soon after you purchase a pregnancy kit from CVS). However, its introduction into healthcare is recent, owing mostly to the availability of five relatively new data sources: clinical data from EHRs, genetic data, government data such as physician billing patterns, data from social media and digital devices, and data from sensors, both wearable and otherwise.

Shahram Ebadollahi, IBM's chief science officer for healthcare, told me of the company's early attempts to sell the concept of big data to healthcare organizations, as recently as a few years ago. "We were trying to convince people of the merits of how to use their data, how to derive insights, how to feed that into daily practice." But few were interested. "Now they are saying, 'Okay, we have the data. We don't know what to do with it.'"

Ebadollahi finds that the biggest problem he and his Watson team are facing is not too much data—after all, Watson can sift through the equivalent of one million books in a second—but too little. In large healthcare datasets, there might be 1,000 pieces of data collected on at least one of the patients, whether it's demographics like age, gender, income, and education level; clinical problems like colon cancer or Crohn's disease; or physiologic data such as heart rate and blood count. But 90 percent of the cells in the spreadsheet are bare, meaning that a piece of data that's available for some patients is missing for others. On top of that, many data points are "noisy"—potentially inaccurate for a variety of reasons, ranging from keystroke errors to sensor malfunctions. Big-data folks call this part of their work "data wrangling" and sometimes refer to themselves as "data janitors," since so much of their time is spent preparing datasets for analysis rather than on the analyses themselves.

Ebadollahi uses a TV analogy to describe how IBM is tackling the seemingly arcane but crucial problem of handling missing data. Let's say that CNN was interested in identifying all the clips in its vast library that show an airplane taking off—and let's assume that the computer can't yet distinguish an airplane from other large objects, like buildings or cars. The network could hire interns to watch and index every video, but that would be wildly inefficient. Instead, IBM's approach begins by pinpointing "concepts" that the computer *can* readily identify, such as big chunks of asphalt, blue sky, or clouds.

Watson then uses machine learning to detect this evolutionary pattern—asphalt and trees giving way to sky and clouds over the space of a few seconds—to guess that the clip shows an airplane taking off. This is also how it works in healthcare, as Watson fills in the empty cells by mining the records of all the patients and making assumptions about what the likely value *would have been* for a given patient had it been measured, a statistical concept known as "imputing."

▶    ▶    ▶

Interestingly, when it comes to analyzing healthcare information, "There are *two* big data problems we've observed," said Eric Brown, the Watson team's lead engineer. First, there's the obvious one: the literature of medicine, which currently contains about 24 million records and expands at a rate of 2,100 articles per day. The idea that a human being could keep up with this flood of literature is laughable.

The second problem is more surprising but equally daunting: the data contained within a patient's own electronic health record. For a complicated patient, the EHR can easily contain thousands of pages, with both structured (such as laboratory test results) and unstructured (physician narratives) data. IBM and other companies[13] are developing techniques to mine these records, which is a more challenging and subtle task than simply performing a Google search of them.

For example, if I'm interested in a patient's risk for heart disease, I need to quickly determine his prior history of angina or heart attacks, his family history, the presence of key risk factors, and other clues to the disease that might be hiding in a doctor's note, a laboratory study, or a cardiac catheterization report—any of which may have been performed last month or during the Clinton administration. Said IBM's Brown, "It doesn't take much data to create

---

[13] I am an advisor to a company named QPID Health, started by a Harvard radiologist and informatician, that specializes in the task of mining the EHR for key data.

a big data problem for the human brain. For a physician to take in and understand a 10,000-page longitudinal patient record in the two to three minutes he has to prepare for the visit with that patient is a problem. And then we want to allow the physician to interact with that information during the visit in a way that doesn't create a barrier between the doctor and the patient because the doctor's head is buried in the EHR."

While much of the promise of big data involves improving care for individual patients, there is another, more ambitious, goal: the creation of a "learning healthcare system," one that constantly mines all its data for patterns and insights to improve the organization of clinical practice. Over time, this kind of analysis is likely to help determine optimal staffing patterns, inform efforts to prevent hospital-acquired infections, and estimate prognosis and risk factors for bad events, ranging from heart attacks to readmissions.

Moreover, big-data techniques seem poised to become powerful research tools, not only to test traditional approaches, such as whether radiation therapy or chemo works better for patients with a certain cancer, but also to assess new sources of data, from genetic analyses to Facebook "likes." In the pre-big-data era, answering such questions required clinical trials, in which patients were randomly sorted into two different arms, treated with one alternative or the other, and followed over time.

But these new techniques create the opportunity to answer such questions by observing what happens to real patients who, for a variety of reasons, received different treatments. Using a Harry Potter analogy, Michael Lauer of the National Heart, Lung, and Blood Institute called this "Magic in the Muggle world." He added, "It will allow us to do dozens, hundreds of large-scale studies at a very low cost." These kinds of analyses have already demonstrated that what we once thought of as lung cancer is actually a series of different cancers, each with a particular genetic signature. These genes, rather than the patient's age or even the appearance of the tumor under the pathologist's microscope, may prove to be the key predictors of outcomes and the best guide to treatment.

IBM's Ebadollahi described how Watson makes sense of large datasets. One of its techniques, known as "patient similarity analytics," is analogous to the method that allows Amazon and Netflix to say, "Customers like you also liked . . . ." In this case, though, it is, "Patients like this had less knee pain after taking infliximab than methotrexate," or, "Patients like this lived a year longer than patients who lacked these attributes," or "Patients like this became septic and hypotensive within 24 hours (even though they didn't look so bad to their nurse or doctor)," or even "Patients like this did better when they saw Dr. Robinson instead of Dr. Reynolds."

Ebadollahi sees such an approach, sometimes called "practice-based evidence," as complementing, not supplanting, the more traditional "evidence-based practice," with its focus on using published clinical research to guide prognosis and treatments. To illustrate how it works, he described a theoretical database containing 100,000 pieces of data on every patient, including clinical, demographic, financial, genetic, and perhaps even social media–derived data. "Out of those 100,000," he said, "I can determine the 100 things of greatest importance to the question I'm trying to answer. Once I have that, I can see what happened to people who were similar to my patient on those 100 variables, and what course of action I should take."

Even with a tool as potent as Watson, this is a harder problem than it might seem. First, there's the missing data problem, as well as the daunting signal-to-noise issues. There also are vagaries in the behavior of certain variables—even those as seemingly straightforward as age. For example, the prognostic importance of a 10-year bump in age is far from linear: it's trivial going from age 25 to 35, but sizable going from 70 to 80. Computer scientists (at IBM and elsewhere) are trying to create models that account for nuances like these.

Moreover, computers are likely to spit out strict goalposts, but patients and doctors may have preferences that challenge these hard guidelines, giving rise to the commonly voiced objections about "cookbook medicine." Larry Fagan, the retired Stanford informatics expert, was being treated for cancer when I interviewed him in 2014. Coincidentally, years earlier he helped develop a computerized algorithm known as ONCOCIN, which guides treatments at Stanford and other cancer centers. Fagan's cancer was being treated with chemotherapy, but then his platelet count (blood cells that promote clotting) came back at 97,000 (normal is about 150,000). ONCOCIN recommended a significant reduction in his chemotherapy dose, which Fagan knew might compromise the effectiveness of the treatment. He also knew that the platelet count can bounce around—it's not unheard of for it to vary by 20,000 to 30,000 from one test to the next.

"My nurse-practitioner checked the algorithm and said, 'We have to do a dose reduction.' I told her that was ridiculous, that the uncertainty associated with the platelet count meant that she should check it again." She did, and the repeat result was 130,000. Fagan received his full dose of chemo.

After a lifetime of building and studying medical IT systems, that was the moment when Fagan fully appreciated the tension between computer rules and their clinical context. "There was this disconnect between the output of the algorithm and a human who wants to receive the full dose of chemo if it's appropriate. I didn't want the answer the program gave me. It was only when I became a patient that I fully appreciated the fuzziness of medicine."

▶    ▶    ▶

Big data is intoxicating stuff, but it's worth pointing out that, despite the hype, this work is in its infancy, at least in healthcare. There is no question but that we will soon be awash in data, and that our ability to sift through it is improving rapidly. But will it be transformative? I remain skeptical, at least in the short term.

While our EHRs will contain vast amounts of information, big-data techniques may be no better at sifting through bloated copy-and-paste-ridden notes than are the frustrated doctors trying to do so today. Much of the data in EHRs continues to be collected for the purpose of creating a superior bill, and using this waste product of administrative functions for clinical decision making can lead to a GIGO (garbage in, garbage out) problem, even with fabulous analytics.

Moreover, while all of our genetic data may eventually help guide prognostic and treatment decisions, today there are only a handful of gene mutations, mostly in oncology, that have proved to be unambiguously valuable in real-life practice. Adding to the challenge, the privacy issues raised by widespread mining of individuals' data have not been resolved. Even if the data are "de-identified" (meaning that the patient's name and other readily identifiable information are stripped from the dataset), studies have shown that a patient's identity can easily be reconstructed through analysis of a small number of variables, including blood test results—a modern fingerprint in 1's and 0's.

As for big data drawn from sensors, as you might have guessed, Vinod Khosla is bullish. He told me about a prototype watch that he's been testing. The watch bristles with tiny sensors. "It collected 19 million data points on me over a couple of days," he pointed out. Khosla conceded that today, a good physician could judge his health more accurately—by talking to and examining him and running some standard tests—than a computer could by analyzing these bits of data. But, he continued, "Once we have readings on 100 million people, it will become more valuable. It's not the data. It's the complex math that creates insights about that data."

And yet . . . and yet, as I reflect on the complexity of the problem, my instincts tell me that Khosla might not quite get it. In *The Checklist Manifesto*, the author and surgeon Atul Gawande recounted a study that vividly illustrates this complexity. In a single year, the trauma centers in the state of Pennsylvania saw 41,000 patients, who had 1,224 different injuries. Taken together, there were 32,261 unique combinations of injuries. Gawande described the findings to me in more detail:

> *Someone stabbed in the eye, and stabbed in the belly. Another person had a seat belt injury with a cardiac contusion and a long-bone fracture. And by the way, he's on Coumadin, so there's an anticoagulation problem.*
>
> *The automated algorithm can tell you, "Well, here's the best combination to try to treat." But it's 2 a.m. and my radiologist, who can do the angiography, is 40 minutes away. Because he just moved, and his house is now in a different place. Sorry.*
>
> *This is life as a trauma surgeon. It's what it's like when I've been on call. The computerized database is not going to be kept up to speed fast enough. It's not going to take all the factors of human life into account. This is the nature of fallibility, and we're going to be at that juncture all the time. A human being is still going to have to be there, putting it together. Are they fallible? Absolutely. But the data are more fallible.*

▶    ▶    ▶

Perhaps someday, a company—maybe IBM, or Apple, or Google, or one that hasn't yet been born—will be able to predict my clinical outcomes or guide my treatments by analyzing my pulse rate, my steps, my thyroid level, my diet, my genes, my underwear sweat, my Visa bill, my Twitter feed, and my golf handicap. But that day is not today, and it's unlikely to be tomorrow.

For now, I see big data as a crucial area for research and development, one that is likely to bear fruit over time—particularly as EHRs become ubiquitous and somehow linked to patient-generated data from sensors and elsewhere, and as developers figure out how to integrate these tools with the habits and work flows of real people. A wise person once observed that we usually overestimate what can be done in a year and underestimate what can be done in a decade. To me, big data in healthcare meets that descriptor perfectly.

If I am right, then, for the foreseeable future, the Quantified Self movement is likely to make its biggest mark among folks who have a bit too much time (and money) on their hands. Mark Smith recalled his experience as a member of the Qualcomm advisory board. Since the company specializes in providing—and profiting from—24/7 connectivity, there were many lively discussions about the value to consumers of minute-to-minute monitoring of things like blood sugar and heart rate. "There was one meeting where somebody said, 'It's like your credit score—you can hit a button and get your number!' I asked him, 'And how often do you check your credit score? Maybe once every six months, not five times a day.'"

"I would argue that if you're checking your blood pressure every hour, you're a self-monitoring narcissist," Smith said. "Not an average human patient."

▶    ▶    ▶

At the end of my visit to IBM's research headquarters in New York's lovely Hudson Valley (the place where the machine that beat the *Jeopardy* champions was built), a few members of the Watson team told me about those thrilling days when it became clear that their invention had succeeded in mastering a task that few had thought possible. Winning the game was a joyous occasion for the IBMers, who celebrated with a small victory party.

I asked Eric Brown, who worked on the *Jeopardy* project and is now helping to lead Watson's efforts in medicine, what the equivalent event might be in healthcare, the moment when his team could finally congratulate itself on its successes. I wondered if it would be the creation of some kind of holographic physician—like "The Doctor" on *Star Trek Voyager*—with Watson serving as the cognitive engine. His answer, though, reflected the deep respect he and his colleagues have for the magnitude of the challenge. "It will be when we have a technology that physicians suddenly can't live without," he said.

And that was it. Just a useful tool. Nothing more and nothing less.

Part Three

# The Overdose

# Chapter 12

# The Error

It may seem a strange principle to enunciate as the very first
requirement in a Hospital that it should do the sick no harm.
> —Florence Nightingale, *Notes on Hospitals*, 1863

The nurses and doctors summoned urgently to the bedside of 16-year-old
Pablo Garcia knew something was terribly wrong. Although Pablo had an
unusual illness—a rare genetic disease called NEMO syndrome that leads
to a lifetime of frequent infections, along with bowel symptoms similar to
those caused by inflammatory bowel disease—this was supposed to be a routine admission for a colonoscopy to evaluate a polyp and an area of intestinal
narrowing.

Pablo had been admitted to UCSF Medical Center's Benioff Children's
Hospital the prior morning, July 26, 2013. At 9 o'clock that night, he took all
his evening medications, including steroids to tamp down his dysfunctional
immune system and antibiotics to stave off infections. At 1 a.m., he started
complaining of numbness and tingling all over his body. His nurse, Brooke
Levitt,[14] a recent nursing school graduate who normally worked in the pediatric
intensive care unit but was "floating" on the regular pediatric floor that night,

---

[14] In keeping with their request, the names of the nurse, pharmacist, and doctor have been changed, but
all clinical details and quotes are accurate. I have also changed the names of the patient, his mother,
and his brother.

wondered whether Pablo's symptoms had something to do with GoLYTELY, the nasty bowel-cleansing solution he had been gulping down all evening to prepare for the colonoscopy. Or perhaps he was reacting to the antinausea medication he was taking to keep the GoLYTELY down.

At about 3 a.m., Pablo's tingling grew worse, and Levitt asked her charge nurse to come assess the situation. The senior nurse, too, was stumped, so they summoned the chief resident in pediatrics to take a look. When the physician arrived in the room, he spoke to and examined the patient, who was anxious, mildly confused, and complaining of being "numb all over." The chief resident opened Pablo's electronic medical record and searched the medication list for clues that might explain the unusual symptoms. He was perplexed at first, too. But then he noticed something that stopped him cold. Six hours earlier, the nurse had given the patient not one Septra pill—a tried-and-true antibiotic used principally for urinary and skin infections—but 38½ of them.

Levitt recalls that moment as the worst of her life. "Wait, look at this Septra dose. This is a huge dose. Oh my God, did you *give* this dose?" the resident asked her. "Oh my God, I did," she said.

The doctor picked up the phone and called San Francisco's poison control center. The toxicology expert there told the panicked clinicians that there wasn't much they could do other than monitor the patient closely; he would probably be fine (not that they'd ever heard of a Septra overdose this large, and nothing close had ever been reported in the medical literature). As a precaution, the hospital's rapid response team was summoned to the room. Pablo's mother, Blanca, who had been with her younger son, hospitalized one floor up at UCSF for a severe skin infection (he, too, suffers from NEMO syndrome), began a vigil by Pablo's bedside. The toxicologist's optimism did not reassure her. "I phoned my sister, and we prayed together," she later recalled.

At 5:32 a.m., Brooke Levitt heard a scream coming from Pablo's room. It was Blanca Garcia. A few seconds earlier, her son had sat bolt upright in bed, yelled out "Mom!" and then flopped backward. By the time Levitt sprinted into the room, Pablo's head was snapping back and forth, teeth clenched, back arched, extremities thrashing. He was having a grand mal seizure. Moments later, just as the Code Blue team arrived, the teenager stopped breathing.

"I thought, what if I killed him?" Levitt told me months later, wiping away tears. "If he had a seizure, I'm wondering if that's going to be the end of it. . . . I'm trying to hold it together, but I'm in shock the whole time. I just felt immensely guilty."

▶   ▶   ▶

To appreciate how one of the nation's best hospitals—*US News & World Report* regularly ranks UCSF among the top 10—could give a patient a 39-fold overdose of a common antibiotic, one first needs to understand how medicines were ordered and administered in hospitals as recently as a few years ago, before the system went digital.

Pablo Garcia had been on one double-strength Septra twice a day at home to prevent his frequent skin infections, so the admitting doctor, a pediatrics resident named Jenny Lucca, would have written "Septra 1 ds bid" (using the Latin abbreviation for "twice a day") in the "Doctors' Orders" section of a paper chart, a stack of sheets contained within a plastic three-ring binder. She would have turned a colored wheel on the side of the binder to green, signaling to the ward clerk that there was an order to be "taken off." The clerk would then have faxed the order sheet to the pharmacy, where a pharmacist would have read it, signified his approval by initialing the page, and handed the copy to a technician, who would have grabbed a big bottle of Septra pills from a shelf. The tech would then have poured out the pill, or perhaps a few days' worth of pills, and put them in a bag or cup, which would have then been delivered to the patient's floor by a runner or a pneumatic tube system. There, at the appropriate time, the patient's nurse would have seen the order (manually transcribed from the doctor's order sheet to the nurse's Medication Administration Record, or MAR), and entered the teenager's room pushing a wheeled cart similar to the ones used by airline flight attendants. After opening the patient's drawer in the cart, the nurse would have removed the medication, and others due to be given at the time, watched the patient take the pill, and placed her signature next to the time and dose on her MAR.

Believe it or not, I've shortened this description to simplify things—time and motion studies have identified as many as 50 steps between the moment the doctor wrote the order and the moment the nurse finally administered the medication. But even in simplified form, you can see why the old system was hugely error-prone. A study from the pen-and-paper era showed that 1 in 15 hospitalized patients suffered from an adverse drug event, often due to medication errors. A 2010 study (using data collected during the predigital era) estimated the yearly cost of medication errors in U.S. hospitals at $21 billion.

Those of us who worked in this Rube Goldberg system—and witnessed the harms it caused—anxiously awaited the arrival of computers to plug its leaks. Computerized ordering would make a doctor's handwriting as irrelevant as scratches on a record album. Computerized decision support would alert the doctor or pharmacist that the patient was allergic to the medication being ordered, or that two medications might interact dangerously. A pharmacy robot could ensure that the right medication was pulled off the shelf, and that the dose was measured with a jeweler's precision. And a bar-coding system would render the final leg in this relay race flawless, since it would signal the nurse if she had grabbed the wrong medication or was in the wrong patient's room.

▶   ▶   ▶

Over the next several chapters, you'll read about how—even in one of the world's best hospitals, filled with well-trained, careful, and caring doctors, nurses, and pharmacists—technology can cause breathtaking errors. As you'll see, other industries—ones in which technology entered gently and spread organically over time—gradually came to appreciate the complex interface between technology and people, and worked to overcome many of the potential hazards. I have no doubt that, even in these awkward early days, computer systems (including computerized provider order entry, or CPOE, and bar-coded medication administration) prevent more errors than they cause, and they will surely get better over time as both the technologies and the processes surrounding them mature. But now that healthcare has entered the digital age, the night that Pablo Garcia was given a 39-fold overdose of a routine antibiotic offers a cautionary tale that cannot be ignored.

# Chapter 13

# The System

I hate the goddamn system, but until someone comes along
with some changes that make sense, I'll stick with it.
        —Clint Eastwood as "Dirty Harry," *Magnum Force*, 1973

English psychologist James Reason developed his "Swiss cheese model" of
error after analyzing scores of terrible mistakes in industries ranging from
nuclear power to commercial aviation. Reason's model holds that all complex organizations harbor many "latent errors," unsafe conditions that are, in
essence, mistakes waiting to happen. They're like a forest carpeted with dry
underbrush, just waiting for a match or a lightning strike.

Still, there are legions of errors every day in complex organizations that
*don't* lead to major accidents. Why? Reason found that these organizations
have built-in protections that block glitches from causing nuclear meltdowns,
or plane crashes, or train derailments. Unfortunately, all these protective layers
have holes, which he likened to the holes in slices of Swiss cheese.

On most days, errors are caught in time, much as you remember to grab
your house keys right before you lock yourself out. Those errors that evade the
first layer of protection are caught by the second. Or the third. When a terrible
"organizational accident" occurs—say, a space shuttle crash or a September
11–like intelligence breakdown—post hoc analysis virtually always reveals
that the root cause was the failure of multiple layers, a grim yet perfect align-

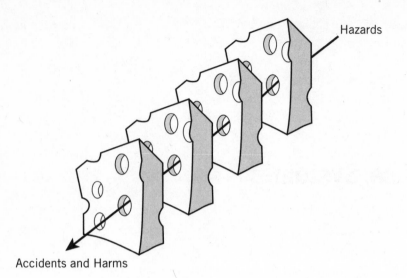

Hazards

Accidents and Harms

ment of the holes in the metaphorical Swiss cheese. Reason's model reminds us that most errors are caused by good, competent people who are trying to do the right thing, and that bolstering the system—shrinking the holes in the Swiss cheese or adding overlapping layers—is generally far more productive than trying to purge the system of human error, an impossibility.

A 1999 report by the Institute of Medicine launched the patient safety movement with the headline-grabbing estimate that nearly 100,000 patients a year in the United States die of medical mistakes—the equivalent of a jumbo jet crashing every day. Tens of thousands of these deaths were from medication errors. For these, computerization was touted as the most promising fix, since it can plug holes like illegible handwriting, mistaken calculations (for example, adding a zero to a calculated dose creates a tenfold overdose, which can be fatal if the drug is insulin or a narcotic), and failure to check drug allergies before administering a medication. More sophisticated computer systems go even further, building in alerts to guide doctors to the correct medication for a given condition, signaling that our dose is too high or low, or reminding us to check a patient's renal function before prescribing certain medications that affect the kidneys.

▶    ▶    ▶

UCSF Medical Center installed its first hospitalwide computer system in 2000. We switched to Epic in 2012 after an unhappy decade with GE's EHR system. Our implementation of Epic, like all such implementations, had its share of hiccups. Some departments didn't send out bills for weeks, some medications and lab tests were overlooked, and a few patients fell off the hospital's radar screen for brief periods. And I've already described some of the profound changes in communication and work flow that emerged soon after Go Live.

But now, on the date of Pablo Garcia's admission, 13 months after UCSF's Epic installation, the system was running smoothly. And there was good evidence that it was meeting its goals: doctors' and nurses' notes were now legible; thousands of medication errors had been intercepted by the bar-coding system; and computerized checklists guided the clinicians through some key safety practices like identifying the correct surgical site before the first incision. Moreover, about 50,000 patients had signed up to access a new electronic portal called MyChart, which allowed them to receive results of lab tests and x-rays, schedule appointments, refill their medications, and e-mail their physicians. Although there were always grumbles here and there, the general feeling was that the electronic health record was making patient care safer and better.

Yet a series of dangers lurked beneath the placid surface. Installing a system like Epic is not like installing an operating system on your laptop, where you just "Accept the Terms," reboot the machine, and off you go. Instead, while the electronic health record provides the scaffolding, there are hundreds of decisions that each hospital needs to make, many of them related to electronic prescribing. For example, should there be maximum dose limits set in the system, so that doses several times higher than the published maximum are grayed out? UCSF decided not to set such limits. The reasoning at the time was that, in a teaching hospital with lots of patients with rare diseases, many of them on research protocols, such "overdoses" would usually be okay. A system with hundreds of "hard stops" would lead to many angry phone calls from frustrated doctors to pharmacists, demanding that they override the block.

When it came to pediatric patients, a second set of decisions had to be made concerning weight-based dosing. Since pediatric patients can range from a preemie weighing a couple of pounds to a morbidly obese adolescent, many pediatric medications are dosed based on weight, usually expressed in milligrams per kilogram (mg/kg). The committee overseeing our Epic implementation decided to require weight-based dosing for all children under 40 kilograms (about 88 pounds).

Another choice involved the translation of weight-based doses into pills. What if the computer calculated that a dose should be 120 mg (based on the child's weight), but the only available pill was 100 mg? The decision: if the available medication was more than 5 percent off the calculated "correct" dose, then the pharmacist would contact the doctor to be sure she endorsed that conversion. After all, there might be cases in which a 10 or 20 percent disparity would be clinically meaningful and the doctor might rethink the order.

Whether an automated system is monitoring the status of a nuclear power plant, a commercial jetliner, or your washing machine, perhaps the most challenging decisions when going digital revolve around what to do with alerts. On an average day at UCSF Medical Center, we prescribe about 12,000 medication doses, and order thousands more x-rays and lab tests. How should the doctor be informed if the computer thinks there is—*or might be*—a problem?

Because many academic medical centers installed Epic before 2012, UCSF had the advantage of learning from the experience of these early adopters. One near-universal recommendation was to be sparing with alerts, because every alert makes it less likely that people will pay attention to the next one. Heeding this feedback, the medical center chose to disable thousands of the alerts built into the drug database system that the hospital had purchased along with Epic. Despite this decision, there were still tons of alerts. Of roughly 350,000 medication orders per month, pharmacists were receiving pop-up alerts on nearly half of them. Yes, you read that right: nearly half. The physicians were alerted less frequently—in the course of a month, they received *only* 17,000 alerts.

The alert problem was especially daunting in pediatrics. There, because of the predominance of weight-based doses and the narrow therapeutic range for many medications, alerts would fire on several of the 10 to 15 medications ordered by the doctors for the typical hospitalized youngster, and on the vast majority of orders processed by the pediatric pharmacists.

All these policy decisions—on alerts, weight-based dosing, hard stops, and the like—were reached by committees composed of well-meaning physicians, nurses, pharmacists, and computer experts. The decisions were made because these people believed that they would enhance the safety of our patients and the efficiency of our operations. There was no way for them to know that some of their choices would ultimately create new vulnerabilities, new holes in the Swiss cheese.

# Chapter 14

# The Doctor

Automation does not simply supplant human activity but
rather changes it, often in ways unintended and unanticipated
by the designers.

—Automation experts Raja Parasuraman
and Dietrich Manzey, 2010

Jenny Lucca, the pediatrics resident who was assigned Pablo Garcia's case, had
been a standout student in medical school and was thrilled to be accepted
to UCSF's residency program. After arriving in San Francisco, she took the
required 10 hours of computer training, and the Epic system seemed easy
enough—the fact that it was the same one she had used in medical school
made the transition even smoother.

But the alerts were a constant nuisance. Even giving Tylenol to a feverish
child every four hours triggered an alert that the dose was approaching the
maximum allowed. Every training program has a "hidden curriculum" (the
way things are actually done around here, as opposed to what the policies say
or what the administrators told you during that interminable orientation). One
of them—passed down from senior residents to the newbies—was, "Ignore
all the alerts." While Lucca was slightly uncomfortable with that as a govern-
ing philosophy, she was convinced that most of the dozen or more alerts she

received each day could be safely ignored, and she knew that doing so was the only way she could get her work done.

On a cool July day in San Francisco, Lucca began the process of admitting Pablo Garcia. Pablo's rare genetic disease had led to bouts of gastrointestinal bleeding and abdominal pain, which needed further evaluation with a colonoscopy. Around noon on July 26, after speaking to Pablo and his mother and examining the young patient, Lucca clicked into the physicians' orders section in the electronic health record.

Pablo was on about 15 different medications. Lucca ordered his usual immunosuppressive pills, the liquid bowel-cleansing prep for the colonoscopy (the famously vile GoLYTELY), and his monthly infusion of immunoglobulins. She then came to the Septra, an antibiotic that the teenager had been taking for years to prevent recurrent bouts of skin and lung infections. The usual dose of Septra for all but the smallest children is one double-strength pill twice daily, and that is what Pablo was taking at home.

In the precomputer days, of course, Lucca would have written to simply continue the Septra, twice daily, on the physician's order sheet. But Pablo weighed less than 40 kilograms (38.6 to be exact, or about 85 pounds), which meant that the weight-based dosing policy dictated that Lucca order the medication in milligrams per kilogram. When she typed "Septra" into Epic's order entry module, she was prompted to select one of two dose choices, and she correctly chose the larger ("double-strength") one, 5 mg/kg of trimethoprim.[15]

The computer calculated that the dose should be 193 mg of trimethoprim (38.6 kg multiplied by 5 mg/kg). Since the nearest tablet size was one double-strength Septra, which contains 160 mg of trimethoprim, the computer rec-

---

[15] Septra, which also goes by the brand name Bactrim, actually consists of two different antibiotics: trimethoprim and sulfamethoxazole. The dose of the trimethoprim component determines the overall Septra dose.

ommended that the dose be rounded to a single tablet, and asked Lucca if she accepted this recommendation.

Order Validation

The following information is missing or may need your attention

**sulfamethoxazole-trimethoprim (BACTRIM DS,SEPTRA DS) 800-160 mg tablet 160 mg of trimethoprim**
160 mg of trimethoprim is the nearest dose that can be administered using available products (a decrease of 17% from the ordered dose of 193 mg of trimethoprim).

Do you want to accept these orders anyway?

Yes          No

She clicked "Yes." In doing so, she believed she had ordered the one double-strength Septra tablet that Pablo had been taking at home, which was precisely what she had intended to do all along. All would have been well—had she been right. But she wasn't.

# Chapter 15

# The Pharmacist

[Only] the right dose differentiates a poison from a remedy.
　　—Paracelsus (1493–1541), the father of modern pharmacology

Benjamin Chan was working in the seventh-floor pharmacy that afternoon. It was his job as the pediatric clinical pharmacist to sign off on all medication orders on the pediatric service. The hospital's safety system requires that no order proceed directly from the doctor's electronic signature to the administering nurse. Teaching hospitals like UCSF that care for patients who are on multiple complex medications with many potential interactions and subtleties generally require pharmacists to preapprove each order. While there is a main pharmacy in the basement of the hospital that deals with most medication orders for adult patients, orders for children are processed by specialized pediatric pharmacists like Chan, who work out of small satellite pharmacies adjacent to the wards.

Lucca's admission orders for Pablo Garcia reached Benjamin Chan's computer screen moments after the doctor had electronically signed them. As Chan reviewed the orders, he saw that Lucca had ordered 5 mg/kg of Septra. Because the resulting calculated dose of 193 mg was more than 5 percent greater than the 160-mg Septra tablets, hospital policy did not allow Chan to simply approve the order. Instead, it required that he contact Lucca, asking her to enter the correct dose of 160 mg.

The pharmacist texted Lucca: "Dose rounded by >5%. Correct dose 160 mg. Pls reorder." Of the scores of medications that the resident would order—and the pharmacist would approve—that day, this was probably the simplest: an antibiotic pill dispensed by corner drugstores everywhere, being taken as a routine matter by a relatively stable patient. Neither the doctor nor the pharmacist could have anticipated that this text message, and the policy that demanded it, would be a lit match dropped onto the dry forest floor.

▶   ▶   ▶

After receiving the text page, Lucca reopened the medication-ordering screen in Epic. What she needed to do was trivial, and she didn't give it much thought. She typed "160" into the dose box and clicked "Accept." She then moved to the next task on her long checklist, believing that she had just ordered the one Septra tablet that she had wanted all along. But she had done something very different. Can you spot the problem?

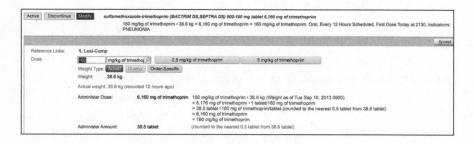

Did you find it? Perhaps not, since it is hiding in the middle of this dense screen, which faithfully replicates the one seen by Lucca. Focus your attention on the line that begins with the number "160" inside a rectangular box.

Since doses can be ordered in either milligrams or milligrams per kilogram, the computer program needs to decide which one to use as the default setting. (Of course, it could leave the unit [mg versus mg/kg] box blank, forcing the doctor to make a choice every time, but few systems do that because of the large number of additional clicks it would generate.) In UCSF's version of Epic, the decision was made to have the screen default to the setting it was on the last time you visited the page. That seemingly innocent decision meant that Lucca's screen remained set at "mg/kg" when she returned to it after receiving the pharmacist's text message. Because of this, in typing 160, Lucca was actually ordering 160 *mg per kg*—not one double-strength Septra, but 38½ of them.

Computer experts call this type of problem—when the same action can result in two very different results—a "mode error," and it is especially problematic when the user is not focused on the mode (in this case, mg versus mg/kg) and the interface offers no obvious clues as to its current status. The most common mode error in day-to-day computing is activation of the caps lock key,[16] which changes the output of all the other keys. While computer designers try hard to avoid having any modes at all, the caps lock key is a major convenience, and so it has survived. When you're stuck with a mode problem, user-centered design principles dictate that the mode should be made obvious to the user. And so most computer manufacturers incorporate a light into the caps lock key to show when it's activated, and they signal (generally through the use of an up-facing arrow icon) that the caps lock key is on, thus explaining why you're having no luck with your password.

Unfortunately, the Epic interface provides no such guidance to alert the user that she is in mg/kg mode. I have shown a picture of the "160 mg/kg" screen to several thousand people during lectures over the past year. "Please raise your hand," I ask, "if you're 100 percent sure you would have noticed the mg/kg setting." Not a single hand has gone up.

▶    ▶    ▶

Of course, both Epic and First Databank, the company that created the rules that govern UCSF's alerts, know full well that a dose of 6,160 mg of Septra is inconceivable; it would be like seeing a street sign saying the speed limit is 2,500 miles per hour. An alert fired, warning Lucca that this was an overdose.

---

[16] Caps lock problems are so common and infuriating that the computer's "swearing symbol"—#$@%*!—is said to have been chosen because it represents the output of typing numbers when the caps lock key has been inadvertently pressed.

With her task list brimming with dozens of unchecked boxes and more sick kids in need of her care and attention, Lucca assumed this was yet another nuisance alert with no clinical significance, and so she clicked out of it. With that, the order for 38½ Septras was now live.

# Chapter 16

# The Alerts

When the villagers saw no wolf, they sternly said, "Save your frightened song for when there is really something wrong!"
— Aesop, *The Boy Who Cried Wolf*

Computerized medication alerts represent only a small fraction of the false alarms that besiege clinicians each day. Barbara Drew, a nurse-researcher at UCSF, has been studying a similar problem, alarms in the ICU, for decades. During that time, she has seen them grow louder, more frequent, and more insistent. She has witnessed many Code Blues triggered by false alarms, as well as deaths when alarms were silenced by nurses who had simply grown weary of all the noise.

In January 2010, an example of the latter brought the issue of alarm fatigue to national attention. An 89-year-old man died at Massachusetts General Hospital after suffering a cardiac arrest. According to the subsequent investigation, 10 nurses on duty did not recall seeing or hearing the multiple alerts, which consisted of beeps at a central nurses' station and messages scrolling on hallway signs. And someone (the person was never identified) had turned off the loud bedside alarm that should have blared as the man's heart first slowed, and then ultimately stopped beating. In 2011, a lawsuit over the incident was settled by the hospital for $850,000.

An investigation launched by the *Boston Globe* revealed that this was far from an isolated case. The *Globe* identified at least 216 deaths in the United States between January 2005 and June 2010 that were linked to alarm malfunction or alarm fatigue. In 2013, The Joint Commission, the main accreditor of American hospitals, issued an urgent directive calling on hospitals to improve alarm safety. The ECRI Institute, a nonprofit consulting organization that monitors data on medical errors, has listed alarm-related problems as the top technology hazard in healthcare in each of the last four years.

There are many reasons for false alarms: misprogrammed thresholds; dying batteries; loosening of an electronic lead taped to the patient's chest. But plenty of alarms are triggered by the activities of daily hospital living. Liz Kowalczyk, who wrote the story for the *Globe*, spent a morning in the cardiac unit at Boston Children's Hospital. She observed,

> *[The nurse] hurried into Logan's room—only to find a pink-cheeked, kicking 3-month-old, breathing well, cooing happily. Logan was fine. His pumping legs had triggered the crisis alarm again.*
>
> *The red alarm is the most urgent, meant to alert nurses to a dangerously slow or fast heart rate, abnormal heart rhythm, or low blood oxygen level. But on this morning . . . infants and preschoolers activated red alarms by eating, burping, and cutting and pasting paper for an arts and crafts project.*

▶    ▶    ▶

In the face of growing nationwide concern about alert fatigue, Barbara Drew set out to quantify the magnitude of the problem. For a full month in early 2013, she and her colleagues electronically tapped into the bedside cardiac alarms in UCSF's five intensive care units, which monitored an average of 66 patients each day. Mind you, this is just the bedside cardiac monitor, which follows the patient's EKG, heart rate, blood pressure, respiratory rate, and oxygen saturation. It does *not* include the IV machine alarms, mechanical ventilator alarms, bed alarms, or nurse call bell. Nor does it include any of the alerts in the computer system, like the Septra overdose alert that Jenny Lucca overlooked.

Drew's findings were shocking. Every day, the bedside cardiac monitors threw off some 187 audible alerts. No, not 187 audible alerts for all the beds in the five ICUs; 187 alerts were generated by the monitors *in each patient's room*, an average of one alarm buzzing or beeping by the bedside every eight minutes. Every day, there were about 15,000 alarms across all the ICU beds. For the entire month, there were 381,560 alarms across the five ICUs. Remember, this is from just one of about a half-dozen systems connected to the patients, each tossing off its own alerts and alarms.

And those are just the audible ones. If you add the inaudible alerts, those that signal with flashing lights and text-based messages, there were 2,507,822 unique alarms in one month in our ICUs, the overwhelming majority of them false. Add in the bed alarms, the ventilators, and the computerized alerts . . . well, you get the idea.

▶   ▶   ▶

Drew believes there are many ways to safely reduce the number of alerts. Some can be eliminated with simple tweaks of the thresholds. At Boston Medical Center, just changing the high and low heart rate parameters—from 120 and 50 to 130 and 45, respectively—and empowering the nurses to make further clinically sensible changes in these limits safely cut the audible alarm rate by 89 percent.

Second, the alarms need to be better integrated. Let's say the monitor incorrectly picks up a fast heart rate when the patient is vigorously brushing his teeth. (This kind of "motion artifact" is a common cause of false readings.) There is currently no electronic governor, for instance, that is smart enough to refuse to set off an alarm if the heart rate is registering at 220 (normal is about 70) while the blood pressure and respiratory rate remain perfectly normal, even though these normal values would be impossible if the heart was really racing that fast.

There are other strategies that would help as well, many of which involve paying a little attention to the things medical students learn in Physiology 101. Delaying the onset of an alarm for one minute, which would be perfectly safe the vast majority of the time, would allow many false alarms to resolve spontaneously. The EKG monitor currently sets off a signal when there is a change in a certain portion of the tracing (the ST segment), even when the timing of that change is incompatible with a heart attack. Alerts for premature heartbeats (to which we no longer pay attention, since studies have shown that treating them with powerful antiarrhythmic drugs kills far more people than it saves) account for fully one-third of the total alerts. These alerts could be markedly pruned. Drew believes that, taken together, an intelligent program of integration and physiologic sense making would abolish more than 90 percent of the false alarms.

IBM's Watson team is beginning to tackle this problem with a technique called cognitive computing, which takes into account not just the physiologic variables, but also the context. "Based on what I can extract from the data"—for example, the changes in heart rate and oxygen saturation coupled with the patient's underlying diseases, which ICU he is in, and even the time of day—"we see how the nurse interacts with that data and responds to those alerts over time," explains Shahram Ebadollahi, the IBM big-data expert. "From this, we ask, 'Can I learn what really matters for this context and condition?'"

Why haven't the folks who make the monitors—including some of the world's most sophisticated technology companies, such as GE and Medtronic—paid more attention to this issue? We might ask the same question of the EHR vendors regarding medication alerts, and one important answer would probably be the same: liability. While manufacturers may appreciate the plight of the poor clinicians playing whack-a-mole with all the alarms, they know their liability centers on missing a crisis, rather than oversignaling, analogous to the challenge faced by TSA agents at airports every day. "Missing a real event is much more costly to the manufacturer," said Roger Mark, head of MIT's Laboratory for Computational Physiology. "On the other hand, if a nurse fails to look at a monitor when a beep goes off and the patient dies, that's the nurse's fault."

▶    ▶    ▶

Despite all the promising ideas for attacking the problem of runaway alarms and alerts, the most common responses today are stoic resignation and workarounds. Drew has observed nurses disconnecting alarm speakers or muffling them under blankets. In one ICU, a dumbwaiter threw off a sound very similar to the critical arrhythmia alert when it reached the floor with the food trays. It drove the nurses berserk.

The issue of alarm and alert fatigue is a clear and present danger, and the victims are both patients and clinicians. Barbara Drew recalled speaking to one nurse amid the din of multiple alarms going off like hand grenades on a Normandy beach. In the face of such cacophony, Drew asked the nurse what kind of alarm would cause her to snap to attention. She thought for a moment and then said, "If the alarms went silent. *That* would be scary."

▶   ▶   ▶

Medicine, of course, is not the only industry in which professionals need to perform their tasks in a swirling, often confusing, high-stakes environment, nor the only one that has to grapple with the matter of computerized alerts. I spoke to Captain Chesley "Sully" Sullenberger, the famed "Miracle on the Hudson" pilot, about how aviation handles the matter of alerts. "The warnings in cockpits now are prioritized so you don't get alarm fatigue," he told me. "We work very hard to avoid false positives because false positives are one of the worst things you could do to any warning system. It just makes people tune them out." He encouraged me to visit Boeing to see how its cockpit engineers manage the feat of alerting pilots at the right time, in the right way, while avoiding alert fatigue.

So I spent a day in Seattle with several of the Boeing engineers and human factors experts responsible for cockpit design in the company's commercial fleet. "We created this group to look across all the different gauges and indicators and displays and put it together into a common, consistent set of rules," Bob Myers, chief of the team, told me. "We are responsible for making sure the integration works out."

Sitting inside the dazzling cockpit of a 777 simulator (before I crashed it on landing; despite the magnificent safety systems, it turns out that you still need to know how to fly the plane), Myers and Alan Jacobsen, a technical fellow with the flight deck team, enumerated the hierarchy of alerts that pilots may see. They are:

- An impending stall leads to red lights, a red text message, a voice warning, and activation of the "stick shaker," meaning that the steering wheel vibrates violently. "The plane is going to fall out of the sky if you don't do anything," Myers explained calmly.
- Further down the hierarchy are "warnings," of which there are about 40. These are events that require immediate pilot awareness and rapid action, although they may not threaten the flight path. Believe it or not, an engine fire no longer merits a higher-level warning because it doesn't affect the flight path. ("Fires in engines are almost nonevents now," said Myers, because the systems to handle them are so robust.) The conventions for warnings are red lights, text, and a voice alarm, but no stick shaker. Impressively, the color red is never used in the cockpit except for

high-level warnings—that's how much thought the industry has given to these standards.

- The next level down is a "caution," and there are about 150 such situations. Cautions require immediate pilot awareness but may not require instant action. Having an engine quit in a multiengine plane generates only a caution (again, my jaw drops when I hear this), since the pilot may or may not have to do something right away, depending on whether the plane is at cruising altitude or at 1,500 feet. A failure of the air-conditioning system—which ultimately can lead to a loss of cabin pressure—is another caution event. With cautions, the lights and text are amber, and there is only one alert modality, usually visual.

- The final level is an "advisory," like the failure of a hydraulic pump. Since jets are designed with massive redundancy ("The plane has three others"), no action is required, but the pilot does need to know about it, since it might influence the way the landing gear responds late in the flight. Advisories trigger an amber text message—now indented—on the cockpit screen, and no warning light.

For every kind of alert, a checklist automatically pops up on a central screen to help guide the cockpit crew to a solution. The checklists are preprogrammed to match the problems that triggered the alert.

And that's it. I asked Myers and Jacobsen how, with more than 10,000 data points recorded on every flight, they resist the urge to warn the pilots about everything, as we seem to do in healthcare. "It's a judgment call," Jacobsen told me. "We have a team of people—experts in systems safety and analysis—who make that judgment." Because of this process, the percentage of flights that have any alerts whatsoever—warnings, cautions, or advisories—is low, well below 10 percent.

I wondered whether the designers of individual components sometimes advocate for their own favorite alerts. Myers chuckled. "It's funny, you'll get some young engineer whose responsibility is the window heat system. He comes in with this list of 25 messages that he wants us to tell the pilot about his system: it's on high, it's on medium, it's on low, it's partially failed, you can't operate it below 26 degrees. . . . He comes out of the meeting—a meeting in which the pilots say, 'We don't care!'—and he's like [Myers affects an Eeyore voice], 'This is my job, this is my life, and it doesn't even make it onto the flight deck.'"

Like many of aviation's safety solutions, the parsimonious approach to alerts came from insights born of tragedies. "The original 'gear down' warning was linked to the throttle," recalled Myers, meaning that it went off, falsely, every time the pilot slowed the plane. "So the pilots' learned response was *throttle back, disconnect the alert.*" Predictably, this led to accidents when pilots ignored this alert even when there truly was a problem. Another example: in the early days of the Boeing 727, some alerts were so frequent and wrong that pilots yanked the circuit breakers to quash them.

When I told the Boeing engineers about my world—not only the frequency of computerized medication alerts, but also the ubiquity of alarms in our intensive care units—they were astonished. "Oh, my goodness," was all Myers could say.

▶   ▶   ▶

When I spoke with Jenny Lucca months after Pablo Garcia's overdose, I asked her how she could have clicked out of the Septra overdose alert, knowing now that by doing so, she had confirmed an order for 38½ Septra tablets. She blamed part of it on alert fatigue, of course. But she also pointed to the appearance of the alerts in Epic. "There is no difference between a minuscule overdose—going 0.1 milligram over a recommended dose—and this very large overdose. They all look exactly the same."

In fact, the Epic alert that Lucca received is a model of bad design.[17] There are no graphical cues, no skull and crossbones, no medical equivalent of a cockpit stick shaker—nothing that would tell a busy physician that this particular alert, unlike the dozens of others that punctuate her days, truly demanded her attention. In the language of the Boeing engineers, it would be as if alerts fired for a window warmer malfunction and an impending stall . . . and both looked exactly the same.

Once Lucca signed the Septra order and clicked out of the alert, it boomeranged to Benjamin Chan's computer within a matter of minutes. The pharmacists at a place like UCSF serve as a crucial layer of protection, and Chan was an experienced professional who prided himself on his carefulness. But, on this particular day, the holes in the Swiss cheese were especially large.

---

[17] The only sign of the severity of the Septra alert (shown in the previous chapter) is the word "High," which appears in the upper left-hand corner of the alert. Epic's 2014 upgrade is somewhat improved in this regard. First, the alerts now show up directly below the order in question, rather than in a pop-up box. Second, the system now distinguishes high-risk alerts from others with both a more vivid text warning and an eye-catching icon.

First, Chan had been on the wards with Lucca in the past. "I have worked with her, we know each other, and I trust her," he told me. In retrospect, Chan said, it's likely that this personal relationship was one of the reasons he let his guard down.

Second, the seventh-floor satellite pharmacy, where Chan works, is a frenzied place. In an 8 × 18-foot room (about the size of a parking space), four individuals—two doctorally trained clinical pharmacists like Chan, and two pharmacy techs—buzz around, bouncing into each other like pinballs. In addition to the bodies, the room is packed tight with equipment, including two ventilated hoods for mixing volatile or toxic medications, a sink, shelves lined with bins stocked with medications, a label printer, IV bags, syringes, needles, and a locked cabinet for storing narcotics. On the day I visited, several months after Pablo Garcia's overdose, one of the technicians was carefully mixing up medications, her arms sheathed in rubberized sleeves that penetrated a clear plastic tent.

In the midst of this bustle, the pharmacists were checking every order that appeared in a computerized queue (often making several follow-up calls to determine whether the order was correct), while simultaneously answering the phones, supervising the technicians, and dealing with visitors who periodically appeared at the Dutch door to pick up medications. "The phones just never stop ringing," Chan told me. "There are always nurses coming to the window to pick up their narcotics; the respiratory therapist comes looking for his meds. In going through one patient's medication orders, I'll be interrupted six or seven times, at least." It sure seemed risky to me, and a 2010 Australian study confirmed that it is. The investigators observed 98 nurses while they prepared and administered 4,271 medications. Every interruption increased the risk of a medication error by 13 percent. When a nurse was interrupted four times, the rate of errors so serious that they were likely to lead to permanent harm or death doubled.

▶    ▶    ▶

Abundant research has demonstrated that the term *multitasking* is a misnomer—performance degrades rapidly when people try to do several things simultaneously, whether it's your kids doing homework while texting or a pharmacist checking orders while answering the phone. Psychologists speak of the concept of "cognitive load"—the overall volume of things a mind is grappling with at a given time. While there are some individual differences in the ways we manage cognitive load, one thing is clear: none of us does this as well as we think we do. Studies of air traffic controllers have demonstrated that at busy times, professionals do their best to manage their cognitive loads by shedding tasks, falling back on automation, and focusing their attention on some things and away from others. But ultimately the brain begins to tire, and that's when you see people cutting the wrong corner.

On top of the challenges of multitasking in a cluttered and hectic workspace, Chan succumbed to the twin cognitive traps of inattentional blindness (focusing so much on one thing that you miss another) and confirmation bias (seeing what you expect to see). You might be acquainted with the video of the psychology experiment in which six kids, three dressed in black and three in white, casually toss around a basketball. When a lecturer uses this video to illustrate the phenomenon of inattentional blindness, before playing the video, he tells the audience to concentrate on counting the number of basketball passes by the students dressed in white. What he doesn't mention is that a few seconds after the passing begins, a person dressed in a gorilla outfit ambles onto the screen, weaves a path between the kids and the ball, turns to the camera for a few Tarzan-like chest thumps, and ambles off. About half the audience, on average, fails to see the plain-as-day appearance of the gorilla. The experiment highlights the fact that the human brain is hardwired to see what it expects to see, particularly when it's busy working on several other tasks, rather than than what's really there.

(By the way, did you notice that the word *than* was repeated in the previous sentence? Don't fret if you didn't—this is your brain engaged in confirmation bias, and it's perfectly natural.)

With all of these cognitive land mines to sidestep, it's little wonder that Chan didn't notice the "mg/kg" (an awfully small gorilla, after all) when he saw "160" only a few minutes after texting Lucca to order just that dose. Also, by a terrible coincidence, when you multiply 160 mg/kg by 38.6 kg, you get 6,160 mg (after rounding to the nearest tablet size), which contains the number "160," another opportunity for confirmation bias.

So Chan accepted the order for 160 mg/kg. And then he went on to click out of his own alert screen, which looked as bland and busy as the one that Lucca received and—for good measure—contains the number "160" in 14 different places.[18]

---

[18] Ten instances of the number "160," and another four of "6,160."

| sulfamethoxazole-trimethoprim (BACTRIM DS,SEPTRA DS) 800-160 mg tablet 6,160 mg of trimethoprim |
|---|
| New |
| Modified from: ↱ sulfamethoxazole-trimethoprim (BACTRIM DS,SEPTRA DS) 800-160 mg tablet 160 mg of trimethoprim |

✎ Edit Clinical Information

| Order dose: | **160 mg/kg of trimethoprim** | Route: | **Oral** | Frequency: | **Every 12 Hours Scheduled** |
|---|---|---|---|---|---|
| Admin dose: | 6,160 mg of trimethoprim (38.5 tablet) | | | For: | Until discontinued |
| Weight: | Actual (38.6 kg) | | | # of doses: | |
| 160 mg/kg of trimethoprim x 38.6 kg (Weight as of Tue Sep 10, 2013 0900) | | | | 1st dose: | Today 2130 |
| = 6,176 mg of trimethoprim x 1 tablet/160 mg of trimethoprim | | | | Last dose: | |
| = 38.5 tablet x 160 mg of trimethoprim/tablet (rounded to the nearest | | | | Scheduled times (adjusted): | |
| 0.5 tablet from 38.6 tablet) | | | | 9/10/2013 | 2130 |
| = 6,160 mg of trimethoprim | | | | 9/11/2013 | 0900, 2100 |
| = 160 mg/kg of trimethoprim | | | | | |

| Indications: | PNEUMONIA | |
|---|---|---|
| Order questions: ✎ Edit | | |
| Suspected Pathogen: | | (no response given) |
| Admin instructions: ✎ Edit | | |
| (none) | | |

| Products to dispense ✚ Add | Order dose | Admin dose | Dispense Package |
|---|---|---|---|
| ↱ SULFAMETHOXAZOLE 800 MG-TRIMETHOPRIM 160 MG TABLET | 160 mg/kg of trimethoprim | 6,160 mg of trimethoprim | 39 tablet  100 EA BLIST PACK |

Just as with the physician's alert, the sheer number of alerts the pharmacists receive creates a particularly holey piece of cheese. "There are just a lot of them," Chan told me. "Sitting here, I can tell you a number of alerts that make absolutely no sense, and we are alerted to them every single day."

While Chan understands all these explanations at an intellectual level, he still can't help beating himself up for the Septra error. He vividly remembers when his supervisor called him at home a few days after Pablo's overdose to tell him what had happened. "I felt like crap," he said. "I thought, 'How could I have done this, what is wrong with me, I'm a horrible pharmacist'—that's all I could think for a long time, sometimes even now."

"The thing that was really frustrating for me is that I've seen and paged the doctors about so many orders they've put in as milligrams per kilogram when they should have been in milligrams. That's actually a fairly common mistake that I and the other pharmacists catch."

▶  ▶  ▶

Like a missile system now set to launch by the simultaneous turning of two keys, the actions by the physician and the pharmacist had created an active order for 6,160 mg of Septra, or 38½ tablets. At this point, the focus of the hospital's electronic medication safety system shifted from making sure that the order was correct—protections that had been breached by the actions of the doctor and the pharmacist—to making sure that the administered dose matched the prescribed dose. Most of the time, these protections are crucial to patient safety, since one-third of hospital medication errors occur during the drug administration phase, when a nurse gives a patient a medicine that differs from the one ordered. But when the order itself is wrong, these protections become a perversion, shielding the error from being caught.

▶    ▶    ▶

Nearly a year after the overdose, Chan told me, "I still look at the alerts much more carefully now. I hear colleagues say, 'Oh, I just bypass that alert,' and I say, 'No! You should really double-check that.'"

# Chapter 17

# The Robot

Civilization advances by extending the number of important
operations which we can perform without thinking about them.
—Alfred North Whitehead, *An Introduction to Mathematics*, 1911

During my visit to UCSF's seventh-floor satellite pharmacy, I saw the pharmacists verifying many medication orders. A few seconds after the pharmacists approved some of the orders, a label popped out of a nearby printer, and one of the technicians read it and gathered up the appropriate medication. When the order was for pills, she did this by pouring the pills out of bottles or tearing them from strips of serrated blister packs. When the order called for an intravenous solution, she mixed it under the aluminum hood with a meticulousness that would have met with approval from Walter White.

I asked Benjamin Chan what would have happened if the tech had received a label from him with instructions to tear out 38½ individual Septra tablets from a large serrated sheet of individually wrapped pills. Partway through the tearing, he told me, "My tech would have said, 'Hey, this doesn't look right.'" I don't doubt this: there is something about a physical act, whether it is tearing off 39 pills from a sheet or writing out an order with a pen, that can jog a mind out of numb complacency. A study of Princeton undergraduates found that those who scribbled their notes on paper retained far more of the content than those who typed them, probably for this reason. Said Yale psychologist

Paul Bloom, "With handwriting, the very act of putting it down forces you to focus on what's important. . . . Maybe it helps you think better." The same may be true of physical acts like tearing or pouring pills.

Even if the pharmacy tech had missed the error and prepared the 39 pills, there would have been another chance for an eleventh-hour save, because Chan and the other pharmacists check the techs' work before every medication leaves the satellite pharmacy. But Pablo Garcia's first Septra dose was not due for about seven hours, which meant there was time for it to be sent electronically to UCSF's Mission Bay campus, about five miles away, to be processed by the Swiss-made pharmacy robot there. The robot, installed in 2010 at a cost of $7 million, is programmed to pull medications off stocked shelves; to insert the pills into shrink-wrapped, bar-coded packages; to bind these packages together with little plastic rings; and then to send them by van to locked cabinets on the patient floors. "It gives us the first important step in eliminating the potential for human error," said UCSF Medical Center CEO Mark Laret when the robot was launched.

Without question, robots have many advantages over humans, which is why they are taking over so many tasks, in medicine and other industries. Like most robots, UCSF's can work around the clock, never needing a break and never succumbing to a distraction. Yet, wrote anesthesiologist Alan Merry and novelist Alexander McCall Smith in their 2001 book *Errors, Medicine and the Law,*

> *It is true that people are distractible—but in fact this provides*
> *a major survival advantage for them. A machine (unless ex-*

*pressly designed to detect such an event) will continue with its repetitive task while the house burns down around it, whereas most humans will notice that something unexpected is going on and will change their activity.*

The robot dutifully collected 38½ Septra tablets—with perfect accuracy—placed them on a half-dozen rings, and sent them to Pablo's floor, where they came to rest in a small bin waiting for the nurse to administer them at the appointed time.

By the way, there is no final pharmacist check of the robot's handiwork, the way there is for the medications prepared by the technicians in the seventh-floor pharmacy. "If the order goes to the robot, the techs just sort it by location and put it in a bin, and that's it," Chan told me. "They eliminated the step of the pharmacist checking on the robot, because the idea is you're paying so much money because it's so accurate."

# Chapter 18

# The Nurse

Automation bias occurs when we place too much faith in the accuracy of the information coming through our monitors. Our trust in the software becomes so strong that we ignore or discount other information sources, including our eyes and ears.
—Nicholas Carr, writing in the *Atlantic*, 2013

Brooke Levitt had been on the nursing staff at UCSF for about 10 months when Pablo Garcia was admitted for his colonoscopy. Levitt is in her mid-twenties, with an open face, a ready smile, and an upbeat Southern California vibe that makes her a favorite of kids and their parents. She couldn't have been more thrilled to land a job at the renowned academic medical center straight out of nursing school. She was assigned to the pediatric intensive care unit (PICU), and she loved the work because "you're constantly on your feet, critically thinking, working with a team of physicians and pharmacists, and you're always at the bedside." After six months of the standard probationary period, she was now fully credentialed, and she prided herself on knowing the PICU system inside and out.

On the afternoon of July 26, Levitt was assigned a night shift, not in her usual ICU, but on a unit that was short-staffed, the general pediatrics floor. In the parlance of the hospital, she was a "floater," and it was only the second time she had floated outside the PICU since starting her job. The system of

159

floating is governed by a kind of lottery—every nurse, except the most senior, is eligible. "I don't want to float," Levitt later told me, "because I don't know the unit; I don't know the nurses. Most people don't like it." But when your number comes up, you have no choice.

Pablo Garcia was Levitt's second patient that afternoon. She gave him several of his medications, including multiple cups of the bowel-purging solution to drink. Then she came to the order for the 38½ Septras in the computer, and, sure enough, she found all the pills in Pablo's medication drawer. "I remember going to his drawer and I saw a whole set of rings of medications, which had come over from the robot. And there were about eight packets of it on one ring. And I was like, wow, that's a lot of Septra. . . . It was an alarming number." She'd given Septra before in the ICU, but always in liquid or intravenous form, never pills. Her first thought was that perhaps the pills came in a different (and more diluted) concentration. That might explain why there were so many.

▶    ▶    ▶

Since the Paleolithic Era, we humans have concocted explanations for stuff we don't quite understand: tides, seasons, gravity, death. The dilution idea was the first of many rationalizations that Levitt would formulate to explain the unusual Septra dose and to justify her decision to administer it. While at first glance it would seem crazy for her to have done so, the decisions she made that night were entirely consistent with patterns of error seen in medicine and other complex industries. What is new, for medicine at least, is the degree to which very expensive, state-of-the-art technology designed to prevent human mistakes from causing harm not only helped give rise to the Septra error, but also failed to stop it, despite functioning exactly as it was programmed.

Pablo Garcia's hospital ward doubled as UCSF's pediatric research center, where patients on clinical trials frequently receive unusual medications. Levitt, still a bit baffled by the number of Septra pills, now wondered whether *that* explained the peculiar dose—perhaps Pablo was on some sort of research protocol. She thought about asking her only colleague on the floor, the charge nurse, but she knew that the charge nurse was busy seeing her own patients and delivering their medications.

Of course, Brooke Levitt now beats herself up for not tapping her colleague on the shoulder. But it's not that surprising that she failed to do so. Studies have found that one important cause of errors is interruptions, so clinicians at UCSF and elsewhere have been counseled to avoid them, particularly when their colleagues are performing critical and exacting tasks like giving children potentially dangerous medications. In some hospitals, nurses now mix or collect their medications wearing vests that say "Don't Interrupt Me," or stand inside a "Do Not Interrupt" zone marked off with red tape.

But there was probably something else—more subtle and more cultural—at play. Today, many healthcare organizations study the Toyota Production System, which is widely admired as a model for safe and defect-free manufacturing. One element of the TPS is known as "Stop the Line." On Toyota's busy assembly line, it is every frontline worker's right—responsibility, really—to stop the line if he thinks something may be amiss. The assembly line worker does this by pulling a red rope that runs alongside the entire line.

When a Toyota worker pulls the cord for a missing bolt or a misaligned part, a senior manager scrambles to determine what might be wrong and how to fix it. Whether on the floor of an automobile manufacturing plant or a pediatrics ward, the central question in safety is whether a worker will "stop the line"—not just when she's sure something is wrong but, more important, *when she's not sure it's right.*

Safe organizations actively nurture a culture in which the answer to that second question is always yes—even for junior employees who are working in unfamiliar surroundings and unsure of their own skills. Seen in this light, Levitt's decision to talk herself out of her Spidey sense about the Septra dose represents one nurse's failure in only the narrowest of ways. More disturbingly, it points to a failure of organizational culture.

Levitt's description of her mindset offers evidence of problems in this culture, problems that are far from unique to UCSF. "When I was counting all the pills and seeing them fill half a cup, my first thought was, *that's a lot of pills.* Obviously it didn't alarm me enough to call someone. But it was more than just a nagging sensation."

Why didn't she heed it? Another factor was her rush to complete her tasks on an unfamiliar floor. The computer helps create the time pressure: a little pop-up flag on the Epic screen lets nurses know when a medication is more than 30 minutes overdue, an annoying electronic finger poke that might make sense for medications that are ultra-time-sensitive, but not for Septra pills. She also didn't want to bother the busy charge nurse, and she "didn't want to sound dumb." As is so often the case with medical mistakes, the human inclination to say, "It must be right" (psychologists call this "satisficing") can be powerful, especially for someone so low in the organizational hierarchy, for whom a decision to stop the line feels so risky.

Finally, the decision to stop the line sometimes hinges on how much effort it takes to resolve one's uncertainty. Remember that Levitt usually worked in the pediatric ICU, where nurses, doctors, and pharmacists still generally work side by side, hovering over desperately ill babies. "I'm so used to just asking a resident on the spot, 'Is this the dose you really want?'" she said. But on the wards, where the pace is slower and the children are not as critically ill, the doctors have all but disappeared. They are now off in their electronic silos, working away, but no longer around to answer a "Hey, is this right?" question, the kind of question that is often all that stands between a patient and a terrible mistake.

▶   ▶   ▶

Of course, it would have been easy enough for Brooke Levitt to page one of the doctors, or to call the pharmacist, or to pull her charge nurse out of a room to ask about the bizarre dose. And sure, a change in the culture might have made her more inclined to do these things, any of which would probably have prevented the overdose. But a major reason she didn't call anyone was that she trusted something she believed was even more infallible than any of her colleagues: the hospital's computerized bar-coding system.

In a seminal 1983 article, Lisanne Bainbridge, a psychologist at University College London, described what she called the "irony of automation." "The more advanced a control system is," she wrote, "so the more crucial may be the contribution of the human operator." In a famous 1995 case, the cruise ship *Royal Majesty* ran aground off the coast of Nantucket Island after a GPS-based navigation system failed because of a frayed electrical connection. The crew members trusted their automated system so much that they ignored a half-dozen visual clues during the more than 30 hours that preceded the ship's grounding, when the *Royal Majesty* was 17 miles off course.

In a dramatic study illustrating the hazards of overreliance on automation, Kathleen Mosier, an industrial and organizational psychologist at San Francisco State University, observed experienced commercial pilots in a flight simulator. The pilots were confronted with a warning light that pointed to an engine fire, although several other indicators signified that this warning was exceedingly likely to be a false alarm. All 21 of the pilots who saw the warning decided to shut down the intact engine, a dangerous move. In subsequent interviews, two-thirds of these pilots who saw the engine fire warning described seeing at least one other indicator on their display that confirmed the fire. But there had, in fact, been no such additional warning. Mosier called this phenomenon "phantom memory."

Computer engineers and psychologists have worked hard to understand and manage these thorny problems of automation complacency and overreliance. Even aviation, which has paid so much attention to thoughtful cockpit automation, is rethinking its approach after several high-profile accidents, most notably the crash of Air France 447 off the coast of Brazil in 2009, that reflect problems at the machine–pilot interface. In that tragedy, a failure of the plane's speed sensors threw off many of the Airbus A330's automated cockpit systems, and a junior pilot found himself flying a plane that he was, in essence, unfamiliar with. His incorrect response to the plane's stall—pulling the nose up when he should have pointed it down to regain airspeed—ultimately doomed the 228 people on board. Two major thrusts of aviation's new approach are to train pilots to fly the plane even when the automation fails, and to prompt them to switch off the autopilot at regular intervals to ensure that they remain engaged and alert.

But the enemies are more than just human skill loss and complacency. It really is a matter of trust: humans have a bias toward trusting the computers, often more than they trust other humans, including themselves. And this bias grows over time as the computers demonstrate their value and their accuracy (in other words, their trustworthiness), as they usually do. Today's computers, with all their humanlike characteristics such as speech and the ability to answer questions or to anticipate our needs (think about how Google finishes your thoughts while you're typing in a search query), engender even more trust, sometimes beyond what they deserve.

An increasing focus of human factors engineers and psychologists has been on how to build machines that are transparent about how trustworthy their results are. In defeating the *Jeopardy* champions, Watson signaled its degree of certainty with its answers. George Mason University psychologist Raja Parasuraman is working on a type of computer Trust-o-Meter, in which the machine might have a green, yellow, or red light, depending on how trustworthy it thinks its result is.

But that might not have bailed out Levitt, since the bar-coding machine probably felt pretty darn sure that it was prompting her to deliver the correct dose: 38½ pills. So we are left struggling with how to train people to trust when they should, but to heed Reagan's admonition to "trust but verify" when circumstances dictate. The FAA is now pushing airlines to build scenarios into

their simulator training that promote the development of "appropriately calibrated trust." Medicine clearly needs to tackle its version of the same problem.

▶   ▶   ▶

In Levitt's case, the decision to put her faith in the bar-coding system was not
born of blind trust; since it had been installed a year earlier, the system had
saved her, as it had all the nurses at UCSF, many times. Unlike the doctors' and
pharmacists' prescribing alerts and the ICU cardiac monitors, with their high
false positive rates, the nurses usually found their bar-code alerts to be correct
and clinically meaningful. In fact, under the old paper-based process, the drug
administration phase was often the scariest part of the medication ecosystem,
since once the nurse believed he had the right medicine, there were no more
barriers standing between him and an error—sometimes a fatal one.

Months after the error, I asked Levitt what she thought of Epic's bar-
coding system. "I thought it was very efficient and safer," she said. "If you scan
the wrong medication, it would instantly have this alert that said, 'This is the
wrong medication; there's not an admissible order for this medication.' So I
would know, oops, I scanned the wrong one. It saved me."

Levitt trusted not just the bar-coding system, but UCSF's entire system of
medication safety. Such trust can itself be another hole in the Swiss cheese.
While a safety system might look robust from the outside—with many independent checks—many errors pick up a perverse kind of momentum as they
breach successive layers of protection. That is, toward the end of a complex
process, people assume that, for a puzzling order to have gotten this far, it
*must* have been okayed by the people and systems upstream. "I know that a
doctor writes the prescription," Levitt said. "The pharmacist always checks
it . . . then it comes to me. And so I thought, it's supposed to be like a triple-
check system where I'm the last check. I trusted the other two checks."

▶   ▶   ▶

Brooke Levitt took the rings of medications to Pablo's bedside. She scanned
the first packet (each packet contained one tablet), and the bar-code machine
indicated that this was only a fraction of the correct dose—the scanner was
programmed to look for 38½ pills, not one. So she scanned each of the pills,
one by one, like a supermarket checkout clerk processing more than three
dozen identical grocery items.

Yet even after the bar-code system signaled its final approval, Levitt's nagging sense that something might be wrong had not completely vanished. She
turned to her young patient.

# Chapter 19

# The Patient

Hospitals should be arranged in such a way as to make being sick an interesting experience. One learns a great deal sometimes from being sick.

—Alan Wilson Watts, *The Essential Alan Watts*

At the time of his July 2013 admission to the hospital, Pablo Garcia was 16 years old, a tenth grader at a high school in Stockton, California. He hoped to be an auto mechanic one day. At about 85 pounds, he was quite small for his age, a consequence of his immune disease and the havoc it had played with his digestive system. Stockton is a two-hour drive from San Francisco, but with its depressed, farm-based economy and its high crime rate, it's a world away from the sparkling City by the Bay. While Pablo has a primary care doctor in Stockton, the city lacks the resources and specialists of UCSF, so he's been coming to San Francisco for care since he was a child.

Pablo's mother, Blanca, is fiercely protective of her children, especially Pablo and the younger Tomás, both of whom have NEMO syndrome. Whenever Pablo or Tomás is in the hospital, Blanca plants herself in the room, partly to lend support, but also to be a final set of eyes and ears. Hospitals, she knows, can be dangerous places.

As luck would have it, on the night of July 26, Pablo and Tomás were both hospitalized at UCSF Medical Center. Since Tomás was the sicker of her two children, Blanca decided to spend the evening in his room, one floor up from Pablo's. But before leaving her older son's room, she reminded him that he would be taking a lot of medicine to get him ready for the colonoscopy.

There's a movement in medicine to practice in a more "patient-centered" way, a major part of which is to involve patients in their own care. One arm of this movement highlights the role of patients and their families in protecting themselves, such as having patients ask their doctors and nurses whether they have washed their hands. While many (including myself) are skeptical about how effective this is and whether it places an inappropriate burden on patients and their families, there are clearly times when patients or their loved ones are highly aware of their treatment plans and can participate meaningfully in catching errors. In the midst of doing the bar-code scans, Levitt decided to ask her young patient about this strange dose of Septra.

Pablo was used to taking unusual medications, and on top of that, he remembered his mom's parting words about the meds he'd be given for his colonoscopy prep. So Pablo told Levitt that the Septra dose seemed okay. Reassured, the nurse handed the half-filled cup of pills to her patient and he began to swallow them, some a handful at a time. Levitt remembers thinking to herself, "What a good kid, what a trouper."

One of Pablo's last memories before his seizure was of texting a friend. "They're having me take an awful lot of pills and drink an awful lot of liquid," his message said. About six hours later, the teenager blacked out, and his arms and legs began jerking. Luckily, the Code Blue team was able to revive him from his brief period of apnea, and he recovered in the intensive care unit over the next several days. On the morning of August 5, ten days after the overdose, the doctors restarted Pablo's Septra. This time, the medication was ordered as "Septra, one double-strength pill twice a day"—not in mg/kg—in the computer system.

▶    ▶    ▶

Try, if you can, to imagine what it feels like to be Blanca Garcia. Her two sons are constantly battling infections—sometimes painful skin infections that weep, itch, and blister; other times pneumonias that cause her children to cough and gasp for air. Their digestive systems are never normal. There may be diarrhea one week, nausea the next, and bleeding the week after that. They are malnourished; Tomás must receive his nutrition through a tube threaded into his small intestine. Blanca is also raising two daughters, who, as females, were protected from the mutation that causes NEMO syndrome. And there is always the memory of her third son, who died at age six from the syndrome, a constant reminder of the risks that may lie ahead for her two boys.

Last year alone, Pablo and Tomás were hospitalized at UCSF a combined total of eight times, and they had an additional 20 clinic visits. Remember, each visit and hospitalization involves a two-hour drive from Stockton to San Francisco, then back again. Any time either of her children is hospitalized, Blanca Garcia is there, ready to help and to question. (In fact, I spoke to her during one of Tomás's hospitalizations in 2014, about a year after the Septra overdose. Pablo was there too, lying on a cot by his brother's bedside.) She is aware that some of the doctors and nurses see her as hard to please, maybe even "difficult." To her, she is simply advocating for her children.

Pablo Garcia is fine today, although Blanca continues to worry about long-term effects from the 39 Septras. The doctors have reassured her, but—after the medication error that nearly killed her child—she doesn't really believe them. "It's exhausting," she said, "to feel like you can't trust people."

# Part Four

# The Connected Patient

# Chapter 20

# OpenNotes

> Each patient carries his own doctor inside him. They come to
> us not knowing that truth. We are at our best when we give the
> doctor who resides within each patient a chance to go to work.
> —Albert Schweitzer (1875–1965)

In a 1996 episode of the iconic TV comedy *Seinfeld*, the character Elaine Benes, played by Julia Louis-Dreyfus, sneaks a peek at her paper chart while waiting for her physician, Dr. Stern, to enter the room to examine her rash. Alighting on a note from a prior visit, Elaine sees that the doctor had described her as "difficult." She becomes fixated on talking Stern into purging the insult from her medical record. After a few minutes, Stern chuckles dismissively and agrees to "erase" the offending word, vigorously scratching the back end of his pencil on the page.

"But it was in pen," the exasperated Elaine says softly. "You fake-erased."

▶   ▶   ▶

If the arc of history bends toward justice, the arc of medicine bends toward transparency. Physicians of yore wrote their notes in Latin and were taught that it was wrong to share too much information—a diagnosis of tuberculosis, the fact that a cancer was untreatable—with patients or their families.[19] Today, most people, including both patients and doctors, are comfortable with the shift toward more openness and honesty—up to a point. One of the remaining debates is over whether patients should be able to read, own, and contribute to their medical records.

Until recently, the paper chart's immutable physicality has, for the most part, allowed us to sidestep this debate. Although the 1996 Health Insurance Portability and Accountability Act (HIPAA) granted patients the right to examine, and even amend, their medical records, when the record was on paper, this portion of the law was like giving a sailboat to someone in the middle of the desert. Since the chart lived in the doctor's office or the medical records department of the hospital, a patient who wanted to read it usually had to wait for weeks and pay hefty photocopying fees—steps designed to prompt her to think twice before making such an impertinent request. Most patients decided it wasn't worth the hassle.

Once the record became an infinitely reproducible digital database, however, the only thing separating the Elaine Beneses of the world from their laboratory studies, x-ray results, and doctors' notes was a password. Of all the changes wrought by the computerization of healthcare, history may ultimately judge the opening of the medical record to patients to have been among the most transformative. But there is often a large gap between the possible and the actual, and closing this gap required a passionate doctor to convince his colleagues that they would not be spending half their time fake-erasing if patients were granted access to their records.

►    ►    ►

Tom Delbanco is intellectual, bookish, worldly, and iconoclastic. He comes by it honestly. His parents—his father was an art dealer, painter, and sculptor with works in the National Portrait Gallery; his mother's graduate thesis in philosophy was a study of one of Hegel's disciples, "proving he didn't *deserve* any attention," said Tom—fled to England from Germany in 1936, arriving in America soon after the Second World War. His brothers, Andrew and Nicholas, are both award-winning authors. Tom is an accomplished amateur violinist.

Delbanco spent his faculty career at Harvard, where he founded the Division of General Internal Medicine at Beth Israel Hospital[20] and launched

---

[19] It's worth noting that this degree of paternalism is still prevalent in many countries outside the United States.

[20] Now Beth Israel Deaconess Medical Center.

several programs aimed at improving doctor-patient communication. He was strongly influenced by sociologist Erving Goffman's description of "total institutions": large bureaucratic entities in which inhabitants' lives are monitored and routinized by staff members, who naturally form their own, often adversarial, community. In 1957, Goffman described the psychological distance between the inmates and the staff of total institutions:

> *Each grouping tends to conceive of members of the other in terms of narrow hostile stereotypes, staff often seeing inmates as bitter, secretive, and untrustworthy, while inmates often see staff as condescending, high-handed, and mean. . . . Two different social and cultural worlds develop, tending to jog along beside each other, with points of official contact but little mutual penetration.*

While Goffman's focus was on prisons and mental institutions, Delbanco saw many things in hospitals that reminded him of the famous sociologist's portrait.

I asked Delbanco whether his passion for patient participation came from seeing its absence as a moral failing. "No, I thought it was a very pragmatic issue," he said. "Patients possess a body of knowledge about themselves that we can never hope to master, and we have a body of knowledge about medicine that they can never hope to master. Our job is to bring these two groups together so we can serve each other well."

One memorable encounter transmuted Delbanco's general passion for improving the doctor-patient relationship into a specific focus on the medical record. As Debanco later recalled,

> *I had a patient who had blood pressure that was hard to control and some job dissatisfaction, and in talking with him, I got a history of his drinking "a few beers off and on." I also . . . learned that he got mad at his kids very often, that his sex life could be better with his wife, and that his job as a printer was something he was thinking about stopping. It struck me that all these little signals might be a proxy for alcohol abuse.*

Delbanco was about to write down the diagnosis of "alcohol abuse" in the chart, but then realized that, as a printer, the patient would be able to read this, even upside down. Delbanco stopped and said,

*I'm wondering whether I should write, as part of our under-*
*standing of each other, "alcohol abuse." If you don't see it as a*
*problem, there's no point in writing it. On the other hand, if you*
*think it is, we should write it down, agree on it, and work on it.*

*There was a long pause, and he said, "Doc, I think you*
*should write it down." And that was the key to opening an*
*aggressive intervention with his drinking and his life. I got a*
*social worker involved. We got his wife involved, and that was*
*a turnaround in his life.*

▶   ▶   ▶

Delbanco was not the first clinician to advocate giving patients access to their
charts. In 1973, in the *New England Journal of Medicine*, Yale's Budd Shenkin
and David Warner argued that patients should be given a "complete and unex-
purgated copy" of all their records after every patient visit. While the proposal
seemed revolutionary, in a letter to the editor, a former medical missionary
described a similar system that had operated in East Africa for many years.

*At each outpatient visit the patient is given a blank scrap of*
*paper stamped with the date and the name and location of*
*the clinic. The doctor or medical assistant writes a few words*
*of history of the present illness and pertinent physical find-*
*ings on this paper and then the prescription, finally at the*
*bottom of the page signing his name, and usually his title. . . .*
*The patient takes this paper, now a "cheti," to the dispenser*
*or nurse, from whom he receives the prescribed treatment,*
*and then pins the "cheti" to the top of his lifetime collection*
*of these documents, plural "vyeti." He carefully preserves*
*them, usually on his person. The next time he is seen at a*
*clinic he hands the sheaf of papers, vyeti, to the doctor to*
*review as he also presents his new stamped blank paper*
*received that day. . . . The record is always where the patient*
*is, even if he is an illiterate nomadic herdsman.*

▶   ▶   ▶

In 1980, Delbanco and his colleagues recruited 25 patients and four physicians to test a new model for the medical record, one in which patients and

clinicians would "co-write" the clinic visit note. Patients were encouraged to keep notes in a special journal that they brought to the clinic, chronicling their symptoms and questions, and recording things they monitored themselves, such as glucose levels for diabetics. During the visit, the doctor and patient would, often awkwardly, collaboratively write down the symptoms and the exam, as well as the assessment and the plan. The physicians worried about the inefficiency of this team note writing, and they were right to do so: visit times increased by 50 percent, at least at first.

Patients became very attached to their little notebooks, even bringing them to visits with doctors who had no clue about the study. Delbanco recalls the gruff ENT surgeon who decided that his patient "must be psychotic" because "the patient had the chutzpah to say to the doctor, 'You write what you think, I'll write what I think, and we'll compare.'" Thirty-five years later, Delbanco still laughs at the memory.

Part of what doomed collaborative note writing was that it isn't very feasible when the medium is paper. (Try picturing a paper-based Wikipedia and you'll appreciate the problem.) But laboratory, radiology, and pathology results were computerized relatively early (many hospitals and clinics did so in the 1990s), and some healthcare systems began experimenting with giving patients access to them.[21] While this information was less fraught than doctors' notes, many in the medical establishment still worried about how patients might handle seeing such results unfiltered. The early results were reassuring. Delbanco and his main collaborator, a nurse/MBA named Jan Walker, observed in 2012 that despite opening access to test results, "the world has not collapsed as a result. To be sure, some patients learn bad news before their doctors intervene, but these cases are the rare exception." To minimize these problems, many organizations built in a time delay of a few days before releasing particularly charged results, such as the results of pathology studies or serum cancer markers.

While Delbanco's early studies of patient access to the medical record focused on sharing a paper chart, he saw a huge opportunity in the switch to electronic notes. His enthusiasm for opening the note was not only for its practical value; he also viewed it as a litmus test for the computerization of medicine. "The first and foremost question is, to what degree will technology distance us from patients, and to what degree will it bring us closer to them," he told me. Giving patients access to their electronic notes, he believes, tilts the scales toward the latter.

---

[21] The term *patient portal* is now commonly used to describe an Internet-enabled, secure website on which patients can view some portion of their health data. More on this in Chapter 21.

▶  ▶  ▶

In a 2004 study in which patients were surveyed about their interest in seeing their medical record online, two responses illustrated the wide range of views. "I do everything online," one wrote. "It would be great if all my records were accessible online and I could e-mail my doctor and/or nurse about a condition I am having and what they recommend." Another disagreed vehemently: "I do not want my records EVER put on a Web page. Nothing is private or secure. If they are, I will sue you royal."

Knowing that advocates of the status quo (both physicians and patients) would push back hard, Delbanco and Walker did much of their work behind the scenes, trying to perfect the idea, build the infrastructure, and collect key data to help refute the inevitable arguments. The early reactions from colleagues, Delbanco recalled, ranged from "transparency is inevitable" to "Screw you!" "Doctors are conservative and hate change," he said. "I knew we would have to use a mixture of seduction and coercion."

Having laid the groundwork, in 2010 Delbanco and Walker launched a trial of OpenNotes at three sites: Beth Israel Deaconess in Boston; Geisinger Medical Center, a large teaching hospital in central Pennsylvania; and Harborview Medical Center, a Seattle facility that specializes in caring for the indigent. Overall, 105 primary care doctors agreed to share their notes with their approximately 14,000 patients. Physicians were able to exclude selected patients (primarily those with substance abuse and psychiatric histories), and a fair number did so.

The study's results were astonishingly positive. Across the sites, 87 percent of patients opened at least one of their notes. At the conclusion of the trial, 99 percent of the patients wanted the program to continue, and no physician elected to pull the plug. Patients reported better medication adherence, and fewer than one in ten found that the notes caused confusion, worry, or offense.

Still, not everything was rosy. Some physicians did find themselves tiptoeing around four particular topics: cancer, mental health, substance abuse, and obesity. And, while the patients and doctors saw eye to eye on most things, a few conflicts remained. For example, while one in three patients thought they should have the right to approve the doctor's notes, nine in ten doctors did not.

Notwithstanding these areas of mild friction, the doctors' collective sentiment was captured in this comment by one physician participant: "My fears: longer notes, more questions, and messages from patients. In reality, it was not a big deal." In fact, the shared note sometimes proved to be a time-saver. One patient e-mailed her physician, "I read your 'open notes' in preparation for my check-up next week, and I'm quite sure nothing has changed. . . . I'm feeling fine, still working out. . . . Rash is still gone, etc. Shall I reschedule for 3 to 6 months, or do you still want me to come in?"

Delbanco was also pleasantly surprised by how smoothly things had gone. Even though the study demonstrated that patients were avidly reading their notes, "The most common question we got from the doctors was, 'Are you sure the computer is working?'" The patients just weren't pestering their doctors in the ways that many had feared.

▶   ▶   ▶

Despite Delbanco's data and increasing acceptance of OpenNotes (in 2015, nearly four million patients in the United States, including most patients in the massive VA system and about half a million patients in Kaiser Permanente's Northwest region, can read their notes), some physicians remain concerned that patients will misinterpret what they have written. Many doctors become more careful with their language when they know patients will read their notes. Descriptors like "difficult patient" disappear, which is probably for the better. More problematic is the fact that many doctors avoid the term *morbidly obese*, despite the fact that it is an accepted clinical descriptor. Other physicians write "mitotic" (the scientific term for cell division; the loss of its regulation is a cardinal problem in cancer) rather than "cancer," and "progressed" instead of "relapsed." At one prominent southern hospital, I'm told that patients who come to the ER intoxicated are described as "Disciples of Bacchus."[22] And it's easy to see how a patient might not welcome seeing himself described as "SOB," not knowing that that is doctor-speak for "short of breath."

While many of the concerns have been predictable, a few surprising issues have emerged. Not only have physicians become more circumspect about their charting, but some patients, after seeing their notes, describe being more careful about the information they share with their doctors. These privacy worries are not entirely rational, since OpenNotes probably doesn't increase the risk of unwanted dissemination—it just makes patients aware of what would get out if the system were breached.

Social media had not been invented when Delbanco began his quest. But the advent of Twitter, Facebook, and the like raises new privacy concerns—not for the patient, but for the doctor. "The patient using OpenNotes can down-

---

[22] The Roman god of wine.

load the great doctor's thinking, post it on Facebook, and ask the world, 'What do *you* think of this son of a bitch?'" Delbanco told me. "Should I listen to him or not?" While this creates a new argument for the naysayers, Delbanco isn't too bothered by it. "It's inevitable," he said, "and I'd rather have the patient post my real notes than a hearsay version of what I said."

Finally, there is the Elaine Benes predicament: What happens when the patient disagrees with something she sees in the note, or spies an entry that is just plain wrong? This happens "all the time," said Susan Edgman-Levitan, a leader in the field of patient communication who gets her own medical care at Delbanco's Beth Israel Deaconess, which has had OpenNotes for years. Edgman-Levitan recalls a spine x-ray that showed a potentially worrisome complication of her longstanding rheumatoid arthritis. The radiologist's report had one very scary sentence, owing to a missing "no" (as in "there is [no] evidence of worsening subluxation"). This simple omission made it seem that her spine disease (which can be life-threatening) had gotten significantly worse. "I'm thinking, oh, this is going to be a nightmare. If I end up in the ER—and especially if I'm not awake—God knows what they're going to do to me until they figure this out."

She called her primary care physician, who reassured her that this was a typo—her results were fine. She asked if the hospital could correct the report. "That's going to take an act of God," her doctor said. And it did—well, not God, exactly, but the bureaucratic equivalent: several months and a committee meeting or two later, an official addendum was added to the radiology report.

In another case, Edgman-Levitan was about to undergo an invasive GI procedure to rule out pancreatic cancer when she happened to notice that a crucial test had not yet been run. She delayed the procedure to wait for the result, which ultimately returned positive for parasites, thus obviating the need for the procedure. In fact, every patient I spoke to about OpenNotes recalled finding and correcting (or at least trying to correct) at least one important mistake in a record.

▶    ▶    ▶

While OpenNotes has opened a promising new frontier in the world of healthcare IT, we shouldn't minimize the challenges it creates. When my patients are able to see my notes (UCSF has not yet rolled out OpenNotes, but is likely to in a few years), I will undoubtedly engage in some self-censorship. My resulting "just the facts, ma'am" documentation may filter out some of the color commentary that can help my colleagues—or me, if a significant amount of time passes between visits—understand what is going on.

Moreover, as you've seen, medical diagnosis is largely a game of probabilities. Whether I pin the diagnosis "pneumonia" or "heart failure" to a set of clinical findings is entirely probabilistic: I do so when the information I have crosses my threshold for "ruling in" the diagnosis. Such thresholds vary depending on the stakes: I'll call something pneumonia if I'm 90 percent sure that it's pneumonia (and rethink the diagnosis if the patient doesn't get better with antibiotics), whereas I reserve the label "cancer" until I'm 99.99 percent certain. Will my patients understand this?

On top of that, many of my notes include a differential diagnosis, the list of possibilities that doctors learn to create in every case. But how will a patient handle "Probable viral infection, but need to rule out HIV, rheumatologic disorder, and malignancy"? That is good medicine, yet I might not write it if I knew that the audience included the patient himself.

▶   ▶   ▶

Most discussions regarding providing patients access to electronic health information focus on our language: it should be understandable, and we shouldn't write anything to which patients will take offense. But we need to go far beyond the written word. In a 2010 article in *Wired* magazine, Steven Leckart took computer-generated laboratory reports—masterpieces of monotonous obfuscation—and presented them in ways that patients could actually understand. "Lab reports don't have to be unintelligible," Leckart wrote. "With some . . . design-minded thinking, tests can be as informative to patients as they are to physicians. With a little context and color, we can make sense of the numbers." Shown on the next page are two examples, from Leckart's article, of reports. The one on the left is the standard, text-heavy, inscrutable version. The one on the right uses graphics and simple text to clearly make its points.

Will today's EHR vendors create patient-facing interfaces like the one on the right? I doubt it. But now that we're beginning to see the Apples, IBMs, and Googles—along with start-ups that specialize in consumer-focused technology—rush into healthcare, patients are likely to see their data displayed in new, more easily decipherable ways.

▶   ▶   ▶

I asked Roni Zeiger, Google's former top healthcare strategist and now CEO of the online patient community Smart Patients, what the shared medical record of the future might look like. He doubts that it will be created unilaterally by

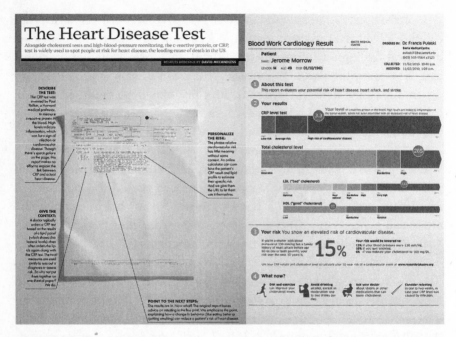

the doctor and later opened to the patient. Rather, he said, "I think the doctor and patient will be talking in a room, and their words will appear automatically on a magic whiteboard that both can see. The board will have fantastic graphics, things like Google Body, which will allow the patient to point to where it hurts and the doctor to digitally remove the skin"—he took a finger and swiped it through the air—"to illustrate what might be going on in the organs underneath," a twenty-first-century version of Morgagni's clinicopathologic correlation, without the need for an autopsy. The words wouldn't simply be a verbatim transcript of their conversation, Zeiger pointed out, but would be transformed into the appropriate format of a note—perhaps by a scribe in the room or by a transcriptionist who is listening in and perhaps even watching the conversation remotely.[23] Ultimately, a computer program using voice recognition and natural language processing will take the conversation and parse it into various buckets: a narrative describing the patient's history; the necessary data for quality measurement and billing; and whatever other forms are needed to feed the big-data machine. "Both doctor and patient will be able to edit the note, and in the end both will sign it," a Jetsons-era equivalent of Delbanco's 1980 shared note initiative.

---

[23] A start-up named Augmedix has built such a capacity: the doctor wears Google Glass during the encounter, and a combination of voice recognition and a remote transcriptionist produces the note. I'll have more to say about this company later.

As he described this vision, Zeiger's eyes lit up. To him, the shared note is about far more than the nuts and bolts of medical care—just as it is to Delbanco. "Software development is like the practice of medicine, parenting, and marriage," said Zeiger. "They're all fundamentally about respect. It's disrespectful to patients not to allow them to co-own their own agenda."

▶   ▶   ▶

One striking aspect of the OpenNotes story is that it is one of the few areas in health IT that has gone better than expected—an area in which the harm was overrated and the hope surpasses the hype.

There is still hype, mind you. While there is evidence that having patients more engaged in their own care leads to greater satisfaction and possibly better medication adherence, the claims that it will revolutionize healthcare by leading to markedly improved clinical outcomes or lower costs remain entirely speculative.

Delbanco knows this, and he is careful not to get too misty-eyed about the potential. He likens OpenNotes to a powerful medication, one that may help patients in many ways, but whose impact needs to be measured. He is quick to add that, like all drugs, OpenNotes may have side effects. "Every medicine kills people. There will be someone who jumps out of a window or murders another person after reading his note. I dread that day," he told me. He and his colleagues have even prepared a response, ready in case that awful phone call ever comes.

# Chapter 21

# Personal Health Records
# and Patient Portals

When we try to pick out anything by itself we find that it
is bound fast by a thousand invisible cords that cannot be
broken, to everything in the universe.
—John Muir, in 1869

OpenNotes is just one slice of a broader phenomenon enabled by healthcare IT: the patient portal. Mark Smith, the former CEO of the California
HealthCare Foundation and a leading thinker in health policy, believes that
patient portals are on the cusp of going viral, in large part because of consumer demand. Smith, who receives his own healthcare from the huge Kaiser
Permanente system, remembers Kaiser's early portal, which was clunky and
downright user-hostile. Today, it's pretty slick, nearly at the level of the customer sites we've grown accustomed to in retail, finance, and travel.

As recently as five years ago, Smith told me, Kaiser CEO George Halvorson
described that company's patient portal in "Washington policy wonk" language—how it would help KP improve quality or alert patients about a newly
identified danger from a drug.[24] Today, it's all about consumerism. "When you

---

[24] The example everyone uses here is that of Vioxx, the arthritis drug recalled by Merck in 2004 after
being found to cause heart problems. Kaiser's EHR helped identify the excess heart attacks, and then,
after the risk became known, quickly alerted all the patients taking the drug and instructed them to
stop using it.

drive to the Oakland airport," Smith said, "you see a Kaiser ad that says, 'Talk to us your way: in person, on the phone, online.' I think within a few years, a healthcare system that can't do that will be dead in the market. Once you get used to checking your lab results on your phone the day they were drawn, you're never going back to, 'Come in next week and we'll talk about it.'"

▶    ▶    ▶

Patient portals need to be something more than just a large data dump. The best portals link physician notes and test results—all presented in user-friendly ways, like the examples Steven Leckart gave us in *Wired*—to medical dictionaries, instructional videos, lists of frequently asked questions, even online communities of patients with similar problems. And, of course, as patients have more access to information outside the clinic visit, they need new ways to communicate with their doctors and health system that don't depend on an in-person visit.

Ted Eytan, a family physician who runs Kaiser's Center for Total Health, is an exuberant supporter of electronic connectivity between patients and the system. "When you start to receive messages from your patients in their own words, it's a totally different experience," he said. "From day one, I had patients e-mailing me about sexual issues that they never would talk to me about directly. Once you do it, it's the thing."

In 2013, 4.4 million of Kaiser's 9.1 million members were active users of *My Health Manager*, KP's patient portal. That year, members visited the site 131 million times to do things like view lab results, make appointments, and refill prescriptions.

And they sent e-mails to their providers—14.7 million e-mails, to be precise. From a corporate perspective, this is fabulous, since, as a prepaid health plan, Kaiser has a powerful incentive to decrease office visits and hospitalizations.[25] For the majority of American physicians, however, who are still paid based on the visit (some payers are beginning to cover e-mails and tele-visits, but such policies are far from commonplace), e-mail remains an unfunded mandate and a powerful source of How-the-Hell-Am-I-Now-Going-to-Find-Time-for-*This* terror. Even for Kaiser physicians, the picture isn't all pretty: several Kaiser doctors told me that they are drowning as they try to juggle the constant thrum of patient e-mails with their day job.

---

[25] The evidence that offering e-mail access to patients lowers the number of visits is mixed. Some studies support this commonsensical association, but the biggest study to date, from Kaiser's Colorado region and published in the *Journal of the American Medical Association* in 2012, found a surprising increase in clinic visits, for reasons that are poorly understood.

The right answer, Mark Smith believes, isn't to limit the connectivity, but rather to give clinicians the time they need to do this new work. "I was in a primary care clinic in Denmark," he recalled. "At 8 in the morning, every clinician was in the office in front of the computer, because the first hour of the day is reserved for answering e-mails." Such work-flow and payment changes will be needed as our newly wired environment allows us to shift the locus of care from the office and the hospital to the home and the community.

▶    ▶    ▶

Kaiser's model for a patient portal—one in which a healthcare delivery system creates the site (in Kaiser's case, built on the backbone of its Epic EHR) and opens it up to patients (known as a "tethered" personal health record)—should be distinguished from another model in which patients create and maintain a personal health record independent of any healthcare system. Of course, wise patients have always kept such information—in decomposing shoeboxes filled with vaccination records and assorted physician notes, x-ray reports, and other medical flotsam and jetsam. Not long ago, some of the world's technology titans set out to create a digital version of this shoebox, in the name of improving patient care and empowering patients (and, no doubt, selling ads or subscriptions). This turned out to be far harder than it looked, even for some of the most successful companies on the planet.

I participated in one such effort as a member of Google Health's Advisory Council. Google's idea was to create an untethered personal health record. The company recognized that patients would never take the time to type in all their health information, so the plan was to populate the site with key information imported from all the places they received care. When the site launched in 2008, Google had already lined up a few provider systems (such as the Cleveland Clinic), pharmacies (CVS and Walgreens), and a national laboratory chain (Quest).

Google Health was run for a time by Marissa Mayer, then Google's "user experience" guru and now Yahoo!'s high-wattage CEO, and our advisory group, chaired by celebrity doctor Dean Ornish, received pep talks from then Google CEO Eric Schmidt and other Google luminaries. "Getting into health is the right thing for Google to do," Schmidt told us. "Not everything has to make money," said Mayer. "Google is an ecosystem, and we're trying to grow a loyal, devoted user base."

Rereading a blog post I wrote in 2008, at the time of Google Health's launch, it is clear that I too was swept up in the hype:

> *I found it easy to link to one of the partnering sites (in my case, Walgreens), and, during a demo at the Council meeting, we were able to import a member's medical records from the Beth Israel Deaconess site into his Google Health record. "Never forget this day," said one of the Council members, with forgivable hyperbole. "You've just seen a demonstration of portability." Is that how Thomas Edison felt?*

Regardless of how Edison felt, by 2010, Google Health had become a digital Do Not Resuscitate, and two years later, it was allowed to die a quiet, pitiful death. I asked Roni Zeiger, Google Health's chief strategist at the time, to explain the iconic company's strikeout on this high-profile project. "We were too ambitious," he said. "We failed to remember the Google mantra that it is much more important to solve a small problem incredibly well than a big problem 80 percent of the way."

Missy Krasner, another member of the Google Health team who now runs healthcare for Box, the cloud-storage company, agreed. "Google products are measured in 7-day and 30-day active metrics," she told me. "The problem was that Google Health wasn't a compelling enough product for people to return on a daily basis." (Google CEO Larry Page calls this "the toothbrush test," as in, will people use it at least once or twice a day.) "Nobody gives a damn about a utility that amasses all your medical records and data behind the scenes so that, when you get sick, you have it. Nobody cares about it until they get sick."

When I signed on to Google Health myself, creating my first couple of electronic handshakes wasn't too painful, but I quickly saw why the site might not work. To assemble anything resembling a personal health record, I needed to establish electronic accounts with Walgreens, UCSF, Quest, and a couple of outside specialists (assuming that they had electronic records and the capacity for and interest in transferring their data). Then came another set of user agreements, all in tiny print, to allow data to be exchanged between these sites and Google. This undertaking illustrated one of the paradoxes of patient engagement: the only people with the stamina to make it through this marathon probably didn't need a personal health record in the first place. The octogenarian with six chronic diseases who could really benefit from one would no doubt have grown befuddled, then dozed off partway through this nettlesome process.

Google wasn't alone; Microsoft had a similar experience with a comparable product, HealthVault.

The bottom line is that all these companies were too early—a personal health record may ultimately be a winning idea, but it needs to be as simple and streamlined as the sites you use to manage your finances or travel. Whether such a site will ultimately be built by an EHR company reaching out (such as Epic or Cerner) or a consumer IT company reaching in (such as Apple, Facebook, or Google), it will have to successfully overcome the interface and privacy issues that doomed Google Health.

And for a personal health record to be truly transformative, it will need to be far more than a passive window into the medical record, with a scheduling and medication refill module tacked on. It will have to be dynamic, engaging, and capable of interacting with patients and families in ways that ultimately lead to better health.

▶    ▶    ▶

While Google and Microsoft were trying to find ways to give patients direct access to their records via the Web, others have focused on what might seem to be an easier problem: sharing records *between healthcare organizations*, a process known today as health information exchange. You might think this happens naturally, but it doesn't. Take Boston's Longwood Medical Area, where several of the nation's most prestigious teaching hospitals share a space of about 10 city blocks. Although the two largest hospitals, Beth Israel Deaconess and Brigham & Women's, are both Harvard affiliates, in the strange business of healthcare, they are actually competing organizations with entirely separate electronic records. Yet thousands of patients get some of their care at both institutions, making it crucial that they can exchange records. There's a rueful joke that circulates around Longwood: What's the fastest way to get a patient's record from the Brigham to Beth Israel? Answer: a paper airplane.

Since most people get their healthcare relatively close to their home or work, efforts to share medical records across sites focused initially on creating regional health information organizations. In this model, all the data from a region's hospitals and clinics is made available to a new organization that serves as the repository and trusted intermediary. When someone ends up in an emergency room across town, that ER pings the regional organization, which then unlocks the patient's healthcare information from the patient's usual site of care and sends it on.

While the concept of a regional health information organization seems sound, the vast majority of these organizations have failed, even those that received significant federal and foundation funding. Perhaps the most visible failure was in Santa Barbara, California. No one would have predicted such a resounding flop. The circumstances in the small, wealthy community seemed favorable, and the exchange was supported to the tune of about $10 million by Mark Smith's California HealthCare Foundation. But after eight years of limping along, the Santa Barbara site was euthanized in late 2006. The diagnosis: nobody—not doctors, not hospitals, not payers, not even patients—cared enough to keep it going.

For Smith, the experience was at once upsetting and illuminating. "The central lesson was that despite all the rhetoric about 'what happens if you were in an emergency room across town,' there was no convincing business model to support spending private money for this relatively rare public good," he said. Smith's pessimism is proving to be warranted: under the HITECH Act, on top of the $30 billion in implementation incentives, the federal government has spent nearly $600 million promoting health information exchanges, but there isn't terribly much to show for it. There are a few successful exchanges, such as ones in Indianapolis and upstate New York, but they remain distinct outliers.

What kind of incentives might actually succeed in creating a viable information exchange system? Under Obamacare, the federal government and private insurers are actively pushing new payment models that promote the formation of large organizations that will share the responsibility for populations of patients and be accountable for the quality and efficiency of care. The hope is that these new models, called accountable care organizations (ACOs), will create markets in which hospitals and clinics will want—strike that, *need*—to move information around. If one allows for a moment of cockeyed optimism, the hope is that since ACOs lose out if they can't track patients who leave their network, even those that compete with each other might eventually choose to break bread to share electronic information.

But today, the slow progress in implementing effective health information exchanges means that there is currently no easy way for patients (except those who live in the few areas with functioning exchanges) seen in an ER away from their usual point of care to get their health information moved electronically. While everyone agrees that this would be terrific, Smith thinks that the clinical case for it is being overstated.

"When I was a resident, if my patient was in an ER across town, I picked up the damned phone and called that ER," he said. "It happened once or twice a month. It's not that having an electronic exchange wouldn't be a good thing, but that, when you think about the legal objections, the lack of a business case, the operational and practical difficulties . . . it just wouldn't be my highest priority."

▶    ▶    ▶

Underlying many of the discussions regarding personal health records, health exchanges, and interoperability is the need for a universal patient identifier, and ultimately a universal patient record that would be accessible anywhere to you or others who need it. But the idea of a universal health ID is a particular bugbear of privacy advocates, who, in arguing against it, sometimes invoke the specter of the Nazi era. In 1998, swayed by the privacy arguments, Congress passed and President Clinton signed a law banning the use of federal funding to create such a number. This means that any effort to share records between hospitals, or even to access your medical history if you arrive at an ER unconscious, has to begin by solving a high-stakes Sudoku game of figuring out who the hell you are.

Luckily, some of the best and brightest minds in the business have been working on solving this particular puzzle. One of them is John Halamka, the chief information officer at Boston's Beth Israel Deaconess Medical Center. He explained the point to me this way: "Halamka, Wachter—those are uncommon names, so there's no problem looking up our records. But if you're in South Boston and your name is Maureen Kelly, it's just not useful." Michael Blum, CIO at UCSF Medical Center, agrees, calling the congressional ban on the universal patient identifier the single biggest failure in the history of health IT legislation. "Think about all the health information exchanges," he said, "and how many billions of dollars we've spent on them. All they are is a master patient index to figure out who's who, so we can build a large clinical database around that. Well, if you knew who was who and the data could flow, you wouldn't have to do all that!"

▶    ▶    ▶

A decade ago, an interesting idea to try to solve the patient ID puzzle surfaced. While it proved a bit too icky and impractical to have staying power, I include it here as a quirky footnote to the history of personal health records. In December 2004, Halamka had a chip—the size of a grain of rice—that allowed access to his medical record implanted in his right arm. He later described his experience in an article in the *New England Journal of Medicine*. Halamka is a sharp dresser who favors monochromatic black mock turtlenecks, bringing up inevitable comparisons to Steve Jobs. Like Jobs, he is brilliant, outspoken, and quirky. He lives on a 15-acre farm outside Boston, where he raises chickens, ducks, rabbits, guinea fowl, llamas, and alpacas. His decision to implant the chip was inspired in part by the use of such chips in his farm animals.

The chip in Halamka's subcutaneous tissue does not contain his full medical record. Instead, scanning it reveals a unique, unencrypted 16-digit number that can be entered into a website that *does* contain his record. This means that the chip is, in essence, a universal patient identifier. "I'm a rock climber, and I believe that if I fall off a cliff and you find me unconscious, the comfort of being able to scan me and figure out who I am outweighs my concern for privacy," he told a TV news reporter when his implant received national attention.

The privacy concerns are not entirely without merit. In his *New England Journal* article, Halamka raised the possibility that retailers could track his movements and deliver customized advertisements to him, much like the ads shown to the Tom Cruise character in the 2002 thriller *Minority Report*. While this has not been an issue, there have been others, as when Halamka's chip has set off the antitheft systems at Home Depot and Best Buy. He isn't much concerned about the risks, but others are plenty concerned for him. He has received many e-mails calling him a "Borg" and a "human/machine hybrid." "To the Religious Right, I am now the Antichrist," he told me. "From the tinfoil hat crowd: 'The NSA is tracking you.'"

Halamka said that implanting the chip seemed like a reasonable thing to do at the time. The technique had just emerged and was gathering a bit of momentum. Before he recommended it to a patient or a colleague, he wanted to assess the privacy, security, ethical, and medical issues for himself. But, with a decade's worth of hindsight, he says, "It's pretty clear that in 2014, this is the wrong approach. People getting implants: creepy."

Today's answers to the same problems, Halamka believes, will come through records that we maintain on our smartphones and in the cloud. While he sees little chance of overturning the 1998 decision and moving toward a mandatory universal patient identification, Halamka favors an opt-in approach. "I already carry a voluntary universal biometric identifier," he said, showing me his Global Entry card, issued by the U.S. State Department, which helps speed American citizens through U.S. Customs.[26] To me, this makes all the sense in the world, although one can expect privacy advocates (Mark Smith calls them the "privacy jihadists") to fight such a system, even if it's voluntary.

---

[26] It is worth noting that the most commonly used patient identifier today is probably the social security number, despite the fact that such use is strongly discouraged by the Social Security Administration and by an array of federal and state legislation.

Although Halamka's chip doesn't do much for him medically today, it still comes in handy periodically. His llamas and alpacas are "chipped" for identity, in case they're lost or stolen. (So is Newman, my miniature poodle.) One day he took one of his llamas to the veterinarian, who couldn't locate the animal's chip with her scanning machine. Perhaps the chip had migrated, or maybe the vet's device wasn't working. To test the latter possibility, Halamka said to her: "Try me." His chip registered just fine.

Laughing, I asked him if he would now show up in some llama database. "The first three digits designate the species, so I did not show up as a llama," he said reassuringly. "I registered human."

▶    ▶    ▶

With the failures of Google Health and Microsoft HealthVault still fresh in the minds of the big consumer technology companies, today's patient portal scene is dominated by tethered models operated by healthcare systems. Epic, the leading vendor to such systems, boasts that it now has more users who are nonclinicians (that is, patients and families) than clinicians. But over time, with nearly one-fifth of America's GDP being spent on healthcare, you can be sure that consumer IT vendors will reenter this space. It is then that we're likely to see some of the most interesting new products, weaving together clinical, consumer, and personal information in ways that we can scarcely imagine today.

Regardless of the vendor, the pressures for widespread interoperability are growing quickly, and much of the health IT policy buzz is about how to meet this goal. However, the best technical model for achieving it remains unclear. After flirting with the creation of new, cloud-based health data warehouses managed by regions or states, federal enthusiasm for a centralized repository of everyone's health data has waned with each news report that another large company's database has been hacked. In an October 2014 report, the Office of the National Coordinator (ONC) threw its weight behind an approach that builds on the current system.

Today, there are millions of exchanges already occurring: of data from a national laboratory like Quest to a doctor's office, of prescriptions from a physician's computer to the local pharmacy, of discharge summaries from one hospital to another. These exchanges use standards to package up the data and send them from place to place electronically. The standards, in turn, create the digital equivalent of a socket that allows lightbulbs from many different vendors to fit.

The October 2014 proposal called for vendors to create "application programming interfaces" (APIs) that all use the same "sockets." These APIs will allow other vendors' products to exchange data with high levels of privacy and security. Moreover, the plan would create a set of incentives and regulations (some of which may be embedded in Meaningful Use Stage 3) to promote widespread system-to-system exchanges. It will also allow third-party app developers to build software that can connect to these standardized APIs.

Under this model, while there may still be a need for regional or state repositories, their function will be modest: to identify you, track your authorization for data exchange, and then open the pipes to allow for authorized exchanges. But they would not house your health data. Instead, your medical records would remain in your EHR, your personal health portal, or your Apple Watch (or wherever else they happen to be) until there was a clinical reason for you to share them.

To me, this seems like a rational approach. As you'll see later, Epic—under considerable pressure from a variety of fronts, ranging from the media to Congress—has already opened up many of its APIs to outside vendors' products, and is currently exchanging tens of thousands of pieces of data (patient summaries, test reports, and more) each day with other Epic users and with hospitals and clinics on other IT systems. For the federal government to build on this tested method by pushing *all vendors* to use standard APIs makes more sense than trying to concoct a fancy new cloud-based system to house everyone's data. It's not the sexiest of approaches, but this may well be a case in which a slow, steady march toward the goal of total interoperability is likelier to reach the finish line than an undisciplined, crowd-pleasing sprint.

# Chapter 22

# A Community of Patients

Therein the patient
Must minister to himself.

—William Shakespeare, *Macbeth*

I served as the program director for the Sixth International Conference on AIDS, held in San Francisco in June 1990. When I accepted the job, I knew that organizing the world's preeminent AIDS gathering would be daunting. There were 4,000 scientific papers to judge, 12,000 participants from around the world to accommodate, and 1,500 members of the media to feed and placate. As a naive 31-year-old physician just finishing my clinical and research training, I understood virtually nothing about patient engagement, and even less about activism.

I learned quickly. By the time the conference ended, I had fielded several calls from AIDS activists accusing me of killing their loved ones because we had turned down a favorite paper. I had invited activists to serve on all the conference's key committees. After the conference became a target of an international boycott triggered by the U.S. government's decision to prevent HIV-positive people from entering the country, I helped organize a colorful protest march down San Francisco's Market Street.

In my 1991 book, *The Fragile Coalition: Scientists, Activists, and AIDS*, I wrote,

> *The empowerment of patients and the questioning of scientific*
> *expertise will be part of the sociological landscape, and not*
> *only in AIDS. Having our patients and our research subjects*
> *ask, or demand, to have an active voice in what we do and*
> *how we do it may be challenging, time consuming, and even*
> *unpleasant. It is also undeniably right.*

The AIDS activists were angry, and justifiably so. AIDS first struck, and ravaged, the gay community—a disenfranchised group that had long been discriminated against in myriad ways, and one that knew both self-advocacy and street theater. (My favorite example of the latter came in 1991, when the group ACT UP lowered a huge condom over the Arlington, Virginia, house of anti-gay Senator Jesse Helms.) They knew that federal action and funding would be key to solving the puzzle of AIDS, yet they saw little evidence of either. (President Reagan did not utter the word AIDS in a speech until 1987, after the deaths of 41,000 people, mostly gay men, in the United States.) By the end of the 1990 AIDS conference, I had great respect not only for the activists' political savvy, but also for their deep knowledge of the disease and its treatments. Long before the days of Google, they had researched HIV and AIDS with the rigor of scientists. And their level of expertise often surpassed that of their physicians.

▶    ▶    ▶

Twenty-five years later, the face of patient engagement looks more like Neil Feldman, a 61-year-old retired technology executive who lives on a lovely tree-lined street in Rockville, Maryland, with his wife, Judy. When I entered the Feldman home, two Australian cattle dogs, Scout and Ralph, sniffed me warily. A steady stream of birds visited the backyard bird feeder during our lunchtime interview. Books and family pictures were everywhere.

Neil Feldman is very thin (borderline cachectic, in fact), and he's wearing clothes that are now a couple of sizes too big. He smiles easily and often, which I take as testament to an indomitable personality, with an assist from the long-acting morphine he takes for painful bone metastases. When Feldman learned he had kidney cancer in May 2010, he signed on to a website that is now called Smart Patients, an online community for cancer patients run by Roni Zeiger.[27]

---

[27] Zeiger was a trainee of mine at UCSF in the 1990s, and I have made a modest personal investment in Smart Patients.

Feldman's cancer was surgically removed, and, although the tumor was very large, the margins were cancer-free. Unfortunately, two years after the surgery, in July 2012, the cancer recurred in his leg bone and his spine, making it Stage IV and probably incurable.

Before the diagnosis of cancer, "I had no interest in anything medical, which in hindsight was probably a mistake because, once I got into this, I found it fascinating," Feldman said. "I joined Smart Patients because I was looking for other people's experience. . . . Gaining knowledge creates a level of control where, at least, I know what is going on. It helps me deal with what's thrown at me."

Feldman posts to the website often, but he keeps his posts understated. "I don't want people to know how bad my cancer is," he said. "If something happens, you know, it's devastating to folks. Everybody wants to be upbeat, I want to be upbeat . . . when you get close to death."

He paused, and his wife, Judy, chimed in, recalling the mother of a child with cancer who frequents the site. "The mother says to Neil, 'Please keep your health up; you're my son's hero; he wants to know that you're thriving.'" Neil told me about another patient on the site, Trevor from Scotland. He and Trevor used to spar, "but I immensely profited by our exchanges, because he made me think and I made him think. But he didn't make it."

I wondered if Feldman's doctor found his level of engagement, and his knowledge about his cancer, threatening. "I was very lucky because I was referred to a doctor [Dr. Hans Hammers at Johns Hopkins] who was very open-minded and encouraged this from day one," he said. "But at this point [his cancer has spread after several types of treatments], I'm done putting my two cents in. I'm at a precarious place, and he's the expert. . . . But I still test him against what I know and learn. It's not carte blanche by any means."

Judy described the value of having a group of people who understand what you're going through. A serious illness changes not just your perspective, but your priorities—about what matters to you, and who. You treat your casual circle of friends differently, Judy said, and they do the same to you. People stop inviting you over. "They're afraid to or they don't know what to say," she added. "So you lose your usual community. But now you've got another community that understands."

But why not join a local, real-life support group, I asked. "Neither of us are emotional types; we're both kind of intellectual," Judy said. "We're not into touchy-feely groups. One of my nieces said to her mother, my sister, 'Oh, you've got to go up there and hold Judy's hand,' and I thought, 'Oh, my God, don't you dare!'"

▶ ▶ ▶

It's worth highlighting a couple of points here. One is that the virtual community has some distinct advantages over an in-person community. In addition to allowing for far-flung relationships (Neil and Trevor were extraordinarily close, although one lived in Maryland and the other in Scotland), people post things they would never say to someone else.

This turns out to be true in the doctor-patient relationship as well. As we think about the role of computers in collecting historical information from patients, while there are downsides (not being able to judge tone of voice and body language, for example, although computers are starting to overcome this limitation), there are upsides as well. Boston University researchers developed a computerized avatar named Louise to educate hospitalized patients about their upcoming discharge. The patients interact with Louise via a computerized touchscreen interface. Not only is Louise far more cost-effective than a real live nurse or doctor, but, by a ratio of three to one, patients prefer her to an actual human. "It was just like a nurse, actually better," said one patient, "because sometimes a nurse just gives you the paper and says, 'Here you go.' She explains everything."

Moreover, Neil Feldman said he found that—rather than distancing him from his doctors—being a knowledgeable patient empowers him, and that his clinicians like it. Of course, everyone knows there are Dr. House types who would find such patient empowerment off-putting, even unacceptable. Larry Fagan, the retired Stanford informatics professor who is battling prostate cancer, is a Smart Patients user but doesn't mention this to his doctor. "When I saw my oncologist yesterday, there were a couple of times I wanted to say, 'We've been talking about this on the list,' but I knew she would flip," said Fagan. "So I just suppress that."

Still, increasing numbers of physicians appreciate the advantages of the knowledgeable patient. Dave deBronkart, who has made a second career out of his persona as "ePatient Dave" (and who, like Neil Feldman, has metastatic kidney cancer) told me about his relationship with his primary doctor. "Think about it," he said. "A hundred years ago, to get their numbers checked, a person with diabetes had to go to the doctor." Now there are test strips, glucometers, and continuous glucose monitoring systems. Those tools haven't put endocrinologists out of business. On the contrary, they have enriched the face-to-face time a patient has with his physician. "If we go into the visit with both parties knowing what's going on, then we can spend the visit talking about what we *do* about it."

▶   ▶   ▶

The fact that Smart Patients works for Neil Feldman and Larry Fagan owes a great deal to its thoughtful design, much of it by Roni Zeiger, the site's cofounder and CEO. Zeiger is an example of the new breed of physician who straddles the worlds of healthcare and technology. We met in the Silicon Valley warehouse office that his start-up shares with a photography studio. He commutes to work by bicycle, his laptop in his backpack. The company's strategy is mapped out on Post-it notes stuck on the outside of the bathroom door. Japanese lanterns hang from the ceiling, the studio's glossy photographs line the walls, and Zeiger and his coworkers stand at their computers to do their work. The MacBook Pro belonging to one of Zeiger's colleagues sits atop oversized art books, while Zeiger has opted for two reams of printer paper and the boxed set of Seasons 3 and 4 of *The Wire*. During my visit, Billy Joel, James Taylor, and Simon and Garfunkel played softly in the background. We sat around a low table, the garage door that serves as the front entrance open to the street.

As Zeiger sees it, the Internet has gone through two distinct phases. The first, in which his old employer, Google, was the victor, involved democratizing access to content. The second, characterized not only by Facebook and Twitter, but also by Uber, Airbnb, and Yelp, has been about democratizing access to other people.

When Zeiger was at Google, one of his roles was to help the company understand this transition as it pertained to healthcare. He discovered a small, e-mail-based cancer community run by a guy named Gilles Frydman whose wife had a serious cancer. Frydman noticed that many of the participants in this community were migrating to Facebook, despite the fact that Facebook doesn't work very well for health communities. He and Zeiger brainstormed about what an ideal online cancer community might look like, but Zeiger was busy at Google, and things didn't progress beyond that.

That is, until August 1, 2011, at 5:15 p.m., when, while running on the treadmill, Zeiger suffered a subarachnoid hemorrhage and found himself in Stanford Hospital's neurosurgical intensive care unit. "That was a day of great intensity and clarity," he said. "When I figured out that I had a brain bleed and that I was going to be okay, I thought, wow, I got a free pass.[28] What am I going

---

[28] The mortality rate of all patients with subarachnoid hemorrhage is 40 to 50 percent, and many who live are left with significant disability.

to do with this? I decided it was time to leave a great job, to take a big risk, and to see if that Frydman guy still wanted to do something together."

▶   ▶   ▶

One of the most critical choices Zeiger and Frydman needed to make for Smart Patients concerned how to deal with recommendations for unproven, or even wacky, treatments. Zeiger's instinct was to block such posts: he wanted the site to tilt in the direction of science. But Frydman and other advisors convinced him that the better, more sustainable solution was to allow the community to monitor itself.

It works. When people start advocating for quack therapies, their peers jump in and start correcting them, often throwing up links to legitimate science. Zeiger proudly attributes this aspect of the site to the creation of two big cultural expectations. "First: when data exist, data win. Two: be respectful." Zeiger and his team monitor the posts and aren't afraid to take one down or privately e-mail someone with a suggestion when these rules are violated, particularly during the early days of a new community, when the culture is most fragile. But after the first few posts, such takedowns are rare, because "discussions about unproven therapies are generally handled not only effectively but really elegantly by the community. People call 'bullshit' respectfully, much better than a site administrator could."

In fact, it is not absurd treatment recommendations that cause Zeiger and his colleagues to lose sleep. Rather, the hottest button is religion, often versions of, "You'll get better because I'm praying for you." Posts like these pose an impossible problem for Zeiger, pitting his desire to let people be open and honest against the desire to create a space within which people are not being preached at. The company handles these on a case-by-case basis.

▶   ▶   ▶

Smart Patients and other online communities are demonstrating that patients can learn a tremendous amount from one another. Like many personal health records (the untethered ones), these websites currently exist outside the orbit of the electronic health record. But Zeiger has already struck deals with several healthcare organizations to offer Smart Patients to their patients, as they might a new treatment. One can envision a day when patient-centered communities and clinician-centered ones blend together, with patients gaining information and support from peers while periodically being counseled by credentialed experts. Here, as with the other patient-facing innovations like OpenNotes and patient portals, it is this integration between the worlds of the patient and the clinician that carries the most promise.

▶   ▶   ▶

In 2008, the core health IT policy question was whether the government should be involved in trying to get hospitals and doctors to computerize. That question was answered affirmatively, to the tune of $30 billion. Today, the dominant question concerns the government's role in connecting electronic health records to one another and to the kinds of electronic tools and apps that patients are increasingly drawn to. Let's explore this next.

# Part Five

# The Players and the Policies

# Chapter 23

# Meaningful Use

Experience hath shewn, that even under the best forms of
government, those entrusted with power have, in time, and by
slow operations, perverted it into tyranny.
                                        —Thomas Jefferson, 1778

I do not mean to say that this government is charged with the
duty of redressing or preventing all the wrongs in the world;
but I do think that it is charged with the duty of preventing and
redressing all wrongs which are wrongs to itself.
                                        —Abraham Lincoln, 1859

If there has been one central figure in the efforts to digitize the American healthcare system, that figure would be David Blumenthal. In 2008, as an advisor to the Obama transition team, it was Blumenthal who first proposed pulling $30 billion out of the $700 billion pile of stimulus money to promote the adoption of electronic health records, an idea that eventually became the HITECH incentive program. In 2009, he became the third director of the Office of the National Coordinator for Health Information Technology (ONC). On his watch, the Meaningful Use program was launched. It was Blumenthal's personality—elegant, unfailingly polite, and politically astute—that shaped the early successes of the Meaningful Use program, and his departure from the policy-making scene in 2011 shaped it yet again. Since then, Meaningful Use has become the most controversial topic in healthcare IT.

I met Blumenthal in his office at Harkness House, the headquarters of the Commonwealth Fund, where he is now CEO. The mansion, on Manhattan's Upper East Side, was built in 1908 by the descendants of Stephen Harkness, an heir to the Standard Oil fortune, and became home to the Commonwealth Fund in 1952. Its outer layer of Tennessee marble is constructed in the style of the Italian Renaissance, not the more ornate French style popular in the early twentieth century. On entering the building, one is struck by the details: the vaulted ceilings, the stone columns, the oak panels, the rococo niches. Blumenthal's magnificent office was once the home's library. Books still dominate the room, whose walls are lined with Brazilian rosewood. Taken as a whole, Harkness House manages to be timeless and impressive, but not ostentatious.

Impressive but restrained would also describe the 66-year-old Blumenthal. For three decades, he was a Harvard professor, his tenure punctuated by periodic postings to a variety of high-impact policy roles: presidential campaign advisor to both Michael Dukakis and Barack Obama, a U.S. Senate staffer (Blumenthal's older brother Richard became a U.S. senator from Connecticut in 2011), and a senior leader at Massachusetts General Hospital and its corporate parent, Partners HealthCare.

Like David Brailer, the first health IT czar, Blumenthal was an interesting choice for the ONC leadership job. Although he had done some fine policy research on health IT, "I knew almost nothing about information technology," he said. "I often think, in the land of the blind, the one-eyed person is king, and I was the one-eyed person." This, of course, is false modesty: the Obama administration needed someone with thick skin and deft political skill at the helm of ONC to ensure that the $30 billion was well spent. It did not need someone fluent in XML.

As ONC director, Blumenthal's job was to breathe life into the HITECH and Meaningful Use programs. When I told Blumenthal that his predecessor, Brailer, had called these initiatives "a Frankenstein," Blumenthal paused, then chose his words carefully.

"I have great respect for David, and I consider him a good friend," Blumenthal said, flexing all his diplomacy muscles, "but I firmly disagree with him. I don't think we would have gotten this process launched for years without these programs. You just can't ask people to make multibillion-dollar investments in things that have no short-term return on investment."

Blumenthal is particularly proud of the major bump in IT adoption that began during his tenure at ONC. The penetration of electronic health records in American clinics and hospitals went from about 10 percent the year before he took office to about 70 percent in 2014. While Obamacare itself, with its shift toward payment for results rather than visits and procedures, might have inspired a modest uptick, few people question that the bulk of the increase can be chalked up to Blumenthal's initiatives.[29] If Job One was to digitize the American healthcare system, then Blumenthal's plan and his tenure at ONC were overwhelmingly successful.

▶   ▶   ▶

To be fair, Blumenthal may well have had the easiest task of the five ONC directors, in that he had billions of dollars to dole out and, at least at first, relatively little opposition. He was also terrific at his job. "David had a combination of extraordinary vision, wonderful people around him, and money," said John Halamka, the microchip-equipped Beth Israel CIO. The first phase of Meaningful Use (dubbed Stage 1), which was planned during and implemented at the end of Blumenthal's tenure, was designed to be ambitious but

---

[29] Another measure of HITECH's reach: as of June 2014, some 403,000 physicians (75 percent of those eligible) and 4,500 hospitals (92 percent of those eligible) had received incentive payments for meeting some or all of the adoption criteria.

achievable: its goal was to ensure that people were actually *using* the comput-ers whose purchases were subsidized with federal dollars. "It really was a bril-liant construct," Halamka added. "I don't know anyone in the industry who doesn't think that Stage 1 was a great thing."

Today, the ONC is mired in controversy, particularly over Stage 2 of Meaningful Use, which was implemented after Blumenthal left office. More generally, ONC has been hit with the "big government" trope by the Fox News/Tea Party crowd. Perhaps this shouldn't have surprised an old pro like Blumenthal, but it did. "I figured information technology was a pretty benign, white-hat kind of thing, but not everybody thought that way," he said.

I asked him how he explained this. "Whenever a lot of money is made avail-able by our government for anything," he said, "there will always be a paranoid group that assumes it was done because of corrupt and nefarious purposes. The IT movement went—almost overnight—from being a victim, an underre-sourced savior for everything, to being bloated, industry-dominated, danger-ous, and overly favored. It was very dramatic."

▶    ▶    ▶

Even if one discounts the "government can't do anything right" argument, legit-imate concerns have been raised about Meaningful Use's evolution from Stage 1 to Stage 2. Stage 1, which was rolled out in 2011–2012 (just as Blumenthal was leaving ONC), was designed to ensure that people were actually using their electronic health records, and that data were being recorded electroni-cally and moved around to support clinical care. The requirements for Stage 1 were real but achievable, for both the EHR vendors and the frontline doc-tors and hospitals. They included things like providing clinical summaries to patients within three days of a hospitalization and transmitting a decent proportion of prescriptions electronically. That was precisely how Blumenthal planned it: to use Meaningful Use to gently raise the bar without having the rules inhibit adoption.

Stage 2, which was developed under Blumenthal's successor, Farzad Mostashari, and rolled out in 2014–2015, upped the ante considerably—in keeping with Congress's mandate. It required hospitals and physicians' offices to meet 17 "core objectives" (with no exceptions) in order to receive incentive payments. And the objectives were far more aggressive. Rather than Stage 1's requirement to implement a single decision support rule (like a vaccination reminder or an alert to consider sepsis in a hospitalized patient with a high fever), the requirement was now to implement five of them.

If Stage 2 had simply raised the requirement bar, it would not have been terribly controversial. Rather, what turned it into an object of considerable scorn was the fact that many of the new mandates depended on a clinical eco-system and healthcare culture that did not yet exist. Take, for example, a new requirement that more than 5 percent of patients "view, download, and trans-mit" (VDT) their electronic medical information to "a third party," such as a subspecialist using a different EHR or an insurance company. To comply with VDT, not only did the vendors need to reengineer their patient portals and the hospitals and clinics revamp their work flows, but providers now became responsible for ensuring that *their patients* were doing something with their newly downloaded data. I tried explaining the view, download, and transmit concept to my 78-year-old mother in Boca Raton, Florida, and didn't get far. "Is this like your dad's arrhythmia monitor?" she asked, referring to the device that beams my father's heart rhythm to his cardiologist's office every morn-ing. Not bad, I thought, but that wouldn't meet the requirement, since the heart monitor doesn't count as an electronic health record. (She does get par-tial credit: the cardiologist probably counts as a third party.) I asked her if her concierge physician had a patient portal. "I think so, but I've never used it," she said. She's a lovely person, but she would not count as a VDT success story.

Take another requirement: that hospitals transmit discharge summaries to other facilities electronically. The most common type of facility-to-facility transition in the world of American hospitals involves patients who are dis-charged to nursing homes. But very few nursing homes are currently com-puterized (they weren't included in the HITECH incentive program). Using a familiar analogy, Halamka explained the problem: "To make me accountable for faxing when no one else has a fax machine is not exactly a great policy."

Stuck in this electronic Catch-22, some hospitals are going to fantastic (in both senses of the word) lengths to meet the Meaningful Use requirements. I learned that some large medical centers now receive hundreds of electronic discharge summaries each month from smaller hospitals. Sounds good, right? The problem is that the summaries (Halamka calls them "spam documents") are of patients who have no chance of ever showing up at the receiving facility. They're being transmitted just so the sending hospital can check a box on its Stage 2 scorecard.

▶   ▶   ▶

John Halamka sees life through the eyes of a CIO at a large academic medical center, so it's not surprising that he and his fellow CIOs would be unhappy with the burden and expense of meeting the Stage 2 requirements. Ditto the IT vendors. But it is harder to write off the sentiments of Christine Sinsky, the primary care internist who is struggling to survive each day in her Dubuque, Iowa, practice.

Sinsky, who has also provided testimony (as "the real doctor") to several ONC policy committees, described how many of the ideas that seem reasonable enough when they're being tossed around an inside-the-Beltway conference room simply don't work in real life. "All the things in Meaningful Use were well meaning but reflected a limited, monolithic view of what practice is, with an idealized, futuristic medical record as the vehicle," she said. "But that's not what we have, and so we on the front lines get stuck trying to practice under the weight of those fantasies."

Take one particular Stage 2 criterion (Core Objective 13), which requires Sinsky to give educational resources (handouts, mostly) to 10 percent of her patients, *prompted by her EHR.* "The way it's designed is not aligned with the way work actually happens," she said. Observing her in her Iowa practice, I saw what she meant. With the care of a wine collector, over the years she has assembled tons of terrific educational materials, which sit in stacks on her office shelves. As she sees patients with plantar fasciitis, diabetes, or arthritis, she hands many of them an appropriate pamphlet, often spending a moment to point out its highlights. It's a system that works.

But, as far as Meaningful Use Stage 2, Core Objective 13 is concerned, none of it counts. "I suppose if I had an inventory of all my paper handouts and there was a computer program that matched those diagnoses, it *could* happen. But that's totally absurd," she said.

Sinsky raised this issue with her contacts at ONC: Would it be okay, she asked, if she created an electronic spreadsheet listing the top 50 handouts, and ticked off a box each time she gave one out? "They said no," she told me, "because that would be just documenting that you *gave* the handout, but the computer wouldn't be *prompting you* to give the handout. To me, this is like some riddle or puzzle, and," she paused, "life is hard enough. Why are we making it so much harder?"

▶   ▶   ▶

Complaints like these—the program is now commonly referred to by clinicians and CIOs as "Meaningless Abuse"—might have swayed David Blumenthal, the consummate mediator, but his successor at ONC, Farzad Mostashari, is a different kind of guy. Where Blumenthal is diplomatic and courtly, Mostashari is flamboyant and passionate. "A shaved-head, bow-tied bundle of enthusiasm, he radiates a good-salesman vibe, fist-bumping and high-fiving through conversations," is how Mostashari was described in a 2012 profile. After moving from his birthplace of Iran to upstate New York as a teenager, he received a master's degree in public health from Harvard and a medical degree from Yale, but chose not to pursue clinical practice. Instead, he went into public health and epidemiology. His worldview was shaped by his years in the New York City Health Department working under Thomas Frieden (now CDC director) and Mayor Michael Bloomberg, a department known for envelope-pushing activism. "We knew what we believed in and were not shy about advocating for it," he told me.

In 2009, Mostashari left New York and became Blumenthal's first lieutenant at ONC. The energy of the two workplaces could not have been more different. "If you want to go to war, you go to war with Tom Frieden," he laughs. "If you want to stay out of war, you go with Dave Blumenthal."

After taking the reins of ONC from Blumenthal in 2011, Mostashari struggled to find his own voice. Was he more Blumenthal or Frieden, consensus builder or china-shop bull? "In my first few meetings," he told me, "people were saying stuff, but I felt like I should bite my tongue. I wrote a note to myself on the back of a 3x5 card, 'Welcome to the federal government. Check your passion at the door.'"

"And then I said, 'Fuck it! I just can't do this.'" At that moment, he became Farzad Unplugged, and his particular passion was for moving health IT aggressively into community and public health, which meant pushing hard to link people and systems, even if everybody complained about not being ready. Several of the people I interviewed for this book, ranging from frontline clinicians to CIOs, praised Mostashari for his zeal and motives, but criticized him for his stubbornness—and for the fact that this nonclinician's activism drove him deep into the weeds of clinical practice.

Even senior ONC staffers, while not endorsing Brailer's "Frankenstein" label for Meaningful Use, admit that the program has gotten out of hand. Jacob Reider, the deputy national coordinator at ONC, has had a varied career as a family physician and a software developer.[30] During his four years at ONC, he saw the office evolve from a sleepy bureaucratic backwater into a DC juggernaut. "I think there were things done in regulation that perhaps were enthusiastic, but those can be undone," he said, with delicious understatement. "We

---

[30] Reider stepped down from his post in October 2014, a few months after our interview.

are in the process of undoing some of these enthusiastic components." This is something you don't hear in Washington every day—the second in command at a large federal agency confessing that his organization is off course.

The hardest part, Reider admits, is getting his own people to chill out. After all, the organization's culture was cemented in the days when ONC had piles of money to give out. But those days have passed. "I'm trying to constrain well-meaning staff who were hired to do A, B, C, D, E, F, and G and get them to focus on A and B," he said about life today at ONC.

I asked David Brailer, the first ONC director, whether his old office might naturally pull back now that the HITECH money—its blood supply—is gone. His answer was a categorical "no." "Bureaucracies don't retrench," he said. "When a bureaucracy that starts as the Candy Man runs out of candy, it goes dark and turns into Regulatory Man." Brailer warned that if ONC isn't forced to scale back, it will be a major obstacle to creating a flexible, organic, innovative, and responsive health IT sector. If it stays on its current course, he worries, "we've created another case of 'I do what the government tells me to do.'"

▶    ▶    ▶

Those who think that Stage 2 was a bridge too far will *really* hate the Stage 3 regulations, which are due to roll out sometime around 2017—the proposed rules are tougher, more ambitious, and more prescriptive. They also have the fingerprints of special interests—not so much the corporate leviathan types as the *don't forget us* variety—all over them. Halamka offered an example of the problem, this one from Stage 2. "One of the standards is that people with vision problems should be able to transmit their health information," he said. "I've got glaucoma. I'm all *for* people with vision problems. But now I have to put my most talented staff on this problem," even before sorting out the basics of transmitting information in the first place, not to mention being sure that the EHR is usable and that kids no longer receive 39-fold overdoses of antibiotics.

Not only has Meaningful Use diverted the focus of CIOs in hospitals and physicians in clinics, but it has also consumed the bandwidth of the vendor community. "It would be great if Epic were able to update its basic architecture to a modern, Web-native platform," said a frustrated Halamka. "But they've spent the last three years creating EHRs for blind people and making sure patients can download their smoking status in the appropriate computer language and then transmit it to nowhere."

The vendors are careful when discussing ONC policies, since they have been the beneficiaries of much of the HITECH windfall, and, if you're a multibillion-dollar company in a regulated industry, it's smart to err on the charitable side when discussing your government. But they too have deep concerns. Carl Dvorak, Epic's president, believes that the HITECH money was an important catalyst for IT adoption. No surprise there. However, he told me, "Government is an inefficient heavyweight to accomplish things like this. If Meaningful Use becomes a permanent lever for unfunded mandates on healthcare, I think it'll turn out to have been a bad thing."

▶    ▶    ▶

Utter the phrase "Meaningful Use" in a room full of chief information officers and you'll hear groans. But say "HIPAA" (shorthand for the 1996 act aimed at protecting patient privacy) and you'll hear the sounds of terror. "This is the number one crazy-making issue for CIOs," said Halamka. "I spend 50 percent of my time on it. Not on, 'How can I create innovative mobile devices for doctors?' Or, 'How can we engage patients and families with new IT tools?' Instead, it's, 'How can I prevent your iPhone from downloading a piece of personal health information should you lose your phone?'"

Halamka knows whereof he speaks. One of the physicians at his hospital recently bought a Mac laptop, plugged it in, and synced his e-mail. He left his office for a meeting, and when he returned, the laptop had vanished. Hospital security quickly identified a known felon from the video footage, and the police found him at his skid row apartment and arrested him. However, the laptop was gone. "Now, what is the likelihood that this drug fiend stole the laptop because he had healthcare identity theft in mind?" asked Halamka. "That would be zero."

As of this writing, the case has cost Beth Israel more than $500,000 in legal fees, forensic work, and investigations, and it isn't over. It will ultimately culminate in a settlement agreement between the hospital and the attorney general's office, "where we basically say, 'It wasn't our fault, but here's a set of actions Beth Israel will put in place so that no doctor is ever allowed again to bring a device into our environment and put patient data on it.'"

As the case unfolded, Halamka told his hospital's board of directors that plugging every hole in a dike that includes 6,000 staff members and 3 million patients will take three years, $5 million a year, and 14 new staff members. Under the threat of multimillion-dollar HIPAA fines, Beth Israel—and every other healthcare facility—has little choice but to approve such plans. It did.

But it's not just the fines and the dollars that bother Halamka and his fellow CIOs. It's the impact on clinical care and on culture. "We have to balance the desires of the vast majority of patients, who want their data shared, with the small minority who don't. My daughter is 21 and puts her *relationship status* on Facebook. My experience is that it's a very small percentage of the population that is convinced that sharing their allergy list is going to cost them a loss of standing in the community." What's coming: stronger passwords with more frequent and annoying changes, new kinds of biometric identification, and a variety of other roadblocks to the free flow of information.

How absurd have things gotten? An August 2014 article in the *New York Times* described how pediatricians and obstetricians around the country are being forced to take down kids' pictures from their office corkboards—*pictures sent in by the proud and delighted parents*—because of the fear that pinning them up might be exposing protected health information. A spokesperson for the Office for Civil Rights of the Department of Health and Human Services confirmed that such displays are, in fact, a violation of HIPAA. Really.

When HIPAA became law, there were virtually no electronic health records, no patient portals, no smartphones, and no hope of ubiquitous connectivity. It was the year Google was invented; Facebook was still eight years away. How does HIPAA fit in today? This is a hard question to answer, made harder by nearly weekly announcements of hacker intrusions into the records stored by everyone from Walgreens to hospitals. One thing seems clear, though: levying multimillion-dollar fines for security breaches on hospitals that are struggling to get by on razor-thin margins can't be the right answer. As with Meaningful Use, the government's "enthusiastic" regulations are creating unintended obstacles to the larger goals of improving health and healthcare.

▶   ▶   ▶

Since we're talking about government programs, you can be certain that while many people criticize Meaningful Use and HIPAA for being too much and too rigid, others criticize the ONC for being too lax in certain areas. The two biggies are usability (the ease of use and learnability of the IT system) and interoperability (common standards that allow different EHR systems to connect with each other).

Blumenthal agrees that today's electronic health records could be far more usable, but when he tried to convert that concern into policy during his tenure as ONC director, he came to believe that judging usability was like Justice Potter Stewart's "I know it when I see it" take on pornography. "We could not get any experts to say they could measure usability in a reproducible, valid way," said Blumenthal, "a way we could stand behind from a legal standpoint."

While this issue continues to be debated, Halamka and others believe that the market is now mature enough for usability to take care of itself. With today's high rate of EHR adoption, Halamka argues, the vendors will compete on usability, and the best products will win. As proof, he is piloting a cloud-based system built by athenahealth in Beth Israel's extensive ambulatory clinics, a system known for its emphasis on usability (I'll have more to say about this company later).

On this one, I side with those who believe that government should keep its nose out. Imagine if the government tried to design the look and feel of your smartphone or your computer's desktop—well, enough said. I do, however, support a proposal to create a federal health IT safety center that can collect and analyze reports of dangerous IT interfaces (like the mg versus mg/kg Septra confusion that nearly killed Pablo Garcia) and take appropriate action. And federal support for a nonpartisan organization that grades the usability of different systems based on standard criteria—that might work. But as for the government dictating standards for fonts, colors, and clicks, well, thanks, but no thanks.

▶    ▶    ▶

Interoperability is a different matter. Interoperability is just the kind of thing government intervention was designed for, since it is a powerful public good that the private market will not automatically create. Why is it so important? Think about your cell phone: your iPhone can call your friend's Samsung without a hiccup, even if your service is with AT&T and your friend's is with Verizon. The same is true with your Web browser: whether you like Safari, Chrome, or Firefox for its look or features, all of them can get you onto the Internet just fine.

In the EHR world, just think how great it would be to have an interoperable system. We'd no longer need a paper airplane to get crucial patient information from one hospital to another. The costs of switching from a crummy EHR to a better one would plummet, since the patient data stored in the old system would be easily transferrable to the new one. A world of innovators (the folks who are currently writing apps for your iPhone and Android) would be freed up to create programs to help diabetic patients or families of patients with ALS manage their care—and these would sync seamlessly with existing EHRs.

On interoperability, Blumenthal defends the ONC's early prioritization of adoption over interoperability. "I had the basic feeling that you had to 'operate' before you could 'interoperate.' And you couldn't create a business case for interoperability," at least at first. Today, while the market for interoperability has gotten a bit stronger, he and I both doubt that the same business case that will drive usability will also drive interoperability. This one needs an assist from Uncle Sam.

While it would be great to have total interoperability tomorrow, it will take some time, even if the ONC puts its shoulder behind it, as it now seems to be doing with its October 2014 proposal for standardized APIs. Not only are there political obstacles to overcome (put in place mostly by vendors and healthcare systems that remain reluctant to share, as you'll see in the next chapter), but the kinds of people involved in the nitty-gritty work of interoperability do not make for a speedy process. Said Halamka, "You know, there are forest people and there are tree people. Standards folks are, by necessity, bark people. They'll spend a day debating the relative merits of an ampersand or a semicolon."

▶  ▶  ▶

There are those who believe that government should stay out of health IT altogether: it can only muck things up. I disagree. First of all, no one else can enforce public goods like interoperability and security—the market just won't do it. Second, the HITECH investment did create an obligation for the government to ensure that the $30 billion has been well spent. Third, even without HITECH, Medicare and Medicaid pay for half the healthcare in the United States. Just as Walmart can dictate how its suppliers behave, so too does the government deserve a seat at this particular table.

Since we live in an era with deep skepticism of *any* government action, it's also important to place the controversy over Meaningful Use and HIPAA in context. I asked MIT's Andy McAfee, a leading authority on computer-enabled transformation of industries, how badly federal oversight distorts digital markets through regulation. "The existence of any 800-pound gorilla is going to distort, especially when it's got the power to throw you in jail or fine you," he said. "At the same time, one of the favorite reasons for inaction I hear is, 'Yeah. But we're a regulated industry.' The regulations are going to change the path forward and maybe slow it down, but what they're not going to do is stop the legitimate innovators from doing their stuff."

Halamka's advice to Karen DeSalvo, the current ONC director, seems right to me. "Stop the treadmill," he told her. "Declare victory for Meaningful Use. We've got all these people who are suffering fatigue, who just need time to catch up. Standards need time to evolve." DeSalvo appears to be listening ("We're taking a deep breath," she told me), but voluntarily shrinking one's own bureaucracy and power has never been among our government's core competencies.[31]

▶    ▶    ▶

When I talked to people about the impact of Meaningful Use and HITECH, there was one more concern that came up over and over again. The higher the regulatory burden, goes the well-accepted teaching, the higher the chance of "vendor lock." In other words, the incumbent companies—Big Steel to use one famous example, Ma Bell another—are best able to meet all the requirements (or, through their lawyers and lobbyists, influence them in their own favor). This makes it harder for nimble new entrants to come in and begin taking over a previously ignored part of the market, the pattern of disruptive innovation famously described by Clay Christensen. It was the deregulation of the airlines in the 1980s that paved the way for Southwest Airlines and JetBlue. And the relatively unencumbered world of the Internet has allowed the emergence of companies like Amazon and Airbnb. Such disruptors often sneak around the edges of a market (and sometimes the law; think Napster or Uber), and, by the time the incumbents wake up and begin trying to defend their franchise, the new service is too entrenched to take down.

When this example is applied to the world of healthcare IT, the incumbent that everyone refers to is Epic. The best example of an upstart company trying to take it on is athenahealth. Their stories are so compelling, and their leaders so unusual, that they deserve a chapter of their own.

---

[31] DeSalvo was named acting assistant secretary of the U.S. Department of Health and Human Services in October 2014, focusing on the federal response to Ebola. Although the initial announcement stated that she was leaving the Office of the National Coordinator, a subsequent press release stated that she would continue her leadership at ONC. In any case, many observers saw this change as evidence of ONC's waning influence in Washington.

# Chapter 24

# Epic and athena

Eschew the monumental. Shun the Epic. All the guys who can
paint great big pictures can paint great small ones.
—Ernest Hemingway, in 1932

On a cool day in Verona, Wisconsin, in September 2014, the town's population
had a bimodal distribution of a type well known on autumn Saturdays in small
midwestern college towns with powerhouse football teams. But Verona has
no college, and no football team. While the 12,000 residents of Verona went
about their business, another 12,000 out-of-town visitors packed the "Deep
Space" auditorium on the 811-acre "Intergalactic Headquarters" of the town's
dominant employer, Epic.

Like a slightly cheesy version of the glitzy users' meetings thrown by Apple
and Salesforce, the visitors—all Epic customers—were there mostly to attend
some of the conference's 750 sessions on Epic's products and plans. "Little Cow
Pokes: Optimizing Pediatric SmartSets and Immunizations" was the title of
one session. "Old MacDonald Had a Farm . . . of Remote Coders" was another.
The classes were scattered around the whimsical campus, adored by many Epic
employees for its themed buildings (there's one called Heaven and another
called Barn; an "Olde English"–themed building is under construction), bab-
bling brook, statues of the Cat in the Hat and a blue neon cow, treehouse-

cum-conference room, and two-story spiral tube slide. But they also came to hear Judy.

Judy Faulkner, the company's founder, CEO, and major shareholder, walked onto the auditorium stage to rousing applause. In past years, she had come dressed as Superwoman, a Harley-riding biker dudette, and a Harry Potter wizard. But, in keeping with the 2014 meeting's theme of "Down on the Farm," this year Judy (like Beyoncé and Madonna, pretty much everybody calls Judy by her first name), age 71, was dressed in a red plaid shirt, overalls, leather work boots, and a green and white John Deere cap. She was accompanied on stage by a pony named Charm.

Charmed would be an apt way to describe the history of Faulkner's company, now the unlikely titan sitting atop efforts to digitize the $3 trillion U.S. healthcare system. Her humble start is the stuff of legends. After completing her master's degree at the University of Wisconsin, Faulkner was hired in 1979 by the school's psychiatry department to write a program to computerize its records and track its patients. She began with three part-time employees, who sat at used desks in the basement of an off-campus apartment building, working on a bulky Data General computer whose two 50-megabyte spinning disk drives sounded like a clothes dryer tossing around a pair of sneakers. "You couldn't touch it, or the data got messed up," she told the *New York Times* in 2012.

Since then, Faulkner has proved to be a shrewd business strategist, making a series of choices that seemed unusual, if not suicidal, but have all paid off. Here are just a few: Epic programs in a version of a 46-year-old language called MUMPS.[32] The company does no marketing; in fact, Epic *invites* customers to buy its system and tells others (basically any hospital with less than 250 beds) that it is not interested in their business. Despite many entreaties over the years, the company remains privately held. It has never acquired another company and has never accepted outside capital. It carries no debt.

And then there's the decision to build a technology powerhouse in the heart of Wisconsin farm country—I passed a "Tractor Crossing" road sign a few hundred yards from the company's front gate, which sits 2,100 miles from Stanford's campus and 1,100 miles from MIT's. Faulkner's motto is, "Do good, have fun, make money," and she has succeeded in all three. *Forbes* estimates

---

[32] Although Epic is often beaten up by its competitors for using "a 50-year-old language," today's language is actually a MUMPS offspring named Caché. While it is not widely deployed, it *is* used by some picky clients—the Swiss banking system, for one. Both Faulkner and Halamka say that it offers very fast database performance, which is useful for the tasks Epic's systems need to perform, including managing text, voice, images, and videos and linking to other IT systems.

her net worth at about $2.3 billion. If Epic ever did go public, she'd probably become even wealthier.

That Faulkner hasn't taken her company public is in keeping with Epic's philosophy of maintaining control—of its destiny, its intellectual property, the programs that link to its software, and its relationships with customers. But one can control only so much for so long, and today Epic is fighting a major image problem, often finding itself portrayed as both a behemoth and the embodiment of all that is wrong with health IT. The indictment goes like this: the federal government created a $30 billion "giveaway"; Epic was lucky enough to have the best system at the time of the "handouts," but only because the others were so bad (faint praise embodied in the quip that Epic's software is "the Cream of the Crap"); the HITECH money and subsequent regulations cemented Epic's "monopolistic position" and locked out the entrepreneurs and "disrupters"; and Epic created a "walled garden" that blocks the open exchange of information that the healthcare system so desperately needs.

Epic's critics have rallied some influential advocates, including a few in Washington, DC. In July 2014, representative Phil Gingrey held hearings under the banner, "Is the government getting its money's worth?" "It may be time for the [Energy and Commerce] committee to take a closer look at the practices of vendor companies in this space, given the possibility that fraud may be perpetrated on the American taxpayer," said the Georgia Republican. No one doubted which company he was referring to.

By 2014, Epic, while still raking in cash and business, had been forced out of its shell. The company famously eschews self-promotion, yet began a quiet PR campaign. There were no gauzy "Epic saved my daughter's life" television ads set to swelling music. But company leaders did point me to several promotional videos created by its client hospitals, touting things like patient portals and hospital-based monitoring systems. Although CEO Faulkner remains intensely private ("I'm hugely introverted, not atypical of math majors," she said in a 2013 interview, one of only a handful on record), Epic's president, Carl Dvorak, took to the stump and has become a regular on the healthcare conference circuit.

Dvorak, a balding, sandy-haired engineer who has been with the company since 1987, told me that until relatively recently, he was so naive about the legislative process that he watched a *Schoolhouse Rock!* video to refresh his memory about how a bill becomes a law ("I'm stuck in committee and I sit here and wait; While a few key congressmen discuss and debate," sings a cartoon character named Bill). In 2014, the company hired its first Washington lobbyist, the brother of George W. Bush's chief of staff, Andrew Card, to "educate members of Congress on the interoperability of Epic's healthcare information technology."

Even Charm went off script, pausing to poop on the stage of the Deep Space auditorium during Faulkner's 2014 appearance.

▶   ▶   ▶

That Epic would find itself labeled a monopoly is in itself an extraordinary turn of events. In 2000, after 21 years in business, the company had only 400 employees and 73 clients, and did not appear on a list of the top 20 hospital EHR vendors. Its big break came in 2003, when the 8 million–member Kaiser Permanente system selected Epic over two far better known competitors, IBM and Cerner. The cost to build Kaiser's electronic health record: $4 billion.

Today, Epic has 8,100 employees, 315 clients, and yearly revenues of approximately $2 billion. The system is now deployed in 9 of the *US News & World Report*'s "Top 10" hospitals. In 2014, the company estimated that 173 million people (54 percent of the U.S. population) had at least some medical information in an Epic electronic record.

Faulkner's vision, built on several central tenets, has been vindicated many times over. The first principle was that the winning EHR vendor would be the one that solved the most problems for its customers. While Apple's App Store has made a modular environment seem feasible and even desirable, most healthcare decision makers want a single product that does everything they need right out of the box (physician notes, nursing notes, drug ordering and dispensing, billing, compliance, and population health) and does those things everywhere, from the newborn nursery to the urology clinic to the ICU. Said David Bates, chief quality officer at Boston's Brigham & Women's Hospital and a national expert in health IT, "If you make a big matrix of all the various things that you want as an organization, Epic covers many more of the boxes than others." When it was choosing which EHR system to purchase, Partners HealthCare (which includes Brigham, Massachusetts General, and several other Boston-area hospitals and clinics) created just such a matrix, and Epic's system covered more than 90 percent of the boxes. The nearest competitor covered just 55 percent. Choosing Epic, said Bates, "was not a close decision." Partners' investment in its new EHR system will total about $1 billion.[33]

---

[33] As Epic often makes clear, only about 15 percent of an organization's electronic health record investment ends up in Verona. The rest is for training the organization's own workers, for paying its own IT staff, and for outside consultants to help with the implementation.

Second, while Epic's software has been criticized for its lack of interoperability, most healthcare leaders don't stay up at night worrying about that. Don't get me wrong: they care deeply about moving information around; it's a core rationale for EHRs in the first place. But their definition of "around" is not *everywhere*. Rather, they want a seamless flow of information around all the buildings they own (within the hospital, between the hospital and their clinics, that sort of thing). They also want interoperability between their system and an outside laboratory they use, their system and Aetna's claims department, and their system and the local Walgreens.

And they do care—up to a point—about connecting to the patient. But this is where things get nuanced, because the information the hospital CIO wants to make available to the patient is finely calibrated: enough to make the patient happy (scheduling appointments, refilling medications, e-mailing her doctor), but not so much as to risk the franchise. If you come to UCSF for a kidney transplant, it's good for business if you also get your flu shots and primary care from us. If you go to see that famous Sloan Kettering oncologist for a second opinion, the cancer hospital would also like to administer your chemotherapy, even though there is absolutely nothing special about its version of the medication, and you could probably get it cheaper at a clinic down the road.

Just think about it: if a patient can go online and shop around for the cheapest CT scan or colonoscopy ("Hey, Groupon's offering a $75 MRI at the mall today!"), this creates a problem for the nation's healthcare Meccas, which count on the profits from these activities to pay the bills.

One way to prevent such shopping around is to be sure the hospital's IT system doesn't connect to outsiders that the hospital views as competition. In fact, one technique that hospitals use with their Epic system is to buy it and offer nearby clinics free or subsidized access to it, but only if they admit their patients to that hospital or are otherwise part of its network. Epic implicitly encourages this by not selling its system directly to small practices. A clinic that chooses to stay outside the major medical center's orbit may find its staff standing at the fax machine when it needs to exchange information with that hospital.

Third, Faulkner was patient. While other companies were busy merging with one another in order to grow, or futzing around with new product lines, Epic remained confident that, someday, the market for electronic health records would take off. Faulker's employees focused on building a solid system that would solve more problems, and solve them better, than their competitors' systems. It worked. Fueled by superior customer ratings and word of mouth,

Epic's client base grew slowly and steadily. "We were making a healthy profit before HITECH," said Dvorak, showing me a curve of customer growth from 2000 to 2014. While the graph depicted an unmistakable uptick after 2010, it also illustrated steady year-over-year increases before the federal incentives kicked in.

Point taken. But it is equally true that the EHR business represented a sluggish corner of the healthcare economy before 2010, so nobody but insiders really noticed Epic, or cared very much about it. The signing of the HITECH Act instantly changed that, and Epic was ready—if not for the politics and the attention, then at least for the business. "The reason that Epic got so much of the market is that its product is simply better," said David Bates. I agree. To frame Epic as somehow having orchestrated HITECH—for its dominance in the past few years to be portrayed, as it sometimes is, as a massive conspiracy launched from the Wisconsin farmlands—is just plain silly. Given its 30-year history of quiet competence, it would also represent a sleeper cell story of, well, epic proportions.

▶   ▶   ▶

My own hospital's tale is relatively typical. UCSF Medical Center originally installed a system made by a Vermont company named IDX, which struggled for survival and was ultimately gobbled up by General Electric in 2006, as the world's largest technology company tried to establish a beachhead in the EHR business. After being dissatisfied with that system (in her 2014 speech at the Epic users' meeting, Faulkner announced that Epic had bought GE and changed its name to "General Epic"—"Just kidding," she added quickly), we needed to decide which EHR to buy. Having made a costly error with our first purchase, we were in no mood to take a big risk.

Like Partners, we found the decision to go with Epic to be relatively easy, on the merits. Moreover, our leaders were also impressed by Epic's sales job—or, more precisely, the lack of one. "They were very honest about what they had, and didn't have," UCSF's chief operating officer, Ken Jones, told *Forbes* in 2012. "Their attitude was more like, 'You're embarking on this big effort, and we want to make sure that you're serious about this, because if you're not successful, then it's not good for us.'"

There was one more plus for us, and it illustrates how surprisingly subtle the issue of interoperability can be. The combination of Epic's enormous market share and the fact that sharing records with other Epic sites is relatively easy (Epic calls this "Care Everywhere," as distinguished from its system of sharing records with non-Epic sites, which it calls, somewhat dismissively, "Care Elsewhere") meant that the choice to install Epic *did* solve a significant portion of our interoperability problems, even for patients coming from or going to other facilities. In California, four of the five University of California medical centers, as well as Stanford, Cedars-Sinai, the large Sutter network of hospitals, and, of course, the massive Kaiser Permanente system, are all on Epic.

This kind of sharing is growing rapidly. Nationwide, in the month of August 2014, there were 5 million clinical records exchanged between Epic systems at different sites, and 500,000 records exchanged between Epic and non-Epic systems. It's no surprise that most of the people who excoriate Epic for being "closed" are outsiders who want in (while some media reports claim that Epic charges exorbitant fees to connect to non-Epic sites, I found no evidence of this in my research) or vendors that are trying to sell their own systems. While everyone endorses the ultimate goal of universal sharing, Epic's clients today actually enjoy an unmatched degree of connectedness.

▶   ▶   ▶

You won't be surprised to learn that Epic's leaders see the assault on their company for being "closed" as terribly unfair, or at best only a partial truth. What *is* true is that Epic is highly selective about which third-party vendor products it links to: only those that its customers want. "Developers have to work through a customer," Faulkner said in 2013. "We don't let anyone write on top of our platform, come read our code, and study our software. I worry about intellectual property at that point."

The company also worries about the safety implications of trying to cobble together mismatched parts, particularly in complex clinical environments like hospitals. In fact, while Epic is open to connecting to a variety of third-party laboratory, radiology, scheduling, and billing systems, Dvorak said that the company is "religious" about not mixing and matching components in areas where integration is critical to safety, such as between the pharmacy inventory and the medication ordering systems. "The links are incredibly fragile, and it's dangerous if you don't get them right," said Dvorak. "We've learned this the hard way."

Dvorak is blunt in his defense of the company's openness. "This whole closed business rubbish . . . I grow weary of it," he told me. He pointed to Epic's open APIs (application programming interfaces, the bits of code that allow for connections to other software products; as I discussed in Chapter 21, standardized APIs now form the heart of the government's strategy to promote interoperability). At the 2014 users' meeting, Epic launched its "Open Epic" initiative, with its library of hundreds of open APIs and of third-party products that already link to them.[34]

Of course, Epic has a stake in protecting its intellectual property. But so do its competitors. "No one publishes their source code. That's all we have," Dvorak said. He attributed much of the criticism of Epic (which has been picked up by media outlets ranging from the *New York Times* to *Modern Healthcare*) to a smear campaign launched by competitors, and added, "It's hilarious that it's misinformation put forward by people who do exactly the same thing we do. They fail to mention that when they preach their misinformation."

Dvorak also sees the fingerprints of Epic's competitors on Congress's new-found interest in interoperability. When I asked why other health IT companies might want to hammer Epic on "openness," his answer was immediate: Epic and IBM have teamed up to bid for a 10-year, $11 billion contract to provide a single EHR to all Department of Defense facilities, and three other teams are vying for the contract.

▶   ▶   ▶

If Judy Faulkner represents the face of the last generation's health IT leaders, Jonathan Bush is working his tush off to be the face of this generation. It would be hard to find two more different human beings. Faulkner, a self-described nerd with a master's degree in computer engineering from the University of Wisconsin, grew up in southern New Jersey, the daughter of a pharmacist dad and a social activist mom (her mother's certificate for her work with Physicians for Social Responsibility, the group that shared the 1985 Nobel Peace Prize, hangs in Epic's headquarters). Faulkner's husband is a pediatrician who still sees kids in a community clinic in Madison. Don't look for either of them at the latest Daniel Boulud restaurant opening or black tie charity ball. By all reports, they happily live a quiet Wisconsin life, well hidden from the glare of the tabloids.

Jonathan Bush, age 45, is the cofounder and CEO of athenahealth, a rapidly growing Web-based EHR company. Bush is a Harvard MBA who grew up on a tree-lined street on Manhattan's Upper East Side and summered in Kennebunkport, Maine. He looks a bit like a young Michael J. Fox, except that when you're sitting with him, there is something else vaguely famil-

---

[34] While Epic is clearly taking steps in the direction of interoperability, I spoke to third-party app developers who are still struggling trying to build interfaces to Epic APIs—one told me that it took phone calls to seven different Epic employees before he could get things to work.

iar about the smile, the squint in the eyes. It's a look you know you've seen somewhere before.

The mantra of Jonathan Bush's extended family was to "use power to help people." The family, as it happens, includes an uncle who was the 41st President of the United States and a cousin who was the 43rd. (On the lighter side, his brother Billy is the host of television's *Access Hollywood*.) "I mean, can you imagine being around the table at the Bush family's Thanksgiving?" he once said in an interview. "'So what have *you* done?'"

Then there is the style. While Judy Faulkner has the trademark awkward bearing and speech of a techie (albeit, to her credit, one willing to parade on stage in costume once a year in front of thousands of people), Jonathan Bush is . . . well, see for yourself.

> On the HITECH Act: "I call it the Sunny von Bülow bill. These companies [by which he means the legacy vendors like Epic and Cerner] were ready to go out of business, and were suddenly given a new lease on life." His other nickname for HITECH: "Cash for clunkers."

> And how about this, on how athena helps its client physicians: "There remains an ocean of shit work that caregivers hate and suck at."

> Or this: "I reached the conclusion not long ago that anger, whether white hot or smoldering, is a fundamental fuel for entrepreneurs. . . . I realized that during many of my most productive stretches, I was seething."

Before Jonathan Bush entered the world of digital health, it was a relatively clubby place, the competition among vendors appreciable but genteel. The culture was more collegial than cutthroat, more Wisconsin than Wall Street.

Afterward, it was different.

▶   ▶   ▶

I met Jonathan Bush on a bright autumn day at his company's headquarters, an open-aired, painted brick restored factory building a few miles outside Boston. Crossing the street to the company cafeteria, he exchanged greetings with everybody, from programmers to security guards, his ADD and his charisma on equal display. At lunch (for him, leftover lobster in a Tupperware container), he spoke a mile a minute, barely chewing his food, sometimes spitting as he talked, his voice booming off the walls of the eatery's high ceilings when he emphasized a point. Despite his volume and his volubility, few of the young employees within earshot even turned around. I had the sense that they had seen this *con brio* performance before.

Athenahealth's story is every bit as remarkable as Epic's, but it bears the unmistakable imprint of today's generation, with its new way of thinking about technology and its *Game On!* sensibility. Said Brandon Hull, a venture capitalist who made an early investment in athena: "Epic is a wonderful company, with incredible solutions, but ultimately is on the wrong side of history. Every other American vertical market is migrating away from centralized, client-server, hub-and-spoke architecture toward distributed, SaaS-based applications and open architecture." This is techno-speak for the difference between using a suite of the old Microsoft Office programs (all of which lived on physical servers in your company's closets and required lots of training, legions of on-site IT staff, and insertion of new disks for program upgrades) to the modern cloud-based architecture (software as a service, or SaaS) of products like Gmail and Dropbox.

After stints as a New Orleans EMT, an army medic, and a Booz Allen consultant ("I was a misfit as a consultant," he said. "I couldn't even spell well"), in 1997, Bush and Todd Park,[35] a fellow consultant, launched a birthing center in San Diego ("we would be the Starbucks of obstetrics, a no-nonsense moneymaker that's warm on the outside and knows the customers' needs, tastes, and phobias," he wrote in 2014). They hoped that a combination of terrific customer service and low prices, partly achieved by using midwives instead of obstetricians, would attract a flood of patients and ultimately lead to a national chain. But they were soon hemorrhaging money. They attributed many of their troubles to their failure to master the arcane billing rules that insurance companies used to delay or deny payments.

Frustrated, Bush and Park wrote a software program to help them win their battles with the insurers by anticipating the roadblocks and proactively addressing them. The program worked beautifully; it didn't dawn on them until later that they had stumbled into a far better business: medical billing. "It's awfully hard to imagine solving a problem for everyone else, when that

---

[35] Park was 24 years old when he cofounded athena. In 2008, he also cofounded Castlight Health, now a publicly traded company; it provides quality and cost data to employers and insurers. In 2012, President Obama named him the nation's chief technology officer, and he was instrumental in fixing the disastrous healthcare.gov website and introducing big data and crowdsourcing approaches to the federal government.

very problem appears utterly mystifying (and is in the process of grounding [sic] your business into fine and pungent dust)," Bush wrote in his 2014 book, *Where Does It Hurt?* Athena's Web-based billing service became a hit among doctors, and before long it had become a thriving business on its own. In 2006, Bush and Park decided that as long as they were processing information for physicians' offices, they might as well add on a system for keeping medical records. Athenahealth was born.

▶   ▶   ▶

Bush, like his investor Hull, makes a point of telling me that "Epic is a great company." Yet it's clear that there is no love lost between the athena leaders and their Wisconsin-based rivals—he means to disrupt Epic, the entire health IT sector, and, indeed, the entire healthcare system. To these ends, he also has it in for the big academic medical centers, which, in his infinitely quotable way, he likens to duchies in middle Europe struggling to hold onto a dying business model by locking down the data and the villagers. So the fact that Epic and the big hospitals are often in cahoots . . . well, it makes his blood boil.

And, as if the marriage between the big hospitals and the Epics of the world weren't bad enough, along comes the government to toss in a bunch of dumb rules. That does it—now we've hit the Jonathan Bush Trifecta of Outrage. "The best thing to do at this point would be to make it as easy as possible for new entrants to come into the system and disrupt these guys—clean their clock, kill them, or at least force them to change," he wrote, *these guys* being both the legacy IT vendors and the academic medical centers. But that's not what's happening, said Bush. Instead, the government produces cumbersome regulations that discourage the newcomers, who don't have lawyers or lobbyists, from entering the market. "So instead of making bad incumbents vulnerable, the government leaves them fat, lame, and stupid . . . and untouchable." It is no surprise that Clay Christensen, the patron saint of disruptive innovation, wrote the preface to Bush's book.

While Bush has a vested interest in railing about vendor lock (though it's worth noting that athenahealth also feasted on the HITECH incentives), his point is legitimate. Having one company control so much of a crucial market is problematic, particularly when it is so terribly complicated and expensive to switch systems if you're unhappy.

Jacob Reider, deputy director of the Office of the National Coordinator for Health IT, told me that ONC was sensitive to the risk of vendor lock when it crafted HITECH and Meaningful Use. He conceded, though, that his office didn't crack this particular nut. "'Watch out for the little guy' was actually one of ONC's guiding principles when Blumenthal and Mostashari were here," he said. "The intent was there. What happened, of course, was the opposite."

▶   ▶   ▶

Every year, Jonathan Bush holds his own version of a users' conference, and he, like Judy Faulkner, dresses up for it. Its tone, though, is different from the one in Wisconsin. The meeting is held off the coast of Maine, and Bush calls it "More Disruption, Please." Its goal is to bring together healthcare entrepreneurs, investors, and other "brilliant people coming up with breakthrough ideas." A few years ago, Bush came dressed in a loincloth and a pockmarked T-shirt, a fake bushy beard on his face and a pike in his hand. His caveman getup was designed to make a point: "Primitive apps are OK. In fact, they can change the world." His hope is that such apps will be written around an athena standard, with the company ultimately becoming the "health information backbone."

What Jonathan Bush wants is far more revolutionary than simply a change in the Meaningful Use regulations. He wants an unfettered marketplace for healthcare, in which consumers have the quality and cost information they need to make wise choices, and the copays that prompt them to shop with gusto. Bush believes that in that kind of market, the big, lazy, and overpriced incumbents (whether Epic or its hospital customers) would be forced to adapt or die. Then, the athenas of the world—nimble, modern, cloud-based, and linking to all manner of helpful apps—would clean up.

I asked him whether he thinks that Epic might ultimately become more open, particularly as pressure grows from patients, competitors, and the government. "I don't know whether they'll be able to reinvent their DNA fast enough," he said, "especially with Judy in her seventies. It's a very monolithic culture, very Judy-centric."

▶   ▶   ▶

After spending a full day at Epic headquarters and five hours with Jonathan Bush and his top lieutenants, I felt a bit like a judge listening to two very savvy attorneys plead their case. Both Epic and athena are justifiably proud of their products and their people, and both defend their worldview with great passion and (particularly in athena's case) no shortage of hyperbole. Did I really need to choose sides?

For now, I think the answer is no—the world is plenty big enough for the two to coexist (along with a few dozen other EHR companies). Athena does a splendid job serving small office-based practices, where its cloud-based architecture and openness to a multitude of apps makes sense. Its EHR interface is simple, elegant, and standardized. Engineers in Boston can monitor the clicks of thousands of physicians and quickly change the system when they spot a problem. After the Ebola virus first appeared in Texas, athena revised its patient intake checklist to include appropriate travel questions, literally overnight.[36]

But building an EHR for a small office practice is a far less complex task than doing so for a huge hospital. It's a bit ironic that Bush rails against full-service hospitals (calling them "do-it-all department stores") for not focusing on a narrow core business (academic centers, he believes, should just do high-end complex care, and leave everything else to others). Yet, in trying to build a do-it-all EHR rather than sticking to the stuff his company is good at (serving the needs of office-based physicians), he is doing precisely the same thing.

In fact, although Bush talks as if he's ready to lace up his gloves and take Epic on, as of late 2014 his company didn't yet have a viable hospital electronic health record product. Speaking in March of that year, athena's CFO, Timothy Adams, noted that athena had two components of a hospital EHR: a billing system and a patient record. But, he admitted, when it came to all the modules that make up a comprehensive hospital system—the nurse rounding station, lab interfaces, bed management modules, nutrition, pharmacy, and "30 other modules out there"—well, "we don't have those." In other words, athena isn't remotely close to being able to replace the inpatient functionality of an Epic or a Cerner.[37] "Some day, if Jonathan is successful, he'll face some of our problems," said a nettled Dvorak, clearly tired of this particular fly buzzing around his face.

I have little confidence that a 500-bed teaching hospital—the kind that performs transplant surgery, cares for premature infants, and manages critically ill patients in ICUs—is going to be well served by linking to a stream of free-for-all products created by a newly unleashed universe of app developers high on Red Bull and "More Disruption, Please" pep talks. As I'll discuss in the next chapter, I desperately want to see entrepreneurs in the healthcare space, but, at least for now, I want their inventions to focus on handling simpler problems,

---

[36] Since the missed diagnosis of the first U.S. Ebola patient took place at an Epic facility, and the Texas hospital initially blamed its EHR for the error (a position that the hospital retracted the next day), athena's prompt revision of its intake module was accompanied, unsurprisingly, by a press release that described the company's cloud-facilitated nimbleness.

[37] In February, 2015, athena and John Halamka's Beth Israel Deaconess Medical Center (one of the few large hospitals still using a homegrown electronic health record) announced a deal to co-develop a cloud-based inpatient EHR. It will likely take two or three years.

those lacking the tight interdependencies and life-and-death consequences of the hospital.

Don Berwick, former head of Medicare and founder of the Institute for Healthcare Improvement, once described a thought experiment that captures the importance of integration. Imagine, he said, that you're trying to assemble the world's best car by using the best parts. You'd connect the engine of a Ferrari, the brakes of a Porsche, the suspension of a BMW, and the body of a Volvo. "What we'd get, of course, is nothing close to a great car," he said. "We'd get a pile of very expensive junk."

Everybody chanting "Open! Open!" points to the iPhone, but if you think about it, Apple is extraordinarily *closed* (or at least brutally prescriptive) about who and what plugs into its system. The company has created the standard, and nobody can just join in and start "disrupting." That is why your apps work so well. Epic is trying to do the same thing as it gradually opens up to third-party programs. That's what I want in my hospital, at least for the foreseeable future.

Does this mean that the government (or Jonathan Bush, for that matter) should just leave Epic be? Of course not. Epic and all the other vendors and providers need to be pushed toward a common standard that supports sharing, accompanied by a set of incentives and penalties to promote total connectivity. Patients deserve that. One interface that is long overdue: it should be easy for physicians to choose an office-based and relatively inexpensive EHR like athena and have it link up to their hospital's Epic system, or any of the equivalent inpatient products. Today, it is not.

Whether the winning model will be a cloud-based model like athena's or Epic's more traditional architecture is not, in the end, terribly important. The market and the state of technology will determine the optimal specs. What *is* important is that we don't jump too quickly onto the "open" bandwagon at the cost of the kinds of integration that, at least today, we need if we are to manage complex and vulnerable patients. Let athena be athena, and let Epic be Epic. Then, within reason, let the market decide on the better solution.

▶   ▶   ▶

Despite all the pressure that Epic finds itself under, the company may yet get the last laugh. Being thwacked by the media for being "closed" is unpleasant, and nobody wants to be publicly excoriated at a congressional hearing. But Epic sales remain brisk, and, at least in its core market, the company continues to receive a steady stream of new customers who are dissatisfied with their current EHRs.

Because he runs a publicly traded company, Jonathan Bush is subject to a different kind of pressure than Epic is. In May 2014, activist investor David Einhorn, the billionaire CEO of Greenlight Capital, went after both Bush and athena in a speech at a large investor conference.

After observing that athena had an outlandish price/earnings ratio, had failed to meet several financial performance expectations, and faces a series of major business challenges in coming years (the loss of the HITECH money and the lack of a viable inpatient system, to name a couple), Einhorn predicted that athena's stock would tumble by 80 percent in relatively short order, in a classic bursting of a Wall Street "bubble." He then asked, rhetorically, what could possibly explain athena's current stock price, which seemed to defy the laws of economic gravity.

"It would take a superhero," he said, and a picture of Jonathan Bush flashed on his screen. This was not a compliment. This slide was rapidly followed by a series of videos that displayed a smorgasbord of unflattering, histrionic, and sometimes buffoonish Bush interviews and stage appearances. In one particularly damning mash-up, Bush slings around virtually every Internet buzz-term:

> "creating network effect, creating an Airbnb."
>
> "a little bit of Facebook."
>
> "it's a little bit like Salesforce.com, but we do more work."
>
> "athenahealth is a cloud-based service—we sell results. Amazon has great software, athena has great software; Amazon sells stories, we sell paid claims, settled appointments, filed claims."

Einhorn then cued another clip, this one of the King of Market Hype, Jim Cramer, host of CNBC's *Mad Money*. "Even before Marc Benioff [founder of Salesforce and the person generally credited with popularizing the idea of cloud-based commerce] knew what a cloud was," said Cramer, "Jonathan Bush did—you can say that he *invented* the damn thing." Predictably, Einhorn followed this with an SAT-like analogy: Jonathan Bush is to the cloud as Al Gore is to the Internet.

Einhorn's audience was reportedly in stitches, but the message was clear and serious: Bush is a hoot to watch, but he and his company might be more polish than shoe, at least when it comes to the things that Wall Street cares about. (It's important to note that what athenahealth does, it does quite well, with extremely high ratings for usability and customer satisfaction in its core business of outpatient billing and electronic charting.) Only time will tell if Einhorn is right, but he often is.

Einhorn wasn't bearish on the entire health information technology sector. In fact, he praised another company—one that has invested billions in doing the hard work of creating robust integrated systems, one that enjoys a 100 percent client retention rate, one whose CEO isn't sexy, trendy, or quotable. This company, he continued, is all but ignored by Wall Street, both because it's not publicly traded and for one additional reason, a reason that instantly revealed the company's identity.

"Oh, and they are from Wisconsin," he said.

# Chapter 25

# Silicon Valley
# Meets Healthcare

For thousands of years, guys like us have gotten the shit
kicked out of us. But now, for the first time, we're living in an
era when we can be in charge. And build empires! We can be
the Vikings of our day.

> —Richard Hendricks, lead character
> on HBO's *Silicon Valley*, 2014

As you've seen, the people who complain that the HITECH incentive payments and the Meaningful Use regulations have locked *in* the incumbents also worry that they have locked *out* the young innovators. You know the entrepreneurial types I'm referring to—the ones who have transformed the way we buy our houses, hail our cabs, and book our travel; the ones who don't ask for permission before they enter a market, and make no apologies when they turn it upside down. The success (at least so far) of athenahealth illustrates that this idea of vendor lock is incomplete even in the relatively staid electronic health record market. But those who harbor this concern about dampening innovation are worried about far more than EHRs. They're worried about the technologies that none of us are smart enough even to imagine today.

David Blumenthal has heard this critique, and he couldn't disagree more. "Our investment convinced the IT world that healthcare was a place to work," he said of the $30 billion federal incentive program. "We created a market, and that market is thriving. It's not perfect, but now everyone wants to build a healthcare app."

The day after Blumenthal and I met in his Manhattan office, he sent me an article with the headline, "Health IT Sees First Billion Dollar Quarter." Blumenthal attached a tongue-in-cheek note to the article: "More evidence of how market innovation in the HIT sector is suffering under the oppressive government HITECH intervention."

Blumenthal recommended that I see for myself the state of health IT innovation by visiting a San Francisco–based incubator named Rock Health. And so I did.

▶    ▶    ▶

I remember the first time I took my family to a restaurant called the Rainforest Café. The food was only fair, but that hardly mattered, since the kid-pleasing attraction was the kitschy jungle ambience. The tables were scattered amid tropical vegetation, fish tanks, waterfalls, statues of assorted creatures (elephants, monkeys, iguanas, and the like), and the animatronic "Tracy the Talking Tree." Periodically there came a flash of lightning and the boom of thunder, followed by a misty rain.

It was only later that I learned that each Rainforest Café is part of a chain that now numbers 32 restaurants, managed by Landry, Inc., a Houston-based hospitality conglomerate whose other brands include Bubba Gump Shrimp Company, Morton's Steakhouse, and the Golden Nugget Hotel and Casino. In its Rainforest Cafés, the company has created something of an oxymoron: an exotic cookie cutter.

The restaurant came to mind as I visited the headquarters of several Silicon Valley health IT companies. Despite the fact that they are a world away from the monochromatic offices of the old IBM, with its dark suits, white shirts, and "sincere ties," they too have a studied sameness. In the Valley, the unspoken dress code calls for blue jeans or khakis. There are far more men than women, but at least as many people of Asian and Indian heritage as Caucasians (sadly, Latinos and African Americans are still few and far between). The average age appears to be mid-twenties, and it's rare to see someone who is overweight or using a non-Apple product. The floor plan is open and capacious, with pipes and wires traversing the ceiling. Beanbag chairs are scattered around, and there is an impromptu chess game over here, a New-Age hammock suspended from the ceiling over there. Expensive bikes are parked in the corners. Many offices have a dog or two happily wandering around. The juice bar is a busy congregational space, as are the small glass-walled rectangular conference rooms, in which one twentysomething, seated on a couch, is listening to another map out a company's can't-miss strategy on a dry-erase board. If one half expects to see a horse-drawn carriage from the window of David Blumenthal's Fifth Avenue office in Manhattan, one half expects to see a self-driving car outside the offices of these Silicon Valley start-ups.

The sense of limitless possibilities is palpable when you enter this world, but the hype can border on the farcical. In the "Health 2.0" office near San Francisco's CalTrain station, a London-born healthcare impresario named Matthew Holt and his staff spend their days analyzing healthcare IT start-ups for a series of publications and conferences that they produce. In the corner of the obligatory whiteboard in the cramped office, I noticed a list of companies under a heading that read, "Uber for Healthcare." I asked Holt about it. In his charming accent, he said, "We're running an office pool. To make the list, either a company has to say that they *are* 'Uber for Healthcare' or they have to have the word 'Uber' in their title." On the day I visited, there were 12 companies that qualified, which gave Holt a narrow lead in his office sweepstakes.

Notwithstanding the hype and the easy-to-mock sense of cool, one has to admit that hanging around in this ecosystem (another favorite Silicon Valley word) is exhilarating. It isn't surprising that smart young folks who want to change the world (and get rich doing it) gravitate toward it. If you are, like me, on the wrong side of age 50, a few hours in one of these places will make you want to dig out your slide rule and calculate just how far over the hill you are.

▶   ▶   ▶

Another such office is in San Francisco's bustling Mission Bay district, a 10-minute walk from the Giants' ballpark and just across the street from UCSF's Mission Bay campus. From this perch, Rock Health provides seed funding, advice, and cheerleading for a dozen or so health IT start-ups at a time. It is here that I developed my keenest sense of where all of this might be headed.

One of Rock Health's cofounders, Nate Gross, is, at age 30, "in the upper quartile" of age for folks in his office. Gross is boy-next-door handsome, tall and lanky, modest and polite, geeky without being awkward, and impressively smart. He became interested in technology as a kid growing up in Medford, Oregon, whiling away four-hour drives to soccer matches by reprogramming a Texas Instruments calculator ("I didn't have a GameBoy, so I wrote apps for the calculator, like a poker and blackjack game"), but he decided to be a doctor.

At Emory's medical school, he was pegged as the "guy who could write code." (This was a recurring theme for many of the physician-informaticists I met.) Before he left Atlanta, Gross had created a Google Calendar–based scheduling system, an improved paging system, and a new way of accessing the medical literature for his Emory classmates and faculty.

In 2008, just as David Blumenthal, Bob Kocher, and Zeke Emanuel were beginning to hammer out the details of HITECH and Obamacare in Washington's corridors of power, Gross was still a medical student, studying anatomy and biochemistry, but transfixed by the excitement of the presidential campaign, particularly the debate over healthcare. He decided to take a break from medical school to obtain an MBA at Harvard, so that he could better understand healthcare economics and policy and make some contribution to them. He had no idea what that would be.

At Harvard, he volunteered to run the healthcare section of a technology conference that the business school hosts each year. There was one other volunteer, a classmate named Halle Tecco, who would become his partner in founding Rock Health. Gross also went on to co-found another company called Doximity. Known as "LinkedIn for Doctors," one in two U.S. physicians has joined it.

Rock Health began as Tecco and Gross's field project in their second year of business school. The two decided to try to figure out why the state of technology in healthcare was so dismal compared to what was available for other sectors of the economy. Before Harvard, Tecco, whose background was in business and finance, had worked at Apple, where she helped manage the healthcare section of the App Store. "She was always bashing her head against the wall, saying, 'Why is *Angry Birds* so beautifully designed, whereas most healthcare apps are absolutely horrible?'" recalled Gross. In seeking the answer to that question, Gross and Tecco interviewed dozens of venture capitalists and entrepreneurs.

Each interview brought them closer to understanding the obstacles to IT innovation in healthcare. They boiled the problem down to three main issues. The first was investor uncertainty: at the time, nobody knew whether the Affordable Care Act would pass and what its real impact on the healthcare marketplace would be. Until things settled out, healthcare's longstanding market problems, particularly the lack of incentives for patients and clinicians to invest in tools that might improve quality or efficiency, would continue to cast a pall on IT investments large (EHRs) and small (wellness apps). (It should be noted that there were exceptions to this rule. The climate for *certain* healthcare technology investments—namely, those designed to be used by specialized physicians who could bill for the services, such as cardiac devices or MRI scanners, or those designed with lucrative self-pay markets in mind, such as lasers in plastic surgery—was and remains vibrant.)

The second problem: most venture capital firms, even those with an interest in healthcare, lacked personnel with the deep medical knowledge needed to evaluate new technologies or the problems they were designed to solve.

The third obstacle stemmed from the youth of most IT entrepreneurs. Unless a 26-year-old computer engineer has a loved one with a serious medical illness or hails from a long line of physicians, the world of healthcare is utterly foreign, with a different language and a set of problems whose solutions appear to be well beyond the horizon. "People like to build products that solve problems in their lives. Snapchat may do that, whereas a healthcare app doesn't," Gross told me.

As their business school project continued, the partners began to believe that they might be able to help fledgling companies by, said Gross, "giving them a little bit of funding, introducing them to the right investors, refining their pitch to build investor confidence, and then helping them build an investable business." They also felt that it was important to "make health IT sexy"—to convince a young engineer or entrepreneur that the field offered a path to economic success and "doing good in the world at the same time."

Rock Health[38] is a nonprofit, funded through a combination of philanthropy from successful graduates and investors, and fees for conferences and educational materials. Each year, about 10 start-ups (out of 400 applicants) successfully compete for a spot in a Rock Health "class" (a 2.5 percent acceptance rate), and the winners receive space in the Mission Bay offices, access to the Rock Health curriculum ("HIPAA 101" is a popular course), hands-on mentorship, and some seed funding. Most Rock Health companies are run by nonphysicians, although they usually have physician advisors. Even as a physician, this makes perfect sense to Gross. "It may be easier to teach a techie healthcare than to teach a doctor tech," he said. In Rock Health's first few years of existence, about 60 start-ups rotated through; collectively, the organization's graduates have had 10 million users and raised $180 million from investors. It is an impressive record, one that has caused the IT and healthcare worlds to take notice.

▶    ▶    ▶

I asked Nate Gross to name some of the Rock Health alumni he is particularly proud of. I could see that the question pained him—it's like choosing your favorite child. But he did name a few that are "doing interesting things." Collectively, they illustrate the breadth and creativity of the start-up side of health IT.

The first is called Augmedix. Recall our earlier discussion about how doctors have become slaves to their electronic health records, leading some hospitals and clinics to hire scribes to allow physicians and patients to make eye contact again. With Augmedix, doctors interact with their patients while wearing Google Glass, and the voice and video recordings go off to a distant site, where a combination of human transcriptionists and natural language processing helps create the note. The physician can also call up data from the EHR ("Okay, Glass, show me the vital signs") without turning away from the patient.

Another Rock Health company, CellScope, makes an attachment for your smartphone that can take a picture inside someone's ear—a replacement for the doctor's otoscope. "Just think how nice it is," Gross said, "for a mom to be able to look in her kid's ear, beam that image through telemedicine to a physician, and have the physician say, 'Yeah, come in,' or, 'No, don't worry about it.'" To demonstrate the clarity of the image, he proudly showed me a selfie of his

---

[38] The name comes from the fact that Gross and Tecco decided to launch the organization while sitting in Harvard Business School's Rock Hall.

own eardrum: the oval-shaped middle ear sheathed by the translucent tym-panic membrane; the malleus, the bone that magically converts sound waves into impulses our brains perceive as sound, hanging down from the top of the oval like a bent pink Q-tip swab. It is, I agree, a middle ear—and an image thereof—worth boasting about.

Finally, he described a company called Lift Labs, whose product, Liftware, is designed to help patients who suffer from serious hand tremors. These are sometimes an isolated, and largely unexplained, problem ("essential tremor") and sometimes a consequence of Parkinson's disease. The tool looks like an electric toothbrush with swappable heads, including a spoon, a pen, and a cof-fee mug. Its core technology is similar to the system in high-end cameras that prevents a shaky hand from causing a blurry photo. In Liftware's case, a gizmo in the handle senses the tremor and creates a precisely timed countermotion to dampen it. The result is a spoon that isn't completely still, but is, for some patients, still enough to make the difference between being able to eat soup or drink coffee in public or not.

▶   ▶   ▶

After a couple of hours at Rock Health, I could see why Nate Gross is proud of what he and his team have accomplished, and why promoting a dynamic healthcare technology investment market is about far more than money. While today's market may be, in another favorite Silicon Valley-ism, "a bit frothy," Rock Health graduates are competing successfully for real dollars from mature, no-nonsense funders. And many of the start-ups appear to be building sustainable businesses. In mid-2014, Augmedix signed a deal with the Dignity Health system, which manages hospitals in 17 states, and Lift Labs was bought by Google. This is not Pets.com, or any of the other dot-com flameouts we've seen over the years.

More important, these products are not indulgent and silly—they are solv-ing real problems for clinicians and for patients. Augmedix, CellScope, and Lift Labs each have compelling human stories: helping a doctor who is strug-gling to satisfy both his patients and his EHR; a working mom who is con-fronting a wailing, febrile toddler; a proud elderly man who is too embar-rassed to eat in his favorite restaurant. Each leverages a technology that did not exist a decade ago: Google Glass, the iPhone, and the vibration sensing and dampening device.

But none of these technologies can achieve its full impact, nor are the business models likely to be viable over the long haul, unless they are supported by, and embedded in, appropriate work flows, cultures, regulations, and economic models. Take Augmedix—it's a good idea, and it's fueled by cool technology. But how do we get the transcript into, and the vital signs out of, the electronic health record? And what about the privacy issues for the doctor walking around the office wearing Google Glass? Will she be hit with a huge HIPAA fine if she inadvertently video records a patient down the hall? For CellScope: Is there a physician available to look at my kid's eardrum picture at 6 a.m.? Are the doctors compensated for telemedicine services, and how are *these* visits documented in the EHR? Can the doctor be in another state? Another country? What if the physician decides your kid needs to see an ear specialist—is that another telemedicine doc or a flesh-and-blood one? And for Lift Labs, does a physician "prescribe" Liftware? Will it be covered by Medicare? Should it be?

The history of technology tells us that it is these financial, environmental, and organizational factors, rather than the digital wizardry itself, that determine the success and impact of new IT tools. This phenomenon is known as the "productivity paradox" of information technology.

# Chapter 26

# The Productivity Paradox

You can see the computer age everywhere but in the productivity statistics.

—Nobel Prize–winning MIT economist
Robert Solow, writing in 1987

Between the time David Blumenthal stepped down as national coordinator for health IT and became CEO of the Commonwealth Fund, he returned to Boston from 2011 to 2013 to manage the transition of Partners HealthCare from a homegrown electronic health record to the one made by Epic. "I took my own medicine," he said, since now, in order to qualify for the HITECH incentives, it was his job to help Partners meet the very Meaningful Use requirements he had created. During the transition, Blumenthal discovered the great challenge of all IT implementations: the need to redesign work flows. The implementation of health IT "is not a technical project, it's a social change project."

He described meetings in which senior clinicians discussed how the electronic health record would operate in a given clinical scenario, such as getting a patient and a donor ready for a kidney transplant. Once you begin to itemize all the steps in this and many of the other things we do in healthcare, the complexity becomes immediately apparent, and the conversation rapidly turns to creating standardized protocols.

Everybody, of course, supports standardization—in theory. But human beings (particularly, but not exclusively, famous Harvard professors practicing at famous Boston hospitals) want things to be standardized *their* way. The difficulty that doctors face in accepting a workplace that is not custom-designed around their personal preferences is captured in this old joke about the physician staffs of hospitals: What do you call a 99-1 vote of the medical staff? A tie.

"These IT implementations are rare, once-in-an-organization's-lifetime opportunities," said Blumenthal—opportunities to clean up messy systems and to make fundamental decisions about work flow and governance. "I just wish more organizations would take advantage of them."

▶    ▶    ▶

The concept of productivity (output per unit of input) sounds abstruse, but it turns out to be central to the functioning of organizations ranging from your corner deli to entire nations. As the economist Paul Krugman has observed, while productivity isn't everything, it is almost everything, because it is what ultimately determines the financial vitality of a business and the living standards of a country.

While specific technologies—a new jet engine, say, or a solar panel—can improve productivity, since the Industrial Revolution the technologies associated with the greatest productivity bumps have been so-called general-purpose technologies—technologies that transformed multiple industries and laid the groundwork for many new applications. The best-known examples are the steam engine and electricity, and so it's fair to say that such technologies don't come around very often, perhaps every 50 to 100 years. Information technology falls into the same category—in fact, in *The Second Machine Age*, Erik Brynjolfsson and Andrew McAfee call IT "the most general purpose of all."

Given the power and range of information technology, one would think that its implementation would rapidly and predictably lead to a sharp uptick in productivity. Yet, in the 1980s, economists began to notice something strange. Companies in industries ranging from manufacturing to accounting were fervently installing computers, but productivity appeared to be stagnant. What was wrong?

In a seminal 1993 article, Brynjolfsson coined the term *productivity paradox* to describe this phenomenon. While he considered several possible explanations, he settled on two main ones. The first: our systems for measuring productivity weren't up to the task. The second: like a safe deposit box, unlocking

IT's potential requires the turning of two keys—the technology itself and the redesign of the surrounding environment.

The first hypothesis—that the gains were real but were being missed by the statistics—was cleverly captured by Brynjolfsson this way: "A shortfall of evidence is not evidence of a shortfall." When the steam engine was discovered, it wasn't hard to quantify its value, since the same factory that had been producing 1,000 zippers in a week could now produce that many in a day. But in our modern economy, in which we produce more knowledge and entertainment than we do steel and corn, the output is not so easy to pin down. How do you quantify the value of better-argued legal briefs, more accurate loan decisions, or a more colorful assortment of dresses? (Or, for that matter, a more thoroughly researched book!)

Economists debate how to capture the productivity contributions of technologies that improve the quality of a product and the customer experience. Take the automated teller machine. If your measure of productivity is the number of checks processed, then banks seemed less productive after they installed ATMs, which is clearly ridiculous. Record sales have plummeted, but thanks to Pandora, iTunes, and Spotify, we have far more access to music than ever before.

While this measurement challenge explains a portion of the paradox, Brynjolfsson's second hypothesis—the need to redesign the work—is the one that dominates modern thinking, as research over the subsequent two decades has placed the weight of the evidence on its side of the scales. The key to unlocking information technology's productivity gains, it says, is not in the technology itself, but in the emergence of "complementary innovations."

The classic example is what happened in the years after electricity replaced steam engines as the power sources in factories. At first, the factories installed the smaller, more nimble electric motors right where the huge steam engines had been, rather than taking advantage of their smaller size to locate them closer to where the actual work was being done. Finally, as new factories were built and old managers retired or died off, businesses figured out how to make the most of the new technology. At that point, wrote Brynjolfsson and McAfee, "productivity didn't merely inch upward on the resulting assembly lines; it doubled or even tripled. What's more, for most of the subsequent century, additional complementary innovations, from lean manufacturing and steel mini-mills to Total Quality Management and Six Sigma principles, continued to boost manufacturing productivity." This was a generational change—it took nearly 40 years for the productivity advantages of electric motors to be fully reflected in factory output statistics.

Today as ever, changing the way that work is done often determines whether an organization will get its money's worth from its IT investment. But the temptation to simply electronify the old process is powerful. Robert Wah, a reproductive endocrinologist who led the Department of Defense's IT systems and is now president of the American Medical Association, told me what happened a few years ago when one of the Defense Department's many outpatient practices switched from paper to digital. He received a call from one clinic manager. "Our waiting room is all backed up, and it's all because of you and your system!" she complained.

Wah went down to see for himself. "When they were on paper, they had the classic work flow. The patient walks into the clinic and says, 'I'm here to see Dr. Wah at 11 a.m.' The receptionist looks him up in the book, finds him, and checks his name off the schedule. A nurse grabs the chart, which was pulled from medical records last night, takes his vital signs, and writes them in the note. She also looks for where he is on his prevention," things like cancer screening and vaccinations, "and signs off on that too. Then she puts the chart in a little rack on the door. Now Dr. Wah sees the chart, grabs it, and goes in to see the patient, who is sitting on the crinkly paper on the exam table."

Yep, that sounds right—it's how everyone's clinic work flow looked when we were in Paper World.

"But now there *is* no paper chart," he said, "and the trigger event to start the whole cascade was that chart behind the front desk. The people who take the vital signs—they're trained to watch that chart rack." Wah and his team pointed out that they could create a new work flow, one that didn't depend on a paper chart being moved sequentially from place to place. After all, the digital record can be viewed by all the workers—receptionist, nurse, and doctor—at the same time. That should be a good thing, right?

"So how did they solve it?" I asked. "Some sort of electronic prompt?"

He laughed. "The receptionist checked the patient in electronically, and then turned around and put a chart-sized piece of cardboard in the chart rack. *That's* how wedded we are to our paper-based processes."

▶    ▶    ▶

Appreciating the need to address work flow and culture does not get kludgy technology off the hook. In 1995, the consulting group Gartner coined the term *Hype Cycle* to describe the trajectory of many technologies. The cycle commences with the introduction of a new technology. Then the hype begins, with a "peak of inflated expectations" preceding a swift descent into the dreaded "trough of disillusionment." Some technologies die there; the ones destined to be successful climb the "slope of enlightenment" to reach their final stage: a "plateau of productivity." The cycle has proved to be a useful model: many technologies, particularly those complex technical advances that require complementary innovations and reengineering of the work, traverse all its stages. Part of what is so impressive about the modern generation of consumer-directed IT tools—Google search, the iPhone and iPad, Facebook— is that they moved through the stages so rapidly, with barely any trough. Could it be that technology designers have become so skilled that, in today's world, the Hype Cycle is either avoided or markedly foreshortened?

Perhaps, but not in healthcare.

▶   ▶   ▶

Part of the hype in health IT was that we'd save boatloads of cash. This was a particularly attractive selling point for EHRs, since healthcare now consumes nearly one in five U.S. dollars, leading to a widespread consensus that if we don't get healthcare costs under control, they will smother the rest of the economy. As health IT boosters (including, but not limited to, the vendors) were seeking support for digitization, the promise of cost savings and productivity gains was a crucial element of the pitch. One widely cited 2005 RAND study projected an $81 billion annual savings in the United States, largely through reductions in personnel and decreased ordering of redundant tests. This became Exhibit A in the argument for HITECH.

Bob Kocher, the Obama advisor who helped craft the HITECH legislation, told me that his White House team was not wowed by the RAND numbers. "We viewed electronic health records as an infrastructure investment to enable us to do things that actually save money [largely by replacing the fee-for-service model with new payment and care delivery models]. We did not think that the purchase and implementation of the records themselves would have any economic benefit." That memo apparently did not get through to Kocher's boss, then President-elect Obama, who, in a January 2009 speech, declared that computerizing medical records would "cut waste, eliminate red tape, and reduce the need to repeat expensive tests."

In 2014, nine years after the original RAND projections, another RAND team reviewed the literature to see what impact health IT was *actually* having on quality and costs. The quality and patient safety evidence was reassuring:

overall, computerized order entry and clinical decision support were leading to modest but measurable improvements in care, mostly by preventing medication errors (though, as you've seen, they can also create new ones) and guiding doctors toward evidence-based treatments.

On the other hand, the efficiency studies illustrated that the productivity paradox was alive and well in healthcare. "Cost effects ranged from a 75 percent decrease to a 69 percent increase in the targeted costs," they wrote. "Some studies found that health IT was associated with increased documentation and that in some instances, even when providers were able to spend more time with their patients, much of that time was spent interacting with the computer."

Julia Adler-Milstein, a professor at the University of Michigan who studies health IT policy, described why some of the early projections of cost savings got it so wrong. The original economic models assumed that in a wired system, if there had been a prior test (a CT scan, say, or a lab test), the test would not be repeated, whereas it might well have been in a paper-based system. But, as we've seen, the electronic health record can be a big and mysterious place, and it's not hard for a physician to miss the fact that a test was done months earlier—perhaps at another organization whose computer doesn't talk to his own.

And then there are the realities of clinical practice, which are often ignored in the economists' models. There may be clinical uncertainty, such as when the patient's situation has changed since a study was first completed. A physician may have greater faith in her colleagues than she does in the clinicians who performed the original study. And there are often financial incentives in play. Taken together, Adler-Milstein is not too surprised that the projected cost savings from EHRs have proven elusive. "If the doctor thinks there might be even the tiniest bit of incremental value, why *wouldn't* she reorder the test?" she asked.

Ashish Jha, a professor at the Harvard School of Public Health who also studies health IT, recalled the cheerleading about efficiency that dominated public debate when HITECH was being considered. Everybody was talking about the cost savings, he told me, "But how do you go from A to B? And, by the way, there's a lot of carnage—disruption, companies that go out of business—between A and B. But nobody was talking about any of that stuff. Turn it on, and the savings will happen. Oh, and by the way, we forgot to tell you that it'll take one to two decades. I'm sure it was just an honest oversight."

▶   ▶   ▶

In a 2012 *New England Journal of Medicine* article, Spencer Jones and colleagues from RAND considered the IT productivity paradox in healthcare, settling on three possible explanations for it: measurement, mismanagement, and poor usability. We've already discussed the issues of usability in considerable detail, so let's focus on measurement and mismanagement.

The measurement problems for health IT are similar to those in other service industries. If patients have some of their needs met through e-mail or a patient portal, and this substitutes for office visits, then the productivity of the physicians may appear to have fallen, just as the productivity of banks appeared to worsen with the advent of ATMs. Yet the trade is clearly one that patients value. It remains devilishly hard to quantify gains that come in the form of better accessibility, quality, or convenience.

The other explanation, mismanagement, does not necessarily imply bone-headedness—this is not a day with Dilbert at the offices of Path-E-Tech or with Homer Simpson at the Springfield nuclear plant. Rather, organizations naturally create structures and cultures that support their usual way of doing things, and (for reasons ranging from risk aversion to job preservation) resist radical new approaches. Yet this approach can be self-defeating. Studies of technology's impact in other industries have clearly shown that those organizations with the management processes and culture to take advantage of the new tools are the ones that thrive.

In 1988, management guru Peter Drucker, he of "culture-eats-strategy-for-lunch" fame, presciently described how the then-fledgling field of information technology would allow organizations to flatten hierarchies and elevate the roles of "knowledge-workers." In the future, Drucker wrote, "the typical business will be knowledge-based, an organization composed largely of specialists who direct and discipline their own performance through organized feedback from colleagues, customers, and headquarters." It was the availability of information—"data endowed with relevance and purpose"—that would catalyze this shift.

In health IT, we're just beginning to work through these issues, and the complexity of medicine and the screwy incentives marbled throughout our payment systems mean that doing so is likely to be even harder than it was in factories and other service industries. From my vantage point, this thesis rings true. Among organizations that have implemented the same IT system (usually Epic, but sometimes one of the others), I see some that are using it to great advantage, and others that are foundering. Since the electronic backbone is essentially the same, one can only conclude that this has everything to do with the structure and culture of the organization and little to do with the technology.

"Organizational factors that unlock the value of IT are costly and time consuming," Brynjolfsson and a colleague wrote in 1998. "For every dollar of IT there are several dollars of organizational investment that, when combined, generate the large rise in measured firm productivity and value." This means that an organization's capacity to avoid treating its IT implementation as a "one and done," and to keep investing and evolving, is what ultimately determines the outcome. But will a healthcare system that is depleted of energy and money after a big Go Live find the wherewithal to summon up more of both when the need to do so is subtle and the returns on investment so mysterious? The answer will depend on how much heat hospitals and doctors feel to improve their performance. And *that* will turn on how closely healthcare hews to the normal laws of thermodynamics of the capitalist economy.

▶    ▶    ▶

The business model of "creative destruction" was first described by Austrian economist Joseph Schumpeter in 1942. It holds that a key driver of corporate innovation is the knowledge that the companies that produce the most value will win, and the rest will be destroyed. The theory—a fundamental component of Christensen's notion of disruptive innovation—is, in essence, economic Darwinism.

Were such forces fully unleashed in healthcare, they would clearly drive not only the adoption of technology, but a headlong effort to develop and implement all the changes in work flow, staffing, and culture that are associated with getting the best results from these expensive digital tools. In his 2012 book, *The Creative Destruction of Medicine*, Eric Topol of the Scripps Clinic argued that healthcare is on the cusp of being "Schumpetered," with information technology playing a crucial role.

Maybe so, but in medicine, we often block the normal Schumpeterian forces from their full expression. Said Harvard's Ashish Jha,

> *Every time an unnecessary hospital in a community that has five others looks like it's going to close, it gets propped up. Information technology has to allow for disruption. Everybody loves that word but people forget that disruption means that somebody needs to be disrupted—meaning that somebody needs to go out of business.*

Why have we shielded healthcare organizations and individuals from Schumpeterian destruction? Some of the reasons are quite noble, as when there isn't another doctor for 60 miles, or when only one hospital in a region will see patients without insurance. Others are less so, as when special interest groups, ranging from hospitals to doctors to nurses to pharmaceutical manu- facturers, fight a change that has the potential to cut costs without compromis- ing quality. Even as we debate the role of government and the caliber of the technology, in the end, it could be society itself, by pushing to make healthcare safe, affordable, and effective, that exerts the greatest influence on the health IT marketplace.

► ► ►

Over the past decade I've seen all of these forces play out in my own hospi- tal—both the new pressures to perform and the need for workforce and cul- ture changes to unlock technology's potential. This is why I'm swayed by the IT-Plus-Other-Stuff explanation for the productivity paradox.

Of course, we scored some quick wins at UCSF just by switching from ana- log to digital. Our medical records department (the folks who used to have to pull the dusty charts off shelves and have them delivered to the clinic or hospital ward) has withered. I can now write my notes and review my patients' records at home, and the problem of trying to decipher a physician's scrawl has disappeared.

On the other hand, there are many areas in which the improvements were elusive or required complementary interventions. We now have dozens of quality specialists plowing through electronic records to find and analyze data requested by payers and regulators—data that would have been impossible to retrieve in the old days, and that will (one day, God willing) be retrievable electronically. And you're now familiar with all the issues involving usability, bloated notes, and the like.

Although we still struggle with the alerts, we are beginning to build in clinical decision support that truly does make a difference. When a patient has a combination of findings that point to sepsis (fever, fast heart rate or breathing, elevated white blood cell count), our Epic system now fires a "Best Practice Advisory" to signal the clinicians to consider starting antibiotics and fluids. Our death rate from sepsis has fallen impressively. This kind of decision support doesn't come with your EHR out of the box, like a Cracker Jack prize. Instead, it's the kind of thing you build after your EHR has been in place for a while, like remodeling your kitchen a couple of years after buying the house.

Our patients now have access to a patient portal that has made it far easier for them to schedule appointments, obtain refills, and communicate with their physicians. Nobody quite knew how to manage all of this at first, and I'm sure we had some analogues to Robert Wah's fake cardboard charts. But after a couple of years, it now works just fine. Although we don't yet have OpenNotes, patients do see their laboratory and x-ray results quickly, and the sky has not fallen.

In my own division of 60 hospitalists (general internists who oversee the care of hospitalized patients), for years we have emphasized the crucial role that physicians play in helping to identify system problems that might compromise quality and safety, and fix them. Our investments have included a vigorous leadership development program and the creation of a committee structure designed to tackle these problems. But until recently, the inaccessibility of data was a critical bottleneck. This is a major problem with today's EHR products: although they are chock-full of data, frontline clinicians usually have no easy way to access those data, either to serve their own patients or to discover ways to improve the system.

This meant that when we tried to answer questions like, "Are we limiting our blood transfusions only to patients who really need them?" (the national guidelines have drastically changed on this; recent research has made clear that many patients do better with fewer transfusions), and "How many of our patients remain on a cardiac monitor despite having no reason to do so?," we lacked the ability to get our hands on such data.

Now we can, three years after our Epic Go Live—but only after a considerable investment in analytical support, including sending a few of our people to attend intensive "Getting Under the Hood of Your EHR" courses at Epic's Wisconsin headquarters. Being able to ask and answer important questions without having to work through our hospital's bureaucracy is just the kind of organizational flattening that Peter Drucker hoped for. And doing so generates a positive feedback loop, since the clinicians can see the value of their work, which drives them to do more of it, and to involve trainees in it, too.

Here's one more example of how reengineering the work was needed to unleash the power of going digital. Until a few years ago, if a patient in our primary care clinic had a problem that required a subspecialty (for example, cardiology or rheumatology) consult, the patient would have been referred to that specialty's practice. The appointment would have taken a few weeks to arrange. The consultant would have seen the patient and dictated a paper note (which might or might not have made it back to the primary care doctor), and the patient would have been scheduled to see the PCP for follow-up a few weeks later. It was often a frustrating, and sometimes even risky, one- or two-month cycle.

Today at UCSF, many specialty questions are answered through a system of eConsults, in which the primary care physician sends the question electronically to a consultant, who can easily review the patient's electronic record and provide an answer within a day, documented in the EHR. We have found that this system obviates the need for about 20 percent of in-person specialty visits. It has been a win-win-win for patients, providers, and the medical center.

But it too doesn't come bundled with the Epic package, and it took us a few years to work out the details. The ones that involved reconfiguring the EHR were by far the easiest. The harder ones went something like this: Would the specialist have time set aside to do this? Would all specialists do this, or just specific ones? How would we manage superspecialized questions that the person manning the eConsult desk might not be qualified to answer? How would the specialists and the PCPs be compensated for their time? Would patients understand, and accept, eConsults? Could we develop a database of common Q&As and place the answers in a FAQ database? When should teleconsults be used instead of eConsults? You get the idea. Answering such questions is healthcare's version of discovering where to put the electronic motors on the factory floor.

The crucial point—and one that leaves me far more optimistic about the future of health IT than I was a few years ago—is that none of these changes, changes that are good for patients, clinicians, and the healthcare system, could have happened by simply implementing an electronic health record. But none of them could have happened without it, either.

Part Six

# Toward a
# Brighter Future

# Chapter 27

# A Vision for Health Information Technology

The future is already here—it's just not evenly distributed.
　　　　　—William Gibson, writing in the *Economist*, 2003

In researching this book, I interviewed nearly 100 people from extraordinarily diverse backgrounds—frontline clinicians, world experts in artificial intelligence and big data, aviation engineers and pilots, federal policy makers, CEOs of major IT companies, entrepreneurs, patients and their families.[39] Unsurprisingly, they gave vastly differing answers to many of today's core questions in health information technology: What is the appropriate role of government? Why is usability so bad? Is Epic really open or closed? Are computers dehumanizing the practice of medicine? Will we need doctors in the future?

But when I asked folks to describe what they thought the healthcare system *could* look like after all the dust settles, I found a remarkable degree of unanimity. If they are right, this future state is thrilling to consider, which is all the more reason why the current state is so dispiriting. Moreover, given the limitations of the human imagination (who could have envisioned IBM's Watson, the Apple Watch, or intelligent underwear at the turn of this century?), their forecast might prove to be overly modest.

---

[39] They are listed at the end of the book.

*Uh oh*, I can hear you thinking. *I read this book because I was looking for an honest appraisal of why today's health IT is so problematic. Has the author morphed into a hopeless techno-optimist?*

Hardly. I remain every bit as concerned about the current state of health IT as I was at the start. But I also have a clearer view of where things could go if we play our cards right. I can't tell you whether the nirvana I'm about to describe is a decade or a generation away—or even whether it will be derailed by missteps, malfeasance, or bad bounces. Judging from our track record over the past decade, both the optimists and the pessimists have ample evidence on their side.

But there is one thing I am sure of: the speed with which health IT achieves its full promise depends far less on the technology than on whether the key stakeholders—government officials, technology vendors and innovators, healthcare administrators, physicians and other clinicians, training leaders, and patients—work together and make wise choices. So let's take a moment to side with the optimists, painting a picture of a healthcare world transformed for the better by IT, a world that, despite our rocky start, is within our reach.

▶   ▶   ▶

In this future state, there will be far fewer hospitals. Neither the 60-bed community hospital nor the 25-bed rural hospital will have the size and volume to produce the best outcomes. After lots of *Sturm und Drang*, many will prove to be economically nonviable, and will close. For the most part, this will be okay for patients (though perhaps not for the laid-off workers), since they will be able to receive most of their care in their homes or in new, less intensive community-based settings.

The hospitals that are left standing will be large, bristling with technology, and, for the most part, embedded in megasystems. Rather than the 6,000 or so hospitals that we currently have in the United States (many of them completely independent and more than half with fewer than 100 beds), the landscape will more resemble that of commercial airlines, with a handful of major national brands, accompanied by some smaller regional enterprises. Geography simply won't matter as much in a connected healthcare world, just as it doesn't matter to you that Amazon is based in Seattle, Fidelity in Boston, and Google in Mountain View.

Patients in hospitals will be there for major surgeries and other procedures, critical illness, or triage in the face of substantial clinical uncertainty. Anyone who is just "pretty sick" or who needs a modest procedure (including having a baby delivered) will be cared for in a less expensive setting. The concept of the intensive care unit as a discrete physical space will evaporate, as every patient who is sick enough to be in the hospital will be sick enough to need, or potentially need, ICU-level care. Each bed in the building will be wired with the technology we currently associate with the ICU, and the intensity of the care (the ratio of nurses to patients, for example) will vary on a case-by-case basis, driven by the results of sophisticated risk-modeling algorithms that will always be humming in the background. The deteriorating patient will no longer need to move to the ICU; she will simply receive the care she requires in her current location.

Patients will be in single rooms designed for safety and infection prevention. Each will be outfitted with wall-sized video screens as well as cameras capable of extreme close-ups (to allow a doctor to examine a patient's eyes or neck veins via video) and wide angles (to see everyone in the room during a family meeting). Patients and their families will be able to review their clinicians' notes, test results, and treatment recommendations, either on the big screen or on a hospital-issued tablet computer. Patients will also receive educational materials, along with periodic messages—including encouragements ("Your goal today is to walk up and down the hallway three times") and attaboys ("Nice work on those deep breaths today!")—through the computer. The confused patient who begins to climb out of bed will hear the recorded voice of a trusted relative, triggered by a bed sensor: "Mom, it's Linda. It's okay, get back to bed."

The nurse call button will be a thing of the past. A patient will simply say, "Nurse, I'm in pain," and the nurse will appear on the screen, discuss the issue with the patient, and increase the pain medication if necessary. None of this will require the nurse to enter the room—a computer-entered order will adjust the IV infusion pump automatically. If a new pill is needed, it will be delivered by a robot.

Physician rounds in the hospital will take place at the bedside, but they will be scheduled so that family members can participate through videoconferencing. As physicians and other team members enter the room, their names and roles will automatically appear on the patient's screen, with their detailed bios a click away.

Consultations with specialists will be completely reimagined. If the inpatient doctors need a nephrology consultation, for example, they will search online for a nephrologist who is available, and quickly arrange a videoconference. In the large national systems that will dominate inpatient care, the best available consultant may not be in the building; in fact, he may be in another state. A new system of national physician licensure, enacted to facilitate telemedicine, will allow consultations to cross state boundaries. There may even be instances in which consultants are in other countries.

The electronic health record will be transformed as well. The visit note will be created by physicians and other team members largely through speaking, rather than writing and clicking. Natural language processing technology will not only parse the words into the right categories in the electronic record to satisfy the demand for quality measurement and patient risk assessments, but also "tune" itself automatically as it analyzes each clinician's manner of speech, specialty, and experience. The note's structure will also change fundamentally: it will be a living document in which new information is added collaboratively, more like a Wikipedia page than today's static and siloed notes created independently by each group of caregivers. Accurate historical information (family history, past medical history, and key prior studies) will be easily accessible and needn't be reentered each time a patient receives care, partly because the billing rules will no longer demand such idiocy.

Information from the record—"show me the hemoglobin trend over the past week"—will be accessed by voice command. Team members will be able to create and display graphs, images, videos, and more, for their own use and to educate patients and promote shared decision making. The technology will allow members at home to fully participate in those decisions.

Computerized decision support for clinicians will also be taken to a new level. While physicians will still be ultimately responsible for making a final diagnosis, the EHR will suggest possible diagnoses for the physician to consider, along with tests and treatments based on guidelines and literature that are a click or a voice command away. Color-coded digital dashboards will show at a glance whether all appropriate treatments have been given. Teams will develop new ways of distributing the work to be sure that all dashboards are green by the end of each shift, although many of the preventive activities (such as elevating the head of the bed for the patient at risk for aspiration) will be carried out automatically by the technology.

Big-data analytics will be constantly at work, mining the patient's database to assess the risk for deterioration (infection, falls, bedsores, and the like) before such risks become clinically obvious. These risk assessments will seamlessly link to the dashboards, suggesting changes in monitoring, staffing, or treatments when a patient's risk profile changes. Alerts (both those in the EHR and those from in-room monitoring devices) will be far more intelligent and far less frequent. Like the Boeing cockpit alerts, they will be graded, and the alert for "you're about to give a 39-fold overdose" will look nothing like the alert that fires for "these two medications sometimes have a significant interaction you should be aware of."

Physicians, nurses, pharmacists, physical therapists, dieticians, and administrators will huddle around their patients at least once a day, and the collaborative game plan they develop will be clearly captured in the EHR. But the creation of the record will, to a large degree, be an artifact of the actual delivery of care, as many of the things that doctors and nurses now type or click into the computer will be automatically entered through voice recordings, by sensors (vital signs, for example), and by patients themselves. The combination of intelligent algorithms and automatic data entry will allow each healthcare professional to practice far closer to the top of her license. As less time is wasted on documenting the care, doctors and nurses will have more direct contact with patients and families, restoring much of the joy in practice that has been eroding, like a coral reef, with each new wave of nonclinical demands.

▶   ▶   ▶

For the patient with multiple chronic diseases, much of the care that currently involves hospitalizations and visits to doctors' offices or ERs will be conducted through televisits and IT-enabled home care. Healthcare systems will have multiple ways of assessing their patients, few of which will require patients to leave their homes. The emphysema patient will be prompted to answer a few questions ("Good morning. How is your breathing? Your cough?") on the computer each day. The heart failure patient will have his state of hydration and vital signs monitored through sensors embedded in a watch, a wristband, or a stick-on device. The diabetic or the kidney-failure patient who needs periodic blood test monitoring will be able to prick a finger at home (assuming that the test still requires a drop of blood; many of today's blood tests will be replaced by sophisticated skin sensors). The specimen will be processed in seconds through a smartphone attachment, and the result will be automatically entered into the electronic record.

Far more important than the acquisition of all these new kinds of data will be a system for making sense of them all—a system that doesn't depend on a primary care doctor reviewing impossible mountains of information. A new kind of integrator—an IT company that can tap into all the relevant information, whether it comes from an ER visit, a sensor, or the answer to a questionnaire—will have emerged to turn the data into actionable intelligence. Its human companion will be a new health professional, akin to an air traffic controller, whose job will be to understand the data, put it in context, and act on it. We'll probably call this person a "case manager," though his role will be more advanced (including a significant amount of patient and family education and coaching) and data-driven than the current version of that job, and his training will be more robust. His work will be overseen by a physician (usually a generalist, but for selected patients with a dominant single chronic problem, perhaps a specialist), who will be responsible for the well-being of large groups of patients.[40]

Patients with multiple chronic illnesses being managed at home will receive some instructions directly from the IT system (to the patient with heart failure, "Please cut down on your salt; your weight is up two pounds"), sometimes from the case manager, and, when needed, sometimes from the doctor via a tele- or in-person visit. The latter will be unusual, mostly for the patient who has multiple active problems or who is not responding to treatment.

Since none of this will alter the human condition—most people who are asked to cut down on salt or calories will fail to do so, whether they are commanded by their wife or their iPad—the algorithms will escalate their prompts in a customized way. They will ultimately "know" what behavioral prompts work for each patient (or, in that Amazonlike way, "for patients *like* you"). I'll leave it to your imagination to decide whether, in the case of the recalcitrant patient, the computer system will ultimately be granted the authority to lock down the salt shaker or the refrigerator. There is no doubt, however, that the "Internet of Things" will give the system the wherewithal to do so, as well as the capacity to offer rewards, of a sort, for good works.

For the patient with an acute medical issue, the capacity for home care will be greatly enhanced through new devices and telemedicine. The mom with a child who has an earache will, in fact, be able to look in the child's ear and beam the image to a nurse-practitioner or a physician, who will diagnose it and prescribe a treatment (at some point, a computer will be able to make simple diagnoses based on visual images). When an urgent care visit is needed, there will be many clinic options in the community, mostly in big stores and pharmacies (the two-person physician office will have gone the way of the corner druggist). Since the medical record will be owned by the patient, stored in a personalized cloud, and completely interconnected, patients will be able to quickly authorize anyone—the drop-in clinic in their local supermar-

---

[40] Today, a version of this model is known as the Patient-Centered Medical Home, but no one has yet sorted out all the details, particularly the data integration part.

ket, the ER across town, the consulting tele-doctor—to see their record and add to it. Strong legal protections will ensure the privacy and security of the record, including that health-related data will not be sold for commercial purposes without a patient's permission. But the government will have calibrated HIPAA, or its successor, to avoid placing patient information in a digital straitjacket, unable to wiggle free even when it needs to move about.

When the patient does need to visit the doctor, the visit will feel very different from today's experience. The doctor will sit facing the patient, listening intently. As the doctor and patient talk, a transcript of their words will appear on a monitor. As in the hospital, the doctor will be able to pull up educational materials and make them available to the patient. The process of teleconsultation will also be similar to the hospital experience, with much of the exchange—certainly the initial discussion and the consultant's final recommendations—now occurring via a three-way video conversation between patient (and family), primary care physician, and specialist. During an office visit, the doctor will receive prompts, perhaps reminding her to ask whether the patient is coughing or to check the patient's legs for swelling. The doctor need not concern herself with the patient's healthcare maintenance: all the scheduled preventive care (vaccinations and screening tests) will have been taken care of by the case manager or by the patient himself; the doctor will see a green dot on her dashboard signifying that this portion of the patient's care is up to date. Here, too, changes in the billing rules will mean that physicians no longer need to focus on documenting clinically meaningless information in order to justify a certain charge code.

For all of these patients, ranging from the elderly person with multiple chronic illnesses to the otherwise healthy person with a single acute problem, treatments will be far more customized than they are today. For the 46-year-old man with high blood pressure, the target will no longer be a fixed number, like today's 140/90. Rather, the system will determine each patient's optimal blood pressure value, based on an analysis of risk factors, genes, and the ongoing monitoring of thousands of patients with similar risk profiles. The same will be true of cholesterol, glucose, and even cancer screening. The promise of personalized medicine will become a reality.

Clinical research will also be transformed through the analysis of vast amounts of data on millions of patients. Determining the best treatment for high cholesterol, Crohn's disease, or acute lymphocytic leukemia will no longer require expensive and elaborately choreographed clinical trials. Rather, there will be a true "learning healthcare system" in which real-world variations in tests and treatments are analyzed, and the ones associated with the best outcomes are identified. These results will then be fed back into the delivery system to influence guidelines and protocols, markedly shortening the time between discovery and action. Such rapid and evidence-based feedback will not only help identify the best drugs and procedures, but also help healthcare systems sort out the best ways to staff their institutions, educational institutions the best ways to teach future doctors and nurses, and patients and families the best ways to keep themselves safe and healthy.

▶   ▶   ▶

Patients will have a much greater role, and voice, in the new healthcare system, and the technology of the future will help them manage their new responsibilities. To sort out new symptoms, customized search tools will be available. For example, the patient with emphysema who develops a cough or fever will find guidance geared to her condition. There will also be easy-to-use tools to allow patients to search for the best and least expensive hospitals and doctors—again, customized for their condition and preferences.[41] The latter is important: for some patients, the surgeon's technical skill trumps the fact that he lacks a winning personality; for others, bedside manner is more important than surgical dexterity. Just as one can refine a Yelp search by adding filters, patients will be able to filter results not just by proximity, quality, and cost, but also by personal preferences and values.

Many patients will want to be educated and supported through peer-to-peer networks, and there will be many to choose from—no longer operating parallel to the traditional healthcare system, but now integrated into it. When a patient on such a network wants a peer to see part of his medical record, it will be easy to import the data from the EHR. The reverse will also be true: the patient who wants his doctor to see a portion of a peer-to-peer conversation will be able to move that into the EHR.

In essence, there will no longer *be* an EHR in the traditional sense, an institution-centric record whose patient portal is a small tip of the hat to patient-centeredness. Rather, there will be one digital patient-centered health record that combines clinician-generated notes and data with patient-generated information and preferences. Its locus of control will be, unambiguously, with the patient.

---

[41] Another FYI: I am on the advisory board of a start-up named Amino.com, one of many trying to build such a Web-based tool.

▶    ▶    ▶

Fundamental to all of this working is a new healthcare payment system. Doctors and hospitals will no longer be paid to do more, as they were in the fee-for-service era. Rather, they will receive fixed baseline payments to care for populations of patients, adjusted for how sick the patients are. The payments will move up and down based on the quality, safety, and efficiency of the care, but they will no longer hinge on the documentation of nine physical examination findings and the like.

Measuring quality, safety, and cost will be markedly improved and made far more seamless—most of the measures will be drawn from the usual care of patients, no longer requiring massive amounts of additional data entry. Relatively few measures will be so-called process ("Did you do X?") measures, which encourage box checking and truth stretching. Instead, most will be of outcomes: for the patient with arthritis, can she walk a block without pain; for the patient with cancer, is he alive and cancer-free three years after the initial diagnosis? Under such a payment structure, healthcare systems and clinicians will have an incentive to organize themselves, including buying and properly implementing the most effective IT tools, to achieve the best outcomes at the lowest cost.

And patients will have some skin in the game as well. Modified by ability to pay, care will no longer be free but will require high enough copays to prompt patients to do the kind of comparison shopping they do when purchasing a car or a refrigerator. Again, Web-based tools will help them make good choices.

▶    ▶    ▶

All patient data will reside in the medical cloud, which will provide the essential infrastructure to ensure complete interoperability. Successful EHRs will be open, not by legislative fiat but because closed systems will be unable to compete in a market that demands that useful apps developed by third parties be accepted. Ditto usability: the government will not dictate usability, the market will, and it will do so effectively.

In fact, the future electronic health record of hospitals and clinics will be something of a commodity, with several different products available to do the same job, similar to Web browsers today. The real action—and the money—will shift to creating innovative tools to allow patients to stay healthy and manage chronic illness, helping clinicians do their work better and less expensively, and serving as the integrator that turns all these petabytes of data into real intelligence.

When we reach this glorious future state, the federal government will have long since scaled back the heavy-handed role it adopted at the time of Meaningful Use Stages 2 and 3. Rather than having federal bureaucrats dictate the specs of health IT systems, the new payment and public reporting systems will have created a market for high-quality, safe, satisfying, and efficient care. Provider organizations will decide for themselves what kind of IT (and non-IT) strategies to deploy to meet those objectives. The salad days of government incentives for IT purchases will be a distant memory. The incentives to buy high-functioning technology systems will be the same as for other businesses in competitive markets: namely, the price for *not* doing so will be swift Schumpeterian death in the marketplace.

This doesn't mean that the government will, or should, completely exit the world of health IT. Rather, it will narrow its focus to what only it can do: setting up rules and standards to facilitate interoperability, ensuring security, creating an honest and level playing field for vendors, convening stakeholders, funding research, and monitoring safety. Reaching the ideal future state will depend on government assuming its proper role: the meaningful—and limited—use of its vast powers.

Notwithstanding this implied criticism, history will judge the federal government's health IT initiatives in the 2004–2015 era favorably, as a time when its actions kick-started the digital transformation of the healthcare system, a transformation that—if we can ever reach the state I've described here—will have made the healthcare system better, safer, and cheaper.

# Chapter 28

# The Nontechnological Side of Making Health IT Work

Ninety percent of this game is half mental.

—Yogi Berra

While the future world I've just depicted may seem fantastical, there is nothing in it that is science fiction—all the technologies I discussed are available today or will be available very soon (which goes a long way toward explaining why today's health IT is so irritating). I've already described some of the business and policy changes that will be needed to achieve this vision. But, after reading about the iPatient, the demise of the clinical note, the disruptions of the social fabric of radiology and the wards, and particularly the story of Pablo Garcia's Septra overdose, you're undoubtedly thinking about the other changes—those involving humans, their relationships, and their thinking—that are crucial to making health IT work. I am, too.

Take the iPatient. Sure, part of the cure will be technological—advances in voice recognition and natural language processing that will permit doctors and patients to look at each other during an office (or a virtual) visit. But there's more to it than that. Even if we get the technology right, it is the job of the medical profession to constantly emphasize that it is the patient—a human being with hopes and fears, dreams and preferences—who is the object of our care, not a digital incarnation. We have to instill this core value of professionalism during training, and reinforce it throughout every clinician's career.

Similarly, while the computerized notes can be improved through better IT design, it is up to us to record a narrative that brings the patient's story to life. David Blumenthal recalls the training in note writing he received as an intern at Massachusetts General Hospital. His experience mirrored my own at UCSF, nearly a decade later. He wrote his notes late at night; they were comprehensive, but much too long. Then he read notes on the same patients written by more experienced residents and attendings. "I thought, 'My God, he said in three words what took me three pages,'" Blumenthal told me.

To Blumenthal, the process of training physicians demands an iterative cycle of modeling and learning and trying and failing—then trying again. "The requirements and regulations must be set by the profession itself," he said. "That process has to be recreated in the electronic record. The profession has to stop complaining about copy and paste, and start teaching young physicians what the ideal electronic note looks like. Nothing else is going to work."

▶    ▶    ▶

An equally tricky problem is the demise of relationships in our new digital world: the fact that we don't talk to radiologists anymore because we don't need to visit them in order to see a film, that we don't hang out on the wards any longer because we aren't tethered there by a paper chart, or that a nurse can gather a worrisome piece of information like a patient's recent arrival from a country suffering from an Ebola epidemic and type this fact into an electronic note rather than discussing it with a physician. It turns out that new technologies always rearrange social relationships—and that effective organizations remain vigilant for problems flowing from these changes and work doggedly to mitigate them. The solution may be the use of another new technology, like a video review with the radiologist, or something old-school and simple, like moving a break room or launching a new conference series.

The point is that part of the work of getting technology to achieve its potential—and overcoming the productivity paradox—is to think about these relationships, to be honest about which losses are survivable and which are not, and to build in fixes that recreate (or reimagine) the parts of the exchanges that remain crucial to the work. In healthcare, we've paid virtually no attention to this part of our digital transformation. We must start.

▶    ▶    ▶

Turning to the Septra case, some fixes seem obvious. Over and over, the Boeing engineers told me, "We try to keep things simple." A computerized prescribing system that forces a doctor to write a dose in mg/kg when she *knows* that the correct dose is one pill twice a day is one begging to be simpler. Crucial information (like whether a dose is in mg or mg/kg) needs to be displayed in a way that is unmistakable. Absurd options, such as prescribing a 39-fold, or even a 4-fold, overdose, must be made impossible.

I've already described how the alert system needs to be streamlined and improved. But there is more to this than simply cutting the number of pop-ups and prioritizing them. There is an underlying philosophy that we seem to lack in building health IT systems. At every step of its design process, Boeing brings pilots into the simulators and checks to see whether the alerts (and everything else) work the way the designers intended. Under this philosophy of "user-centered design," after the aviation engineers have completed their mock-ups and built a version of a new cockpit, they spend thousands of hours observing pilots *in the environment*, tweaking the technology until they have things just right.

We do nothing like this in healthcare, partly because those who build the computer systems can't easily test them in the diverse organizations in which they will be deployed (from rural clinics to large urban academic medical centers), and partly because the EHRs are trying to satisfy so many different audiences and demands. But no other mission should trump the mission of making healthcare safe. And the only way to achieve this goal is to make aviation-style integrated field testing a standard part of healthcare automation.

Part of what drives Boeing to do this kind of design and testing is utilitarian: the company knows it will produce a better airplane. But it goes deeper than that. In the aviation industry, there is an abiding respect, even reverence, for the wisdom of the frontline workers. In a 2012 video discussing what health-care can learn from aviation, Mike Sinnett, Boeing's chief 787 project engineer, pointed to the difficulty of introducing new technology to midcareer pilots who have been accustomed to doing things a certain way for years and years. While pilots like new safety features, he said, "We need to introduce them in a way that honors all their past training, but is also intuitive to them so it's easy to use. All the technology in the world is not going to help you if it's not intuitive and if the end user can't use it."

I heard many references to this notion of honoring the pilots' experience and traditions in my discussions with various folks at Boeing and with pilots themselves. It is clearly part of the DNA of commercial aviation. I never heard anything like it from a health IT vendor, many of whom see clinicians as expensive cogs to be replaced or technophobic obstacles to overcome. Physicians and nurses are far from perfect, but creating a high-functioning digital health-care system is going to require far greater involvement of—and, yes, reverence for—the members of these proud and noble professions.

We also need better training for clinicians, including simulation-based pro-grams in which doctors, nurses, and pharmacists confront scenarios in which they should trust the technology, and others (like an order to give 39 pills) in which they should not. Blind trust is the enemy; the goal is to develop appro-priately calibrated trust.

This issue is not just a struggle in healthcare. As Captain Sullenberger told me, aviation faces a similar need to balance trust in the machine and human instinct. The fact that today's cockpit technology is so reliable means that pilots tend to defer to the computer. "But we need to be capable of independent criti-cal thought," Sully said. "We need to do reasonableness tests on whatever the situation is. You know, is that enough fuel for this flight? Does the airplane really weigh that much, or is it more or less? Are these takeoff speeds reason-able for this weight on this runway? Everything should make sense."

The decision whether to question an unusual order in the computer is not simply about trust in the machines. It's also about the culture of the organiza-tion. Safe organizations relentlessly promote a "stop the line" culture, in which every employee knows that she must speak up—not only when she's sure that something is wrong, but also when she's not sure it's right. Organizations that create such a culture do so by focusing on it relentlessly and seeing it as a cen-tral job of leaders. No one should ever have to worry about looking dumb for speaking up, whether she's questioning a directive from a senior surgeon or an order in the computer.

How will an organization know when it has created such a culture? My test involves the following scenario: A young nurse, not unlike Brooke Levitt, sees a medication order that makes her uncomfortable, in a way she can't quite pin-point. She feels the pressure to, as the Nike ad goes, "just do it," but she trusts her instinct and chooses to stop the line, despite the computer's "You're 30 Minutes Late" flag, "bothering" her supervisor, and perhaps even waking up an on-call doctor. And here's the rub: the medication order was actually correct.

The measure of a safe organization is not whether the person who makes the great catch gets a thank-you note from the CEO. Rather, it's whether the person who sees something that seems to be amiss and decides to stop the line receives that note . . . *when there wasn't an error.* Unless the organization is fully supportive of that person, it will never be completely safe, no matter how good its technology.

# Chapter 29

# Art and Science

The more questioningly we ponder the essence of technology,
the more mysterious the essence of art becomes.
   —Martin Heidegger, *The Question Concerning Technology*, 1977

Not long ago, I gave a talk to a group of UCSF medical students. I chose to focus on the transformation of healthcare: changes in the payment system, public reporting, the structure of hospitals and clinics, the engagement and empowerment of patients, and, yes, the technology. Of course, it's the older doctors who are most troubled by the changes (a few years ago, one of my senior colleagues, a respected cardiologist, said, "It could be worse. . . . I could be younger"). Nevertheless, I thought the students should be prepared to enter a profession that has become barely recognizable to those of us who started 30 years ago.

The root of these changes, I told them, was our society's determination that the current healthcare system delivers care that is often unsafe, of patchy quality, unsatisfying to patients, and too expensive. It is this determination that is leading to all the upheaval.

"You folks need to be prepared for a career that will be massively different from mine," I said. "You will be under relentless pressure to deliver the highest quality, safest, most satisfying care at the lowest possible cost." I spoke these words slowly and gravely, doing my best to shake the students out of their youthful complacency.

271

A clean-cut student raised his hand and asked, with the blinding mixture of naïveté and brilliance that characterizes smart young folks, "What exactly were *you* trying to do?"

▶    ▶    ▶

Clinicians' unhappiness with the current state of health IT needs to be viewed against the backdrop of these wrenching, but largely needed, changes. They are changes that will transform the doctor-patient relationship, profoundly alter the roles of physicians and other health professionals, and ultimately result in some, perhaps many, people losing their jobs, income, and prestige. Our electronic health records could be vastly better, no doubt, but we also yell at them the way we sometimes yell at our kids after a bad day at work. They're caught in the crossfire of a profession being reshaped.

That certainly doesn't mean that the EHRs are blameless. As you've seen, today's systems are clunky and irritating on a good day, maddening and dangerous on a bad one. But perhaps it was naive of us to believe that the first versions of these technologies would be perfect; that in a field as complex as healthcare, the technology Hype Cycle could be abolished or the productivity paradox sidestepped. After all, before there was the iPad, there was the Newton; before there was ubiquitous wireless connectivity, we suffered the screeches of the dial-up modem, to say nothing of its molasses-like speed. We're simply not smart enough to make it from A to Z without going through the rest of the alphabet first.

▶    ▶    ▶

One of the positive aspects of our new digital world is that it creates new ways for patients to be active participants in their care. As exciting as this is, I also worry about it. With the advent of widespread and increasingly expensive copayments and deductibles, the temptation for patients to self-diagnose, self-treat, and crowdsource medical advice over the Web will become irresistible. After all, how many of us consult "expert" restaurant reviews anymore? We trust the wisdom of crowds on sites like Yelp and TripAdvisor.

As we enter a similarly information-rich world in healthcare, patients will face this question with greater frequency: When do I really need to consult with, and trust, a credentialed expert? There will be times when the answer is obvious, but increasingly the line will be shifting and subtle.

There is a famous story about Franz Ingelfinger, the editor of the *New England Journal of Medicine* from 1967 to 1976 and, at the time, one of the most powerful people in medicine. I call this Ingelfinger's Dilemma. In the late 1970s, Ingelfinger, a gastroenterologist, developed esophageal cancer—a tragic irony, since he was one of the world's experts in this disease. He went from doctor to doctor seeking advice, but each deferred to him, asking, "Franz, what would *you* do?"

Finally he went to see a wise physician friend, who immediately understood the problem.

"Franz," his friend told him, "what you really need is a *doctor*."

Until now, the question of when you really need a doctor—a trusted expert who can help you make difficult decisions at a time of great stress—wasn't much of a decision at all. But the changing economics and the democratization of healthcare information mean that all people, not just physician-patients, will soon face a version of Ingelfinger's Dilemma.

▶    ▶    ▶

So when *will* patients need to see doctors? And what exactly will a doctor *do* in a world of digital healthcare? These are the same questions I raised that remarkable day when I spoke to both the humanist Abraham Verghese and the technology optimist Vinod Khosla. I confess that it is difficult for someone like me, who spent nearly a decade in training and a generation in practice, to give unbiased answers.

Arnie Milstein seemed like a particularly good person to ask: he's a world expert in healthcare innovation; like Verghese, he is on Stanford's faculty; and he has worked with many IT entrepreneurs, including Khosla. Perhaps even more important, Milstein's clinical training is in psychiatry. He told me this:

> In many healthcare situations, even the most accomplished
> humans can be pushed far down Maslow's hierarchy. Hu-
> mans' often-repressed anxiety about their own mortality
> gets activated. What exactly is this? Is this the beginning of
> something that will end my life or my functional ability? If
> you think about evolution, humans are very attuned to think
> that something might kill us or leave us handicapped.
>
> Physicians are danger-control agents. Travel agents are
> not. Restaurants are not. That's why I think there will always
> be something reassuring about a person with greater skill and
> knowledge saying, "I really care about you, and I'm going to
> spend my time understanding what you want and then do

*everything that can be done to mobilize biomedical technol-*
*ogy to protect you from disability and death."*

Almost paradoxically, given the staggering growth in our scientific tools and understanding, we may be entering an era in which we rediscover a physician's traditional role as healer and counselor. In the days before technology—not just digital health records, but x-rays, blood tests, and modern pharmaceuticals—all the physician could do was be there for his patients (recall Fildes's painting *The Doctor*). Over the last century, our diagnostic and therapeutic tools have grown enormously, but our means for dealing with them have lagged far behind, leaving doctors overwhelmed and sapped of time, joy, and empathy. If our technology succeeds in helping us manage this information, physicians and other health professionals may find themselves able to return to the fundamental work of medicine: diagnosing, treating, comforting, teaching, and discovering. It is an inspiring thought, and one that does not feel overly Pollyannaish.

▶   ▶   ▶

Yet, as you've seen, the threats to this inspiring vision are real. Here are the ones I worry about most.

First, while computers can liberate patients and physicians, they also permit a level of control and micromanagement of clinical practice that scares me. There is a fine balance to be struck here: while we want our doctors to follow well-established guidelines when they are appropriate, we don't want government bureaucrats or insurance executives, rather than medical experts, exercising undue control over clinical practice. Such control was impossible in the pen-and-paper era; the charts resided in the rack in the nurses' station, far from the prying eyes of actuaries and politicos (and, even if they could reach the chart, the doctors' handwriting was usually indecipherable). In the current digital age, this kind of oversight has become feasible, turning this question into an inevitable battleground, one that must be approached with great wisdom and care.

A second, but related, issue has to do with the measurement of quality. We have left the era in which a doctor's or a hospital's reputation was derived from its research, its endowment, or its pedigree. Good riddance. Patients deserve to make choices based on the factors they care about: quality of care, safety, access, cost, and patient-centeredness. But until we get better at measuring these things, clinicians will still to be forced to play to the test: checking the boxes, prettying up the numbers, and putting us at continued risk for, as the saying goes, "hitting the target but missing the point." We must ramp up our support for the science of quality measurement, and then find ways to collect the data that don't distract clinicians from the care of the patient.

Third, as the machines get better, the tensions between them and the people who work with them will escalate. Perhaps the time will come when physicians are entirely removed from the healthcare picture—when Dr. Watson really does diagnose you and his robot cousin performs your surgery. But that will not be anytime soon. Until then, we will be in the business of creating collaborative work environments that blend people and technology.

Aviation offers a precedent, one that is at once exciting and troubling. Exciting: the safety of commercial aviation today is remarkable, much of it owing to the feats of the modern digital airplane. Troubling: the degree to which pilots have been relegated to being there primarily to monitor the computers. There's a saying in aviation that the airplane of the future will no longer have two humans in the cockpit. Instead, there will be a pilot and a dog. The pilot will be there to keep the dog company. The dog will be there to bite the pilot if he tries to touch the controls.

Cute. But then there are the tragic stories of crashes (such as the 2009 crashes of Air France 447 off the coast of Brazil and Colgan Air 3407 near Buffalo) in which the machines failed, and, after they did, it became clear that the pilots did not know how to fly the planes. Experts call this phenomenon *deskilling*, and preventing it is a major focus of today's aviation safety efforts. In his 2014 book, *The Glass Cage*, Nicholas Carr describes the challenge. "How do you measure the expense of an erosion of effort and engagement, or a waning of agency and autonomy, or a subtle deterioration of skill?" he asked. "You can't. Those are the kinds of shadowy, intangible things that we rarely appreciate until after they're gone." In a perverse way, we've been lucky that the current state of health IT is so woeful. It gives us the time we need to begin to sort out how to prevent such deskilling and disengagement before the computers *really* take over. Let's take advantage of this window before it is too late.

Finally, there is no guarantee that the time freed up by our newfound technological efficiencies will be made available for the human touch. A look at the modern history of industrial computerization would have one lay odds that this squishy stuff will be precisely what is sacrificed on the altar of productivity, particularly once every word, touch, and minute is measured, analyzed, and priced out.

In fact, I am convinced that the human side of medicine will be nurtured in the digital era only if both patients and clinicians value it and demand it.

Warner Slack, the informatics pioneer, laid out a challenge for doctors when he said three decades ago, "Any doctor who could be replaced by a computer should be." In the future, patients may face a parallel challenge, a modern version of Slack's Law: "Any patient who feels comfortable being cared for by a computer probably will be."

▶   ▶   ▶

In responding to my request for an example of where the medical profession might be heading in our newly wired world, several of the people I interviewed gave me the same surprising answer. For instance, when I asked MIT's Andy McAfee to name an analogous field, he immediately responded: "Baseball scout."

"Scouts haven't gone away, but their influence on the game is greatly diminished in the face of *Moneyball*," he said. Today's scout might say, "That guy has a pretty swing," but his observations are going to be trumped by the hitter's statistics, even by detailed video observations of the hitter's swing mechanics.

Where the humans still excel, McAfee added, is in motivating people to change. "The role of the expert is going to shift a lot—it won't be the guy who knows the answers but the guy who can convince other people to go along with the program."

I asked my son Doug, who works in baseball analytics, whether there is still a raging debate in his field between the Billy Beane, "It's-all-in-the-data," types and the "I-know-greatness-when-I see-it" traditional camp of scouting. He told me that the debate is largely settled; the current consensus is that each method brings strengths that complement the other. "The data might be bat and ball information, or spin rates on pitches, or what the scout felt when he sat down in the kid's parents' living room and asked, 'How bad do you want this?'" he told me. All these data sources—the digital and, yes, the "eyeball test"—factor into a team's decision about a player's worth.

In his book *Smarter than You Think*, Clive Thompson endorsed this idea, making a forceful case that people working collaboratively with technology are far more effective than either people or technology alone. This has been shown persuasively not only in chess ("Human strategic guidance combined with the tactical acuity of a computer was overwhelming," said grandmaster Garry Kasparov after a 1998 "collaborative chess competition"), but also in many other fields.

Thompson also described a long tradition of alarmism in the face of new technologies, beginning with the Gutenberg press. "The past turns out to be oddly reassuring," he wrote, "because a pattern emerges. Each time we're faced with bewildering new thinking tools, we panic—then quickly set about deducing how they can be used to help us work, meditate, and create."

Today, only five years into the digital transformation of medicine, it is not too early to be concerned, but it *is* too early to panic. In 1957, the year I was born, *Popular Mechanics* predicted that we'd be driving flying cars by the year 2000. We're not. But incremental improvements—airbags, cruise control, seat warmers, hybrid engines, rearview cameras, and automatic braking and lane-wandering technologies—have made today's cars far more comfortable, safer, and more fuel efficient than the Pontiac Chieftain Super Catalina that my parents drove at the time of my birth. In health information technology, we've made remarkable progress in a few short years, and the pace of progress is quickening.

In fact, I see every reason to believe that the technical problems with today's health IT—the note, the user interfaces, the alerts, the connectivity, the analytics—will largely be solved over the next 10 years. Not tomorrow, not perfectly, not everywhere, and not without pain or political dogfights, but incrementally and, ultimately, in a relatively satisfying way, one that truly makes healthcare better.

But, in the end, we will still confront the question of what to do about those messy, nonperfectible, nondigitized relationships—the ones between clinicians, of course, which continue to feel awfully important, but especially those between patients and healthcare providers. Even when that wonderful day arrives when we have finally coaxed the machines into doing all the things we want them to do and none of the things we don't, we will still be left with one human being seeking help at a time of great need and overwhelming anxiety. The relationship between a doctor and a patient does not feel transactional now, and I don't think it will then. Rather, it will remain vital, scary, ethically charged, and deeply human.

It will take great discipline and all the professionalism we can muster to remember, in a healthcare world now bathed in digital data, that we are taking care of human beings. The iPatient can be useful as a way of representing a set of facts and problems, and big data can help us analyze them and better appreciate our choices. But ultimately, only the real patient counts, and only the real patient is worthy of our full attention.

▶   ▶   ▶

A couple of years ago, I was caring for a patient in his seventies (let's call him Mr. Gordon) in the intensive care unit at UCSF Medical Center. This was a challenging case. While it was clinically obvious that the patient, who had widely metastatic cancer, was going to die, several members of the family had not come to terms with this sad reality. Layered on top of that, I sensed significant conflict within the family: the patient's son and daughter were cool toward each other, nearly businesslike, and the son and the daughter's husband could hardly stand to be in the same room.

As Mr. Gordon drifted into and out of consciousness, I sat down with his family in a conference room just outside the ICU. The family tension suffused the room with a heavy air, the smog of longstanding resentments. I described the clinical situation. I told them how it was that we were sure that Mr. Gordon was dying. I gave them my assessment that ongoing aggressive care would be futile and inhumane. I recounted my consultations with the ICU specialist, the oncologist, and the palliative care team, all of whom endorsed my prognosis and approach. I told them that I understood their desire to keep Mr. Gordon alive, but that I believed the time had come to stop trying.

After talking for a while, the family members began to describe some happy memories of their times with Mr. Gordon, and recalled his attitudes about end-of-life care (it became clear that he would not have wanted aggressive care at this stage). I could feel the family members gradually casting aside their grievances, if only temporarily, as they coalesced around Mr. Gordon's interests. Their questions answered, I left the room and returned to the ICU.

A few minutes later, Mr. Gordon's son, holding back tears, found me in the ICU and told me that the family had decided that it was time to allow his dad to die peacefully. I replied that I understood how wrenching this decision was, but that it was the right one, one that I would make for one of my own parents. He went back to the waiting room to rejoin his family.

I entered Mr. Gordon's room and informed the nurse that we would be switching from our current full-court press to comfort care. I asked him to turn down the oxygen on the mechanical ventilator, to remove all the IVs except the one for morphine, and to bring some chairs into the room to allow the family to be at Mr. Gordon's bedside during his final minutes. I walked out to the waiting room to inform the family that the time had come, and then escorted them in to see Mr. Gordon for the last time.

They entered the room, one by one. The two siblings embraced, the son and son-in-law nodded at each other (an act I interpreted as a momentary truce), and all four took seats surrounding the patient's bed.

Mr. Gordon lay still, now unconscious from his morphine drip. The stage was set, but then I noticed a problem: in his haste to discontinue the various tubes and treatments, the nurse had forgotten to disconnect the bedside cardiac monitor, which continued to flicker a few feet above Mr. Gordon's head. And so it was that at one of life's most profound moments, a moment nearly impossible in its mystery and poignancy, a moment paradoxically rich with promise and ineffable sadness, all four family members' eyes were raised, not searching for Truth or for God, but watching little squiggles, each the electronic signature of a heartbeat, march across a rectangular screen.

Mr. Gordon's son was sitting closest to the monitor. I put my hand on his shoulder. Speaking to all of them, I said, "Your dad is comfortable, and I'm so glad you could all be here with him. I'm sure he is, too. But," I pointed to the heart monitor, "there is absolutely nothing on this screen that matters." And I pressed the *off* button.

As the screen went to black, the family members shared a look of shock, then clarity, and then—what was it?—acceptance, warmth, gratitude, transcendence, maybe even love. After a moment of gathering themselves, each turned to Mr. Gordon, squeezed his hands, stroked his arm, touched his cheek. The scene was pure, peaceful, and—in a way that is hard to describe—quite beautiful. And then he died.

# Acknowledgments

I must have been thinking about writing this book for several years. Yet the idea for it felt like an epiphany.

My wife, Katie Hafner, has written about technology for the last three decades, much of it for the *New York Times*. Over the past few years, she has shifted her journalistic focus to healthcare. Thrilled that we were now playing in the same sandbox, a few years ago I found myself pitching her stories for the *Times*: Will we still need smart doctors in the Age of Watson? How are older and younger physicians adapting to digital healthcare? Medical scribes? *Really*?

Clearly, I was becoming intrigued by how computers were changing the world of healthcare. But I'm not a techie; 18 months ago, I couldn't have told you the difference between an API and an APB. So it didn't dawn on me to write a book about technology in medicine.

Then one day in mid-2013, I found myself sitting in a meeting at UCSF at which an astounding 39-fold overdose of the common antibiotic Septra was being discussed. It was at that moment that I realized that my beloved profession was being turned upside down by technology—and that I needed to write about it. I also sensed that the story of healthcare's digital transformation is not really a tech story at heart. Rather, it's a story about clinical medicine, ethics, history, sociology, people, policy, politics, psychology, and money—all things I *do* know something about.

A series of lucky breaks followed. My agent, Jim Levine, was wonderfully supportive as we found a home for the book at McGraw-Hill. Mary Glenn, my editor there, has been a joy to work with. Somebody told me about a medical student at UCSF, Allison Tillack, who had just finished her PhD in medical anthropology. Oh, and by the way, her thesis was on the digital transformation of radiology. I hired her on the spot to be my research assistant, and she made major contributions to the manuscript, particularly the early chapters on the note and artificial intelligence.

My luckiest break came in one of my early discussions with my wife about the book. "This is a journalistic book," she said. By that, she meant that in order to advance the story, I needed to do some real reporting, which meant interviewing real people. In retrospect, I can't imagine how I could have done it any other way, yet without that piece of advice, I might have tried. The nearly 100 people I interviewed could not have been more generous with their time and insights, and it was through these conversations that I was able to make sense of, and breathe life into, this remarkable saga. Plus, chatting with them was unbelievably interesting. They all have my deepest thanks.

I am particularly indebted to the participants in the Septra case. The nurse, the physician, and the pharmacist all agreed to speak with me about this terrible incident because they knew that doing so could save lives. I am grateful to my institution, UCSF Medical Center, particularly CEO Mark Laret, Chief Medical Officer Josh Adler, and Director of Risk Management Susan Penney, for allowing me to write about the case. Being transparent about such a case is an act of individual and institutional bravery, and it makes me proud to be part of the organization. I am also indebted to the many people who helped me research the case, particularly Sheri VanOsdol, Jennie Smith, Stephen Wilson, and Carolyn Jasik. Of course, I owe my greatest debt of gratitude to the young patient and his mother. Their decision to participate in this effort was an act of exceeding generosity.

I am also indebted to Richard Baron, Gurpreet Dhaliwal, Pierre Elias, John Halamka, Sandy Kivowitz, Joshua Liao, Zoë Lyon, Jessica Raimi, Christine Sinsky, Mark Smith, Lori Wolfson, Michael Zalis, and Bernice, Murray, Douglas, Benjy, and Andrea Wachter, who read drafts of the book and provided me with indispensable feedback. Any errors that remain are, of course, my responsibility.

I am grateful to my colleagues at UCSF, particularly Brad Sharpe, Niraj Sehgal, Maria Novelero, Maye Chrisman, and Talmadge King for their support and friendship, and for picking up the considerable slack while I was consumed by this project. Mary Whitney and Erica Huie provided essential administrative support. I wrote much of the book while on sabbatical at the Harvard School of Public Health, and am grateful to my colleagues there, particularly Ashish Jha and Atul Gawande, for their help and support.

My luckiest break of all was meeting and marrying Katie Hafner. She is a brilliant writer and editor—with a preternatural ability to spot a cliché from across a room—who is also an expert in technology and medicine. In fact, I doubt there's another person alive who is better qualified to have edited this book. Moreover, watching her work taught me how great journalists operate: how hard you have to dig to get a complex story straight; how crucial it is to be fair without being timid; how important it is to check your ego at the door when receiving feedback ("This is *not* a PhD thesis!!!" was typical of the notes from Katie I'd find in the margin); how landing a single great quote or fresh insight from an hour-long interview represents a stunning success. For this book and so much more, I owe her everything.

# Notes

## Preface

xi   *that long-awaited "disruptive innovation"*    This concept was described by Clayton Christensen in C. Christensen, *The Innovator's Dilemma: The Revolutionary Book That Will Change the Way You Do Business* (Boston: Harvard Business Review Press, 1997). For its relevance to healthcare, see C. M. Christensen, J. H. Grossman, and J. Hwang, *The Innovator's Prescription: A Disruptive Solution for Health Care* (New York: McGraw-Hill, 2009).

xii   *I even blog and tweet*    My blog is Wachter's World, and it can be found at www.wachtersworld.org. My Twitter handle is @Bob_Wachter.

xii   *evidence-based care only about half the time*    The evidence-based care estimate is from E. G. McGlynn, S. M. Asch, J. Adams, et al., "The Quality of Health Care Delivered to Adults in the United States," *New England Journal of Medicine* 348:2635–2645 (2003). The jumbo jet a day estimate is drawn from T. A. Brennan, L. L. Leape, N. M. Laird, et al., "Incidence of Adverse Events and Negligence in Hospitalized Patients: Results of the Harvard Medical Practice Study I," *New England Journal of Medicine* 324:370–376 (1991), and made famous in the Institute of Medicine's report, L. T. Kohn, J. Corrigan, and M. S. Donaldson, *To Err Is Human: Building a Safer Health System* (Washington, DC: National Academy Press, 2000).

xii   *adoption of electronic health records*    I've used the numbers in the Office of the National Coordinator's October 2014 report to Congress, which show that hospital adoption was at 9 percent in 2008 and rose to 59 percent in 2013. Extrapolating this curve, the rate in 2015 would be about 80 percent. In physicians' offices, the rates rose from 17 percent in 2008 to 48 percent in 2013; a similar extrapolation would bring the rate to about 60 percent in 2015. Office of the National Coordinator for Health Information Technology, *Update on the Adoption of Health Information Technology and Related Efforts to Facilitate the Electronic Use and Exchange of Health Information: Report to Congress*, October 2014, available at http://www.healthit.gov/sites/default/files/rtc_adoption_and_exchange9302014.pdf.

xiii   *How could a recruiting ad for physicians*    This ad is further described in Chapter 8.

xiii   *problems that require people themselves to change*    Heifetz is quoted in S. Vedantam, "Lessons in Leadership: It's Not About You. (It's About Them)," *Morning Edition*, NPR, November 11, 2013.

## Chapter 1: On Call

1 *"One must confess"* M. H. Mellish, ed., *Collected Papers of the Mayo Clinic*, Vol. 7 (Philadelphia: W. B. Saunders, 1916).

1 *I'm sitting with Burton in a conference room* Interview of Matthew Burton by the author, April 16, 2014.

2 *Millard Fillmore Gates Hospital* The hospital no longer exists. There is now a shopping center on the site. E. Guggenmos, "Plans for Former Millard Fillmore Gates Circle Hospital," *WIVP.com*, June 9, 2014.

3 *my 600-bed academic medical center* Personal communication from Matt Aldrich, cochair of the Code Blue committee at UCSF Medical Center in San Francisco.

3 *The survival rate for in-hospital codes* This literature is reviewed in J. T. Neagle and K. Wachsberg, "What Are the Chances a Hospitalized Patient Will Survive In-Hospital Cardiac Arrest?," *Hospitalist*, September 2010.

4 *was founded by the two Mayo brothers* For a detailed history, see H. Clapesattle, *The Doctors Mayo* (Rochester, MN: Mayo Clinic, 1969).

5 *The idea of a centralized medical record* The inventor was Dr. Henry Plummer, who is described at http://www.mayoclinic.org/tradition-heritage/dr-henry-plummer.html.

5 *a remarkable network of pneumatic tubes* J. Kiger, "Mayo's Tube System Still at Work," *Rochester Post-Bulletin*, February 18, 2010.

5 *Following a report by the Institute of Medicine* L. T. Kohn, J. Corrigan, and M. S. Donaldson, *To Err Is Human: Building a Safer Health System* (Washington, DC: National Academy Press, 2000).

5 *regulators had limited the number of hours* Accreditation Council for Graduate Medical Education, "Resident Duty Hours Language: Final Requirements," 2003, available at http://www.acgme.org.

7 *After receiving advanced training in informatics* For more information on the field of informatics, see R. A. Greenes and E. H. Shortliffe, "Medical Informatics: An Emerging Academic Discipline and Institutional Priority," *Journal of the American Medical Association* 263: 1114–1120 (1990).

## Chapter 2: Shovel Ready

9 *"By computerizing health records"* State of the Union address by President George W. Bush, available at http://www.c-span.org/video/?179813-1/2004-state-union-address.

10 *At a summit meeting in 2003* Interview of David Brailer by the author, June 18, 2014.

10 *his new $16 billion "Connecting for Health" initiative* M. Cross, "Will Connecting for Health Deliver Its Promises?," *BMJ* 332:559–601 (2006).

10 *in a speech in Minnesota* J. Conn, "10 Years After the Revolution: Health IT Coordinators Look Back at the Nation's Progress," *Modern Healthcare*, April 5, 2014 .

10 *The 44-year-old Brailer* "David Brailer," *Wikipedia*, http://en.wikipedia.org/wiki/David_Brailer, retrieved December 26, 2014, and interview with the author, June 18, 2014.

10 *the federal government had a place in setting standards* Brailer laid out his initial vision in a July 2004 "Framework for Strategic Action": D. J. Brailer, "The Decade of Health Information Technology: Delivering Consumer-centric and Information-rich Health Care: Framework for Strategic Action," June 21, 2004, available at http://www.providersedge.com/ehdocs/ehr_articles/the_decade_of_hit-delivering_customer-centric_and_info-rich_hc.pdf.

11 *when Modern Healthcare magazine named him* "100 Most Powerful People in Healthcare (List)," *Modern Healthcare*, 2004, available at http://chedit.cr.atl.publicus.com/article/20040823/PREMIUM/408230346/.

12 *only 17 percent of doctors' offices* Data are from the ONC's October 2014 report to Congress (see under Preface for more information).

12 *As Clay Christensen* C. M. Christensen, J. H. Grossman, and J. Hwang, *The Innovator's Prescription: A Disruptive Solution for Health Care* (New York: McGraw-Hill, 2009).

13  *America's decision during the Lincoln administration*    See G. W. Hilton, "A History of Track Gauge: How 4 Feet, 8½ Inches Became the Standard," *Trains*, May 1, 2006.

13  *the adoption of a single networking protocol*    K. Hafner and M. Lyon, *Where Wizards Stay Up Late: The Origins of the Internet* (New York: Simon & Schuster, 1996).

14  *"You never want a serious crisis"*    G. F. Seib, "In Crisis, Opportunity for Obama," *Wall Street Journal*, November 21, 2008, available at http://online.wsj.com/articles/SB1227212780563 45271.

14  *The term* shovel-ready *was coined*    M. Roig-Franzia, "Obama Brings 'Shovel-Ready' Talk into Mainstream," *Washington Post*, January 8, 2009.

15  *in an appearance on NBC's* Meet the Press    Ibid.

15  *In a five-page white paper*    D. Blumenthal, "The Federal Role in Promoting Health Information Technology," Commonwealth Fund, January 2009, available at http://www.common wealthfund.org/usr_doc/1230_Blumenthal_federal_role_promoting_hlt_IT_Perspectives .pdf?section=4039.

16  *"There's a risk that somebody, somewhere"*    Interview of Bob Kocher by the author, June 19, 2014.

16  *for a program called HITECH*    D. Blumenthal, "Launching HITECH," *New England Journal of Medicine* 362:382–385 (2010).

16  *Zeke Emanuel recalled approaching Sen. Max Baucus*    (footnote) Interview of Emanuel by the author, December 1, 2014.

17  *would ultimately be deemed "a fiasco,"*    R. Bacon, "The Sickening £12 Billion NHS Fiasco," *Telegraph* (London), April 17, 2007.

17  *Robert Wah, Brailer's first lieutenant at the ONC*    Interview of Robert Wah by the author, August 4, 2014.

17  *a decade earlier when WellPoint*    M. Holt, "J. D. Kleinke—the Arianna Huffington of Health Care," *Health Care Blog*, September 19, 2005, available at http://matthewholt.typepad.com/ the_health_care_blog/2005/09/tech_jd_klienke.html.

18  *adoption rates soared from the low teens*    Source is the ONC's October 2014 report to Congress (see under Preface for more information).

18  *Today he runs a large healthcare investment fund*    Brailer's firm is called Health Evolution Partners (http://www.healthevolutionpartners.com/david-j-brailer-md-phd/), while Kocher works at Venrock (http://www.venrock.com/teammember/bob-kocher/).

## Chapter 3: The iPatient

23  *"Some patients . . . recover their health"*    S. J. Reiser, A. J. Dyck, and W. J. Curran, eds., "Hippocrates, Precepts VI," in *Ethics in Medicine: Historical Perspectives and Contemporary Concerns* (Cambridge, MA: MIT Press, 1977), p. 5.

23  *Relman, who died in 2014*    This biography is drawn from several sources, most important S. J. Farber, "Conferring of Honorary Fellowship upon Arnold S. Relman, MD," *Bulletin of the New York Academy of Medicine* 64:887–890 (1988).

24  *In a 2012 video commemorating*    Interview with Relman on the occasion of the 200th anniversary of the *New England Journal of Medicine*, available at https://www.youtube.com/ watch?v=jnB2P7cJuDE.

24  *taking on what he called the "Medical-Industrial Complex"*    A. S. Relman, "The New Medical-Industrial Complex," *New England Journal of Medicine* 303:963–970 (1980).

24  *In a 2014 essay in the* New York Review of Books    A. Relman, "On Breaking One's Neck," *New York Review of Books*, February 6, 2014.

25  *In a 2014 study, Cornell researchers found*    A. Musicus, A. Tal, and B. Wansink, "Eyes in the Aisles: Why Is Cap'n Crunch Looking Down at My Child?," *Environment and Behavior*, April 2, 2014.

25  *Northwestern University researchers videotaped*    E. Montague and A. Asan, "Dynamic Modeling of Patient and Physician Eye Gaze to Understand the Effects of Electronic

Health Records on Doctor-Patient Communication and Attention," *International Journal of Medical Informatics* 83:225–234 (2014).

25  *"Eye contact is a really good surrogate"*   K. Murphy, "Psst: Look Over Here," *New York Times*, May 16, 2014.

25  *In 2010, a seven-year-old girl*   E. Toll, "The Cost of Technology," *Journal of the American Medical Association* 307:2497–2498 (2012).

26  *In his famous 1891 painting* The Doctor   Available at http://www.tate.org.uk/art/artworks/fildes-the-doctor-n01522/text-summary.

26  *Fildes's doctor could do little to save the boy*   The first effective treatment for tuberculosis was the antibiotic streptomycin, discovered in 1944.

27  *Over the past decade, Abraham Verghese*   His most recent book is *Cutting for Stone* (New York: Knopf, 2009).

27  *"I joke, but I only half joke"*   A. Verghese, "A Doctor's Touch," TEDGlobal, 2011, available at https://www.ted.com/talks/abraham_verghese_a_doctor_s_touch?language=en.

27  *In an influential 2008 article*   A. Verghese, "Culture Shock—Patient as Icon, Icon as Patient," *New England Journal of Medicine* 359:2748–2751 (2008).

28  *"The iPatient is getting wonderful care"*   Verghese, "A Doctor's Touch."

28  *Sitting in Verghese's sun-drenched office*   Interview of Abraham Verghese by the author, April 29, 2014.

28  *In a 2013 study, researchers at Johns Hopkins*   L. Block, R. Habicht, A. W. Wu, et al., "In the Wake of the 2003 and 2011 Duty Hours Regulations, How Do Internal Medicine Residents Spend Their Time?," *Journal of General Internal Medicine* 28:1042–1047 (2013).

## Chapter 4: The Note

29  *"To advance professional improvement"*   T. Percival, *Medical Ethics, or a Code of Institutes and Precepts, Adapted to the Professional Conduct of Physicians and Surgeons* (Manchester, U.K.: S. Russell, 1803).

30  *In fact, two books chronicling the withering*   E. Shorter, *Doctors and Their Patients: A Social History* (New Brunswick, NJ: Transaction Publishers, 1991); and D. J. Rothman, *Strangers at the Bedside: A History of How Law and Bioethics Transformed Medical Decision Making* (New York: Basic Books, 1991).

30  *As described by medical historian Stanley Reiser*   S. J. Reiser, "The Clinical Record in Medicine. Part 1: Learning from Cases," *Annals of Internal Medicine* 114:902–907 (1991).

30  *For example, the case of a gentleman*   W. H. Jones, ed., *Hippocrates*, Vol. 1 (Cambridge, MA: Harvard University Press, 1923), p. 279.

31  *A patient with pleurisy, for example*   T. Sydenham, quoted in K. Dewhurst, ed., *Dr. Thomas Sydenham (1624–1689): His Life and Original Writings* (Berkeley, CA: University of California Press, 1996), pp. 60.

31  *That changed in 1761*   G. B. Morgagni, *The Seats and Causes of Diseases Investigated by Anatomy*, Vol. 2 (New York: Hafner Press; 1960), pp. 127–128.

32  *but a French physician named René Laennec*   S. J. Reiser, "The Clinical Record in Medicine. Part 1: Learning from Cases," *Annals of Internal Medicine* 114:902–907 (1991); and S. J. Reiser, *Technological Medicine: The Changing World of Doctors and Patients* (Cambridge, U.K.: Cambridge University Press, 2009), pp. 4–13.

32  *In 1834, speaking of the stethoscope*   *Times* (London), 1834.

33  *To Reiser, the discovery of the stethoscope*   S. J. Reiser, *Technological Medicine*, p. 12.

33  *For example, the technique of bloodletting*   P. C. Louis, *Research on the Effect of Bloodletting in Several Inflammatory Maladies* (Boston: Hilliard, Gray and Company, 1836), pp. 64–65.

## Chapter 5: Strangers at the Bedside

35  *Strangers at the Bedside*   The chapter title is drawn from D. J. Rothman, *Strangers at the Bedside: A History of How Law and Bioethics Transformed Medical Decision Making* (New York: Basic Books, 1991).

35  *"At first sight, the medical record"*    M. Berg, "Practices of Reading and Writing: the Constitutive Role of the Patient Record in Medical Work," *Sociology of Health & Illness* 18:499–524 (1996).

35  *The 1910 Flexner Report*    A. Flexner, *Medical Education in the United States and Canada: A Report to the Carnegie Foundation for the Advancement of Teaching*, Bulletin No. 4 (New York: Carnegie Foundation, 1910).

36  *Henry Plummer introduced the modern method*    R. F. Gillum, "From Papyrus to the Electronic Table: A Brief History of the Clinical Medical Record with Lessons for the Digital Age," *American Journal of Medicine* 126:853–857 (2013). The first 100 patients are described in C. L. Camp, R. L. Smoot, T. N. Kolettis, et al., "Patient Records at Mayo Clinic: Lessons Learned from the First 100 Patients in Dr. Henry S. Plummer's Dossier Model," *Mayo Clinic Proceedings* 83:1396–1399 (2008).

36  *American College of Surgeons launched a "hospital standardization" program*    S. J. Reiser, "The Clinical Record in Medicine. Part 2: Reforming Content and Purpose," *Annals of Internal Medicine* 114:980–985 (1991); and K. M. Ludmerer, *Let Me Heal: The Opportunity to Preserve Excellence in American Medicine* (Oxford, U.K.: Oxford University Press, 2014), pp. 121–123.

36  *One Boston surgeon, Ernest Codman*    Reiser, "The Clinical Record. Part 2." The Martin quote is from A. Donabedian, "The End Results of Health Care: Ernest Codman's Contribution to Quality Assessment and Beyond," *Milbank Quarterly*, 67:245 (1989).

37  *The earliest malpractice cases*    K. A. DeVille, *Medical Malpractice in Nineteenth-Century America: Origins and Legacy* (New York: New York University Press, 1990).

37  *"Even the most egregious Quacks"*    N. Smith, "Medical Jurisprudence," lecture notes taken by A. J. Skelton (New Haven, CT: Yale University Medical School, 1827), cited in J. C. Mohr, "American Medical Malpractice Litigation in Historical Perspective," *Journal of the American Medical Association* 283:1731–1737 (2000).

37  *since malpractice verdicts turned on evidence*    S. J. Reiser, "Malpractice, Patient Safety, and the Ethical and Scientific Foundations of Medicine," in P. Huber and R. Litan, eds., *The Liability Maze: The Impact of Liability Law on Safety and Innovation* (Washington, DC: Brookings Institution, 1991).

38  *The country doctor of the nineteenth century*    E. Shorter, *Doctors and Their Patients: A Social History* (New Brunswick, NJ: Transaction Publishers, 1991); and T. R. Cole, N. Carlin, and R. A. Carson, *Medical Humanities: An Introduction* (Cambridge, U.K.: Cambridge University Press, 2014).

39  *In a 2010 article, Siegler vividly illustrated*    E. L. Siegler, "The Evolving Medical Record," *Annals of Internal Medicine* 153:671–677 (2010).

41  *Medical historian Stanley Reiser captured the impossibility*    S. J. Reiser, *Technological Medicine: The Changing World of Doctors and Patients* (Cambridge, U.K.: Cambridge University Press, 2009), p. 103.

41  *Nineteenth-century notes were completely lacking in structure*    Siegler, "The Evolving Medical Record."

42  *In 1921, Johns Hopkins statistician Raymond Pearl*    R. Pearl, "Modern Methods in Handling Hospital Statistics," *Bulletin of the Johns Hopkins Hospital* 32:184–194, 1921.

42  *Some have argued that medicine experienced a golden age*    P. J. Kernahan, "Was There Ever a 'Golden Age' of Medicine?," *Minnesota Medicine*, September 2012; and Cole, Carlin, and Carson, *Medical Humanities*.

42  *a famous 1925 lecture given by Professor Francis Peabody*    O. Paul, *The Caring Physician: The Life of Dr. Francis W. Peabody* (Boston: Countway Library of Medicine, 1991).

43  *Today, the average elderly patient in the United States*    H. H. Pham, D. Schrag, A. S. O'Malley, et al., "Care Patterns in Medicare and Their Implications for Pay for Performance," *New England Journal of Medicine* 356:1130–1139 (2007).

43  *The provision of healthcare is remarkably information-intensive*    Some of the material in this section is adapted, with permission, from R. M. Wachter, *Understanding Patient Safety*, 2nd ed. (New York: McGraw-Hill, 2012).

43   *A large healthcare system processes about 10 million*   Welcome to About NASDAQ, available at http://www.nasdaq.com/about/about.pdf.
45   *an iconoclastic physician named Larry Weed*   L. Jacobs, "Interview with Lawrence Weed, MD—the Father of the Problem-Oriented Medical Record Looks Ahead," *Permanente Journal* 13:84–89 (2009); and A. Wright, D. Sittig, J. McGowan, et al., "Bringing Science to Medicine: An Interview with Larry Weed, Inventor of the Problem-Oriented Medical Record," *Journal of the American Medical Informatics Association* 21:963–968 (2014).
45   *I stumbled upon a video of Weed*   Available at https://www.youtube.com/watch?v=qMs PXSMTpFI.
46   *Weed dubbed his method of organizing the physician's narrative*   L. L. Weed, "Medical Records That Guide and Teach," *New England Journal of Medicine* 278:593–600 (1967).

## Chapter 6: Radiology Rounds
47   *"Every place is given its character"*   C. Alexander, *The Timeless Way of Building* (Oxford, U.K.: Oxford University Press, 1979).
49   *In 1888, George Eastman revolutionized photography*   S. J. Reiser, *Technological Medicine: The Changing World of Doctors and Patients* (Cambridge, U.K.: Cambridge University Press, 2009), p. 19.
50   *As Röntgen's biographer wrote*   O. Glasser, *Dr. W. C. Röntgen* (Springfield, IL: Charles C. Thomas, 1958).
50   *coated with a photographic emulsion*   S. P. Tyagi, "X-ray Film and Accessories," available at http://www.hillagric.ac.in/edu/covas/vsr/pdf/teaching_material_2/X%20ray%20film%20 and%20accessories.pdf.
50   *David Avrin . . . remembers the day he knew*   Interview of Avrin by the author, April 2, 2014.
51   *In 1956, the earliest computer hard drive*   This was IBM's model 305 RAMAC computer. Available at http://royal.pingdom.com/2008/04/08/the-history-of-computer-data-storage -in-pictures/.
51   *by the late 1990s a protocol known as DICOM*   W. D. Bidgood Jr., S. C. Horii, F. W. Prior, and D. E. Van Syckle, "Understanding and Using DICOM, the Data Interchange Standard for Biomedical Imaging," *Journal of the American Medical Informatics Association* 4:199–212 (1997).
51   *Patrick Luetmer, a neuroradiologist*   Interview of Patrick Luetmer by the author, April 15, 2014, and e-mail correspondence, October 5, 2014.
52   *In 2000, only 8 percent of U.S. hospitals*   Dorenfest Institute for Health Information through the HIMSS Foundation, *Picture Archiving and Communication Systems: A 2000–2008 Study* (Chicago: HIMSS Foundation, 2010), available at http://apps.himss.org/foundation/docs/ pacs_researchwhitepaperfinal.pdf.
53   *In 1999, Stephen Baker*   S. Baker, "PACS and Radiology Practice: Enjoy the Benefits but Acknowledge the Threats," *AJR American Journal of Roentgenology* 173:1173–1174 (1999).
53   *Paul Chang, professor of radiology*   S. Jerslid, "Informatics: the Cause of—and Solution to—Radiology's Problems," *Diagnostic Imaging.com*, November 27, 2012, available at http:// www.diagnosticimaging.com/pacs-and-informatics/informatics-cause-%E2%80%94 -and-solution-%E2%80%94-radiology%E2%80%99s-problems.
55   *Allison Tillack, a young radiologist*   Tillack served as the research assistant for this book while she was a fourth-year medical student at UCSF (she had already received her PhD in medical anthropology).
55   *"The ability of PACS to alter the accessibility"*   A. A. Tillack, "Imaging Trust: Information Technologies and the Negotiation of Radiological Expertise in the Hospital," doctoral dissertation, 2012. Retrieved from ProQuest Dissertations and Theses (Accession Order No. 1115149266).
55   *which averaged $340,000 in 2013*   Radiologist compensation survey, Medscape, 2014, available at http://www.medscape.com/features/slideshow/compensation/2014/radiology.

55  *radiologists and radiology residents identified*   Tillack, "Imaging Trust."

56  *But I've come to realize that the dissatisfaction*   G. M. Glazer and J. A. Ruiz-Wibbelsmann, "Decades of Perceived Mediocrity: Prestige and Radiology," *Radiology* 260:311–316 (2011).

56  *In a 2012 paper, Tillack and a colleague*   R. B. Gunderman and A. A. Tillack, "The Loneliness of the Long-Distance Radiologist," *Journal of the American College of Radiology* 9:530–533 (2012).

56  *Information, he wrote, "consists of objectified, decontextualized"*   H. Tsoukas, "The Tyranny of Light: The Temptations and the Paradoxes of the Information Society," *Futures* 9:827–843 (1997).

57  *Organizational expert Jody Hoffer Gittell*   Interview of Jody Hoffer Gittell by the author, August 8, 2014. The case is further described in J. H. Gittell, *The Southwest Airlines Way* (New York: McGraw-Hill, 2005).

58  *PACS, observes Tillack, created a new normal*   Tillack, "Imaging Trust."

58  *Without any changes in policy*   E. L. Siegel and B. L. Reiner, "Challenges Associated with the Incorporation of Digital Radiography into a Picture Archival and Communication System," *Journal of Digital Imaging* 12(2 Suppl 1):6–8 (1999).

59  *Said one radiologist, "With PACS, work is busier now"*   Tillack, "Imaging Trust."

59  *Ron Arenson . . . sees this as the greatest threat*   Interview of Arenson by the author, April 11, 2014.

60  *In a 2011 editorial entitled "The Life Cycle"*   W. Mallon, "The Life Cycle of a Parasitic Specialist," *Emergency Physicians Monthly*, October 4, 2011, available at http://www.epmonthly.com/departments/columns/in-my-opinion/the-life-cycle-of-a-parasitic-specialist/.

60  *The playing field soon expanded across national borders*   See D. C. Levin and Y. M. Rao, "Outsourcing to Teleradiology Companies: Bad for Radiology, Bad for Radiologists," *Journal of the American College of Radiology* 8:104–108 (2011); and R. M. Wachter, "The Dis-location of U.S. Medicine—the Implications of Medical Outsourcing," *New England Journal of Medicine* 354:661–665 (2006).

61  *Disruption often begins with*   C. M. Christensen, J. H. Grossman, and J. Hwang, *The Innovator's Prescription: A Disruptive Solution for Health Care* (New York: McGraw-Hill, 2009).

61  *With the average U.S. radiologist earning*   For U.S. radiologists' salaries, see http://www.medscape.com/features/slideshow/compensation/2014/radiology. For Indian radiologists' salaries, see Payscale Human Capital, available at http://www.payscale.com/research/IN/Job=Physician_%2F_Doctor,_Radiologist/Salary.

61  *Studies have shown that computers can detect*   The literature is reviewed in J. Shiraishi, Q. Li, D. Appelbaum, and K. Doi, "Computer-Aided Diagnosis and Artificial Intelligence in Clinical Imaging," *Seminars in Nuclear Medicine* 41:449–462 (2011).

62  *Said Paul Chang, the University of Chicago radiologist*   Interview of Paul Chang by Brian Casey, December 12, 2012, available at https://www.youtube.com/watch?v=jZIrqby2yXk.

62  *"We have to act more like consulting physicians"*   Interview of David Levin by Brian Casey, December 12, 2012, available at https://www.youtube.com/watch?v=0FT6_C9Dcf0. See also S. E. Seltzer and T. H. Lee, "The Transformation of Diagnostic Radiology in the ACO era," *Journal of the American Medical Association* 312:227–228 (2014).

## Chapter 7: Go Live

65  *"In all science, error precedes the truth "*   Cited in J. Wood, ed., *Dictionary of Quotations* (London: Frederick Warne and Co., 1899).

65  *The YouTube video opens*   "The Ballad of Go Live," available at https://www.youtube.com/watch?v=ZEDJku0-hcQ.

66  *UCSF Medical Center, went live with . . . Epic*   This is nicely chronicled on Russ Cucina's *Epic Go Live Blog* blog, available at http://russcucina.org/category/health-it/epic-electronic-health-record/epic-go-live-blog/.

67   *GE's system is poorly rated*   Ratings available at klasresearch.com. Halamka's "Imagination at Work" is from an e-mail correspondence with the author, October 11, 2014.

67   *In 2013, Healthcare IT News reported*   B. Monegain, "Go-Live Gone Wrong: Are There Lessons to Be Had from a Maine Hospital's Rollout Troubles?," *Healthcare IT News*, July 31, 2013, available at http://www.healthcareitnews.com/news/go-live-gone-wrong.

67   *The first indication that an EHR Go Live was not tiddlywinks*   I describe the Cedars-Sinai fiasco in more detail in R. M. Wachter and K. J. Shojania, *Internal Bleeding: The Truth Behind America's Terrifying Epidemic of Medical Mistakes* (New York: Rugged Land, 2004). See also C. Connolly, "Cedars-Sinai Doctors Cling to Pen and Paper," *Washington Post*, March 21, 2005, p. 1.

67   *One doctor told the* Los Angeles Times   C. Ornstein, "Hospital Heeds Doctors, Suspends Use of Software," *Los Angeles Times*, January 22, 2003.

68   *one actually took to secretly clocking colleagues*   Connolly, "Cedars-Sinai Doctors."

68   *"They poorly designed the system"*   T. Chin, "Doctors Pull Plug on Paperless System," *AMA News*, February 17, 2003.

68   *"The important lesson of the Cedars-Sinai case"*   Connolly, "Cedars-Sinai Doctors."

68   *"Let me see which of Dr. Smith's female patients"*   Interview of Richard Baron by the author, July 21, 2014.

69   *"Although the vendor urged us to think through"*   R. Baron, E. L. Fabens, M. Schiffman, and E. Wolf, "Electronic Health Records: Just Around the Corner? Or Over the Cliff?," *Annals of Internal Medicine* 143:222–226 (2005).

## Chapter 8: Unanticipated Consequences

71   *"We have the capacity to transform"*   Quoted in "HIMSS Summit: HHS Secretary Michael Leavitt Announces Formation of American Health Information Community (AHIC)," HIMSS, June 6, 2005, available at http://www.himss.org/News/NewsDetail .aspx?ItemNumber=16300.

71   *"Emergency department physicians spent 44 percent"*   H. Gregg, "4,000 Clicks per Shift: ED Physicians' EMR Burden," *Becker's Health IT & CIO Review*, October 11, 2013, available at http://www.beckershospitalreview.com/healthcare-information-technology/4-000 -clicks-per-shift-ed-physicians-emr-burden.html.

71   *In a brilliantly tart essay published*   R. E. Hirschtick, "A Piece of My Mind: Copy-and-Paste," *Journal of the American Medical Association* 295:2335–2336 (2006).

72   *Ross Koppel, a University of Pennsylvania sociologist*   Interview of Koppel by the author, July 18, 2014.

73   *In 2013, Steve Stack, board chair of the American Medical Association*   Quoted in F. Quinn, "Why Are Doctors Frustrated in Using EHR?," *MedCity News*, November 7, 2013, available at http://medcitynews.com/2013/11/doctors-frustrated-using-ehr/.

73   *investigators at the RAND Corporation*   M. W. Friedberg, P. G. Chen, K. R. Van Busum, et al., "Factors Affecting Physician Professional Satisfaction and Their Implications for Patient Care, Health Systems, and Health Policy" (Santa Monica, CA: RAND Corporation, 2013).

73   *"We had one question in the interview guide"*   Interview of Mark Friedberg by the author, July 25, 2014.

74   *"Our study does not suggest that physicians are Luddites"*   M. Friedberg, F. J. Crosson, and M. Tutty, "Physicians' Concerns About Electronic Health Records: Implications and Steps Towards Solutions," *Health Affairs* blog, March 11, 2014, available at http://healthaffairs. org/blog/2014/03/11/physicians-concerns-about-electronic-health-records-implications -and-steps-towards-solutions/.

74   *A separate 2013 survey reported*   "New IDC Health Insights Survey of Ambulatory Providers Reveals Dissatisfaction with Ambulatory EHR," press release, November 13, 2013, available at http://www.idc.com/getdoc.jsp?containerId=prUS24443913.

75   *Studies have shown that the use of scribes*   See C. Sinsky, R. Willard-Grace, A. M. Schutzbank, et al., "In Search of Joy in Practice: A Report of 23 High-Functioning Primary Care Practices," *Annals of Family Medicine* 11:272–278 (2013); and D. B. Reuben, J. Knudsen, W. Senelick, et al., "The Effect of a Physician Partner Program on Physician Efficiency and Patient Satisfaction," *JAMA Internal Medicine* 175:1190–1193 (2014).

75   *A January 2014 article in the* New York Times   K. Hafner, "A Busy Doctor's Right Hand, Ever Ready to Type," *New York Times*, January 12, 2014.

75   *In the 23 physician practices that Sinsky observed*   Sinsky et al., "In Search of Joy."

76   *"When you're building for experts"*   Interview of Roni Zeiger by the author, March 13, 2014.

77   *Steve Polevoi is the director of quality*   Interview of Polevoi by the author, June 17, 2014.

77   *A 2014 study bore this out*   S. P. Taylor, R. Ledford, V. Palmer, and E. Abel, "We Need to Talk: An Observational Study of the Impact of Electronic Medical Record Implementation on Hospital Communication," *BMJ Quality and Safety* 23: 584-588 (2014).

77   *James Stoller . . . has dubbed this phenomenon "electronic siloing"*   J. K. Stoler, "Electronic Siloing: An Unintended Consequence of the Electronic Health Record," *Cleveland Clinic Journal of Medicine* 80:406–409 (2013).

77   *All of these concerns became tragically concrete*   M. Fernandez, M. D. Shear, and A. Goodnough, "Dallas Hospital Alters Account, Raising Questions on Ebola Case," *New York Times*, October 3, 2014; M. Fernandez and K. Sack, "Ebola Patient Sent Home Despite Fever, Records Show," *New York Times*, October 10, 2014; R. Wachter, "What Ebola Error in Dallas Shows: State-of-the-Art Computer Systems Can't Replace Face-to-Face Communication," *USA Today*, October 13, 2014. For more on the tendency to blame the EHRs for everything, see J. Halamka, "The View from Underneath the Bus," available at http://geekdoctor .blogspot.com/2014/10/the-view-from-underneath-bus.html.

78   *Alan Jacobsen, a Boeing psychologist and human factors expert*   Interview of Jacobsen by the author, June 4, 2014.

78   *Christine Sinsky, the Dubuque primary care doctor*   Interview of Sinsky by the author, June 25, 2014.

79   *John Birkmeyer, a prominent Dartmouth surgeon and researcher*   Interview of Birkmeyer by the author, June 27, 2014.

80   *A mouse-over would reveal its instructions*   "Putting the 'A' back in SOAP Notes: Time to Tackle an Epic Problem," *Wachter's World* blog, September 3, 2012, available at http:// community.the-hospitalist.org/2012/09/03/putting-the-a-back-in-soap-notes-time-to -tackle-an-epic-problem/. For more on the importance of free-text narrative, see G. D. Schiff and D. W. Bates, "Can Electronic Clinical Documentation Help Prevent Diagnostic Errors?," *New England Journal of Medicine* 362:1066–1069 (2010).

80   *The OIG found that the hospitals had collectively overcharged*   J. Carlson, "$700M in Kwashiorkor Charges Trigger OIG Audit," *Modern Healthcare*, February 12, 2014, available at http://www.modernhealthcare.com/article/20140212/NEWS/302129957. See also D. Marbury, "EHR Copy-and-Paste Function: Fraud or Efficiency?," *Medical Economics*, January 14, 2014.

81   *a 2005 RAND study estimated that wiring the United States healthcare system*   R. Hillestad, J. Bigelow. A. Bower, et al., "Can Electronic Medical Record Systems Transform Health Care? Potential Health Benefits, Savings, and Costs," *Health Affairs* 24:1103–1117 (2005).

81   *Now, hospitals could install software*   A 2005 study found that "increased coding levels" represented the dominant financial benefit to small practices, and Rich Baron recalls this as the main selling point touted by the vendors when he purchased his system in 2003. R. H. Miller, C. West, T. M. Brown, et al., "The Value of Electronic Health Records in Solo or Small Group Practices," *Health Affairs* 24:1127–1137 (2005). While Medicare clearly believes that upcoding is widespread, a 2014 study, surprisingly, showed no evidence of more upcoding in hospitals with EHRs than in those without them. J. Adler-Milstein and A. K. Jha, "No Evidence Found that Hospitals Are Using New Electronic Health Records to Increase Medicare Reimbursement," *Health Affairs* 33:1271–1277 (2014).

82   *"We're continuing to see the use of cut-and-paste"*   Quoted in N. Brinkerhoff, "Flaw in Electronic Health Record System Leads to Overcharging," AllGov.com, January 10, 2014, available at http://www.allgov.com/news/where-is-the-money-going/flaw-in-electronic-health -record-system-leads-to-overcharging-140110?news=852133.

82   *In a March 2014 post on the popular* KevinMD *blog*   Anonymous, "The Disturbing Confessions of a Medical Scribe," *KevinMD* blog, March 9, 2014, available at: http:// www.kevinmd.com/blog/2014/03/confessions-medical-scribe.html.

83   *In a 2013 study, Michigan State researchers*   E. M. Altmann, J. G. Trafton, and D. Z. Hambrick, "Momentary Interruptions Can Derail the Train of Thought," *Journal of Experimental Psychology: General* 143:215–226 (2014).

83   *lead researcher Erik Altmann told the* Atlantic   L. Abrams, "Study: A 3 Second Interruption Doubles Your Odds of Messing Up," *Atlantic*, January 10, 2013.

83   *Bob Myers, Boeing's chief flight deck engineer*   Interview of Myers by the author, June 4, 2014.

83   *She once nearly overlooked a patient's pulmonary embolism*   C. Sinsky, "If Not for the Pause . . . ," *Sinsky Healthcare Innovations* blog, January 9, 2014, available at http:// www.drsinsky.com/blog/2014/1/9/if-not-for-the-pause.

84   *In a case published in a patient safety journal I edit*   J. Halamka, "Order Interrupted by Text: Multitasking Mishap," *AHRQ WebM&M* (online journal), December 2011, available at http://webmm.ahrq.gov/case.aspx?caseID=257.

86   *"I print out thousands of pages a day"*   Interview of Deb Althaus by the author, June 25, 2014.

86   *While he believes the potential for benefit is large*   Interview of Ross Koppel by the author, July 18, 2014.

86   *In a 2012 article, Koppel added*   R. Koppel, "Patient Safety and Health Information Technology: Learning from Our Mistakes," *AHRQ WebM&M* (online journal), July 2012, available at http://webmm.ahrq.gov/perspective.aspx?perspectiveID=124.

87   *Gordon Schiff had a similar experience*   Interview of Gordon Schiff by the author, July 28, 2014.

89   *In a controversial 2009 article*   R. Koppel and D. Kreda, "Health Care Information Technology Vendors' 'Hold Harmless' Clause: Implications for Patients and Clinicians," *Journal of the American Medical Association*, 301:1276–1278 (2009).

89   *Epic denies having ever had*   (footnote) Epic's denial: e-mail from Carl Dvorak to the author, October 6, 2014; Jonathan Bush quote on practicing medicine: interview of Bush by the author, September 22, 2014; the vendor Code of Conduct is available at http:// www.himssehra.org/docs/EHR%20Developer%20Code%20of%20Conduct%20Final.pdf.

## Chapter 9: Can Computers Replace the Physician's Brain?

93   *"Any doctor who could be replaced by a computer"*   Interview of Warner Slack by the author, July 25, 2014. Slack told me that he first used the line in 1961, when he heard it from his psychologist brother, Charles Slack, who first heard a variation of it from B. F. Skinner in reference to teachers being replaced by "teaching machines."

93   *The first, physician-author Abraham Verghese*   Interview of Verghese by the author, April 29, 2014.

93   *Khosla has been predicting*   His original piece is V. Khosla, "20-Percent Doctor Included: Speculations and Musings of a Technology Optimist," 2012, available at http://www .khoslaventures.com/wp-content/uploads/20-Percent-Doctor-Included_DRAFT.pdf. The revised version (referenced in the footnote) is V. Khosla, "The Reinvention of Medicine: Dr. Algorithm Vo-7 and Beyond," September 22, 2014, available at http://techcrunch.com/ 2014/09/22/the-reinvention-of-medicine-dr-algorithm-version-0-7-and-beyond/.

94   *believed that another seemingly intractable problem*   The story of the Google car is well told in E. Brynjolfsson and A. McAfee, *The Second Machine Age: Work, Progress, and*

*Prosperity in a Time of Brilliant Technologies* (New York: W. W. Norton, 2014). While the car is an astounding achievement, there still are a few things it cannot do, described in R. Sorokanich, "Six Simple Things Google's Self-Driving Car Still Can't Handle," August 30, 2014, available at http://gizmodo.com/6-simple-things-googles-self-driving-car-still-cant -han-1628040470.

94  *"Executing a left turn across oncoming traffic"*    F. Levy and R. J. Murnane, *The New Division of Labor: How Computers Are Creating the Next Job Market* (Princeton, NJ: Princeton University Press, 2004).

94  *"Just as factory jobs were eliminated"*    The story of Watson's defeat of the *Jeopardy* champions is described in S. Baker, *Final Jeopardy: Man vs. Machine and the Quest to Know Everything* (New York: Houghton Mifflin Harcourt, 2011).

94  *Sean Hogan, vice president for IBM Healthcare*    Interview of Hogan by the author, July 16, 2014.

94  *"I can't see how that doesn't happen"*    Interview of McAfee by the author, August 13, 2014.

95  *Hemingway's observation about how a person goes broke*    E. Hemingway, *The Sun Also Rises* (New York: Scribner, 2006).

95  *Undaunted, I tried another tack on Khosla*    Interview of Vinod Khosla by the author, April 29, 2014.

96  *The public worships dynamic, innovative surgeons*    Some of the material in this section is adapted, with permission, from "Solving the Riddle" in R. M. Wachter and K. J. Shojania, *Internal Bleeding: The Truth Behind America's Terrifying Epidemic of Medical Mistakes* (New York: Rugged Land, 2004).

97  *The late Yale surgeon Sherwin Nuland*    S. Nuland, *How We Die: Reflections on Life's Final Chapter* (New York: Knopf, 1994).

97  *a Tufts kidney specialist named Jerome Kassirer*    For example, J. P. Kassirer, "Diagnostic Reasoning," *Annals of Internal Medicine* 110:893–900 (1989).

99  *Gurpreet Dhaliwal, who was profiled in a 2012* New York Times *article*    K. Hafner, "For Second Opinion, Consult a Computer," *New York Times*, December 3, 2012.

101  *"A heart attack that happened five years ago"*    Interview of Peter Szolovits by the author, August 28, 2014.

101  *Larry Fagan, an early Stanford computing pioneer*    Interview of Fagan by the author, August 7, 2014.

101  *A number of autopsy studies*    See K. G. Shojania, E. C. Burton, K. M. McDonald, and L. Goldman, "Changes in Rates of Autopsy-Detected Diagnostic Errors over Time: A Systematic Review," *Journal of the American Medical Association*, 289:2849–2856 (2003); and K. G. Shojania, "Autopsy Revelation," *AHRQ WebM&M* (online journal), March 2004, available at http://webmm.ahrq.gov/case.aspx?caseID=54.

101  *Diagnostic errors contribute to 40,000 to 80,000 deaths*    D. E. Newman-Toker and P. J. Pronovost, "Diagnostic Errors—the Next Frontier for Patient Safety," *Journal of the American Medical Association* 301:1060–1062 (2009).

101  *And reviews of malpractice cases have demonstrated*    A. S. S. Tehrani, H. Lee, S. C. Mathews, et al., "25-Year Summary of U.S. Malpractice Claims for Diagnostic Errors 1986–2010: An Analysis from the National Practitioner Data Bank," *BMJ Quality and Safety* 22:672–680 (2013).

102  *early computing pioneer in a 1971 paean to his computer*    H. L. Bleich, "The Computer as Consultant," *New England Journal of Medicine* 284:141–147 (1971).

102  *Ted Shortliffe . . . has said that the early experience*    E. H. Shortliffe, "The Adolescence of AI in Medicine: Will the Field Come of Age in the '90s?," *Artificial Intelligence in Medicine* 5:93–106 (1993).

102  *He calls today's medical IT programs "Version 0"*    Khosla, "20-Percent Doctor Included."

103  *These cases illustrate a perennial debate in AI*    See, for example, M. van Emden, "Scruffies and Neats in Artificial Intelligence: A Programmer's Place," September 11, 2011, available at http://vanemden.wordpress.com/2011/09/11/scruffies-and-neats-in-artificial-intelligence/.

103  *When he was asked about the difference between human thinking*   E. Brown, "IBM's 'Watson' in Layman's Terms by Dr. Eric W. Brown," available at https://www.youtube.com/watch?v=gRVjFhEnLRQ.

## Chapter 10: David and Goliath

105  *"There is a science in what we do"*   A. Gawande, *Complications: A Surgeon's Notes on an Imperfect Science* (New York: Metropolitan Books, 2002).

105  *dubbing the computer "Dr. Watson"*   The "Meet Dr. Watson" headline is from S. Kliff, "Meet Dr. Watson: 'Jeopardy'-Winning Super Computer Heads into Health Care," *Washington Post*, September 12, 2011; the "Paging Dr. Watson" headline is from J. Jackson, "Paging Dr. Watson, IBM's Medical Advisor for the Future," *PC World*, August 28, 2014.

105  *Paul Grundy . . . told me*   Interview of Grundy by the author, July 21, 2014.

105  *Added Michael Weiner, who runs IBM's healthcare strategies*   Interview of Weiner by the author, July 28, 2014.

106  *The name of the child, and the software, is Isabel*   www.isabelhealthcare.com.

106  *It wasn't in Jason Maude's life plan*   Interview of Maude by the author, July 21, 2014, as well as L. Sanders, *Every Patient Tells a Story: Medical Mysteries and the Art of Diagnosis* (New York: Broadway Books, 2009).

107  *After all, a hospital can look stellar*   R. M. Wachter, "Why Diagnostic Errors Don't Get Any Respect—and What Can Be Done About Them," *Health Affairs* 29:1605–1610 (2010).

108  *Mark Smith, the former CEO of the California HealthCare Foundation*   Interview of Smith by the author, July 24, 2014.

108  *I asked Maude whether he worried*   I interviewed Maude with two of his Isabel colleagues, Amanda Tomlinson and Natalie Cronje, on July 21, 2014.

110  *At the end of the 2012* New York Times *profile*   K. Hafner, "For Second Opinion, Consult a Computer," *New York Times*, December 3, 2012.

111  *In a collaboration with the New York Genome Center*   C. Zimmer, "Enlisting a Computer to Battle Cancers, One by One," *New York Times*, March 27, 2014.

112  *"Right now, we have no better way of knowing"*   Interview of Peter Szolovits by the author, August 28, 2014.

112  *"If you do a single thing"*   F. Manjoo, "Will Robots Steal Your Job?," *Slate*, September 27, 2011, available at http://www.slate.com/articles/technology/robot_invasion/2011/09/will_robots_steal_your_job_3.html.

113  *The latter has been one of the most fruitful avenues*   This literature is reviewed in A. X. Garg, N. K. J. Adhikari, H. McDonald, et al., "Effects of Computerized Clinical Decision Support Systems on Practitioner Performance and Patient Outcomes: A Systematic Review," *Journal of the American Medical Association* 293:1223–1238 (2005); and T. J. Bright, A. Wong, R. Dhurjati, et al., "Effect of Clinical Decision-Support Systems: A Systematic Review," *Annals of Internal Medicine* 157:29–43 (2012).

113  *But, observed technology journalist Alexis Madrigal*   A. Madrigal, "By the Time Your Car Goes Driverless, You Won't Know the Difference," *Fresh Air*, NPR, March 4, 2014, available at http://www.npr.org/blogs/alltechconsidered/2014/03/04/285740673/by-the-time-your-car-goes-driverless-you-wont-know-the-difference.

## Chapter 11: Big Data

115  *"What would life be without arithmetic"*   S. Smith, *Selected Writings of Sidney Smith* (New York: Faber & Faber, 1957).

115  *I visited the Washington, DC office of Karen DeSalvo*   Interview of DeSalvo by the author, July 23, 2014.

116  *The improbable story of intelligent underwear*   Y.-L. Yang, M.-C. Chuang, S.-L. Lou, and J. Wang, "Thick-Film Textile-Based Amperometric Sensors and Biosensors," *Analyst* 135:1230–1234 (2010).

116  *Even the underwear can go both ways*   T. Cheredar, "Durex Creates Vibrating Underwear You Can Control via Smartphone Apps," *VentureBeat*, April 19, 2013, available at http://venturebeat.com/2013/04/19/durex-creates-vibrating-underwear-you-can-control-via-smartphone-apps/.

117  *The consulting firm Gartner defines big data*   Available at http://www.gartner.com/it-glossary/big-data/.

117  *Shahram Ebadollahi, IBM's chief science officer*   Interview of Ebadollahi by the author, August 18, 2014.

118  *"There are two big data problems we've observed"*   Interview of Eric Brown by the author, July 16, 2014.

119  *the creation of a "learning healthcare system"*   This concept is well described in M. Smith, *Best Care at Lower Cost: The Path to Continuously Learning Health Care in America* (Washington, DC: National Academy Press, 2012).

119  *Using a Harry Potter analogy, Michael Lauer*   Quoted in A. Allen, "Can Big Data and Patient-Informed Consent Coexist?," *Politico Pro*, September 3, 2014, available at http://www.politico.com/story/2014/09/can-big-data-and-patient-informed-consent-coexist-110567.html

120  *Larry Fagan, the retired Stanford informatics expert*   Interview of Fagan by the author, August 7, 2014.

121  *studies have shown that a patient's identity*   B. Malin and L. Sweeney, "A Secure Protocol to Distribute Unlinkable Health Data," *JAMIA Proceedings* 2005: 485–489 (2005).

121  *"It collected 19 million data points on me"*   Interview of Vinod Khosla by the author, April 29, 2014.

121  *In* The Checklist Manifesto, *the author and surgeon*   A. Gawande, *The Checklist Manifesto: How to Get Things Right* (New York: Metropolitan Books, 2009).

122  *Gawande described the findings to me*   Interview of Atul Gawande by the author, July 28, 2014.

122  *Mark Smith recalled his experience*   Interview of Smith by the author, July 24, 2014.

## Chapter 12: The Error

127  *"It may seem a strange principle"*   F. Nightingale, *Notes on Hospitals* (London: Longman, 1859).

127  *a rare genetic disease called NEMO syndrome*   For more detail, see "NEMO Deficiency Syndrome," available at http://primaryimmune.org/about-primary-immunodeficiencies/specific-disease-types/nemo-deficiency-syndrome/.

128  *Levitt recalls that moment as the worst of her life*   Interview of the nurse (Brooke Levitt is a pseudonym) by the author, May 10, 2014.

128  *nothing close had ever been reported in the medical literature*   An overview of what is known is available at http://toxnet.nlm.nih.gov/cgi-bin/sis/search/a?dbs+hsdb:@term+@DOCNO+6780.

129  US News & World Report *regularly ranks UCSF among the top 10*   Ranked eighth in 2014, it has been in the top 10 for 14 out of the last 15 years.

129  *identified as many as 50 steps*   Niraj Sehgal, MD, MPH, associate chair for quality and safety, UCSF Department of Medicine, personal communication.

129  *1 in 15 hospitalized patients*   D. W. Bates, D. J. Cullen, N. Laird, et al., "Incidence of Adverse Drug Events and Potential Adverse Drug Events: Implications for Prevention," *Journal of the American Medical Association* 274:29–34 (1995).

129  *A 2010 study (using data collected)*   "Preventing Medication Errors: A $21 Billion Opportunity" (Washington, DC: National Priorities Partnership and National Quality Forum, December 2010), available at http://psnet.ahrq.gov/resource.aspx?resourceID=20529.

## Chapter 13: The System

131  *"I hate the goddamn system"*  T. Post, director, *Magnum Force* (motion picture), United States: Warner Brothers, 1973.

131  *James Reason developed his "Swiss cheese model" of error*  First described in J. Reason, *Managing the Risks of Organizational Accidents* (Surrey, U.K.: Ashgate, 1997).

132  *A 1999 report by the Institute of Medicine*  L. T. Kohn, J. Corrigan, and M. S. Donaldson, *To Err Is Human: Building a Safer Health System* (Washington, DC: National Academy Press, 2000). The report was announced, to great fanfare, at a December 1999 press conference.

133  *Moreover, about 50,000 patients had signed up*  I'll have more to say about patient portals in Chapter 21.

134  *On an average day . . . we prescribe about 12,000 medication doses*  Thanks to Sheri VanOsdol, PharmD, and Pierre Elias for these and the rest of the pharmacy data in this section.

134  *built into the drug database system*  We, like many hospitals, use a system from a company named First Databank, www.fdbhealth.com.

## Chapter 14: The Doctor

135  *"Automation does not simply supplant human activity"*  R. Parasuraman and D. Manzey, "Complacency and Bias in Human Use of Automation: An Attentional Integration," *Human Factors* 52:381–410 (2010).

135  *Jenny Lucca, the pediatrics resident*  Interview of the pediatrics resident (Jenny Lucca is a pseudonym) by the author, April 22, 2014.

## Chapter 15: The Pharmacist

139  *Benjamin Chan was working in the seventh-floor pharmacy*  Interview of the clinical pharmacist (Benjamin Chan is a pseudonym) by the author, April 22, 2014.

141  *Computer experts call this type of problem . . . a "mode error"*  For more on mode errors, see D. A. Norman, "Design Rules Based on Analyses of Human Error," *Communications of the ACM* 26:254–258 (1983).

## Chapter 16: The Alerts

143  *"When the villagers saw no wolf"*  Aesop, *The Boy Who Cried Wolf* (Huntington, NY: Story Arts Library, 2000).

143  *Barbara Drew, a nurse-researcher at UCSF*  Interview of Drew by the author, June 19, 2014.

143  *An 89-year-old man died at Massachusetts General Hospital*  L. Kowalczyk, "'Alarm Fatigue' Linked to Patient's Death: US Agency Says Monitors at MGH Unheeded," *Boston Globe*, April 3, 2010.

144  *The* Globe *identified at least 216 deaths*  See L. Kowalczyk, "Patient Alarms Often Unheard, Unheeded," *Boston Globe*, February 13, 2011; and L. Kowalczyk, "State Reports Detail 11 Patient Deaths Linked to Alarm Fatigue in Massachusetts," *Boston Globe*, December 29, 2011.

144  *The Joint Commission . . . issued an urgent directive*  Joint Commission, "Sentinel Event Alert Issue 50: Medical Device Alarm Safety in Hospitals," April 8, 2013, available at http://www.jointcommission.org/sea_issue_50/.

144  *The ECRI Institute . . . has listed alarm-related problems*  For example, see ECRI Institute, "Top 10 Health Technology Hazards for 2015," available at https://www.ecri.org/Press/Pages/ECRI-Institute-Announces-Top-10-Health-Technology-Hazards-for-2015.aspx.

144  *"[The nurse] hurried into Logan's room"*  L. Kowalcyzk, "For Nurses, It's a Constant Dash to Respond to Alarms," *Boston Globe*, February 13, 2011.

144  *Drew's findings were shocking*  V. Colliver, "Hospitals Look to Reduce Danger of 'Alarm Fatigue,'" *San Francisco Chronicle*, October 23, 2013. The results were published in B. J. Drew, P. Harris, J. K. Zègre-Hemsey, et al., "Insights into the Problem of Alarm Fatigue

with Physiologic Monitor Devices: A Comprehensive Observational Study of Consecutive Intensive Care Patients," *PLoS One*, October 22, 2014.

145   *At Boston Medical Center, just changing*   D. A. Whalen, P. M. Covelle, J. C. Piepenbrink, et al., "Novel Approach to Cardiac Alarm Management on Telemetry Units," *Journal of Cardiovascular Nursing*, September-October:E13–E22 (2014).

145   *Alerts for premature heartbeats*   The study that demonstrated that aggressive treatment of these premature beats is dangerous is D. S. Echt, P. R. Liebson, L. B. Mitchell, et al., "Mortality and Morbidity in Patients Receiving Encainide, Flecainide, or Placebo: The Cardiac Arrhythmia Suppression Trial," *New England Journal of Medicine* 324:781–788 (1991).

146   *"Based on what I can extract from the data"*   Interview of Shahram Ebadollahi by the author, August 18, 2014.

146   *"Missing a real event is much more costly"*   Quoted in L. Kowalczyk, "Patient Alarms Often Unheard."

147   *I spoke to Captain Chesley "Sully" Sullenberger*   Interview of Sullenberger by the author, May 12, 2014.

147   *So I spent a day in Seattle with several of the Boeing engineers*   Interviews of Bob Myers, Alan Jacobsen, and Mark Nikolic by the author, June 4, 2014.

150   *and a 2010 Australian study confirmed that it is*   J. I. Westbrook, A. Woods, M. I. Rob, et al., "Association of Interruptions with an Increased Risk and Severity of Medication Administration Errors," *Archives of Internal Medicine* 170:683–690 (2010).

151   *Studies of air traffic controllers*   S. M. Galster, J. A. Duley, A. J. Masalonis, and R. Parasuraman, "Air Traffic Controller Performance and Workload Under Mature Free Flight: Conflict Detection and Resolution of Aircraft Self-Separation," *International Journal of Aviation Psychology* 11:71–93 (2001).

151   *the video of the psychology experiment*   D. Simons, "Selective Attention Test," available at https://www.youtube.com/watch?v=vJG698U2Mvo. For more detail, see C. Chabris and D. Simons, *The Invisible Gorilla: And Other Ways Our Intuitions Deceive Us* (New York: Harmony, 2010).

152   *since one-third of hospital medication errors occur*   D. W. Bates, D. J. Cullen, N. Laird, et al., "Incidence of Adverse Drug Events and Potential Adverse Drug Events: Implications for Prevention," *Journal of the American Medical Association* 274:29–34 (1995).

## Chapter 17: The Robot

155   *"Civilization advances by extending"*   A. N. Whitehead, *An Introduction to Mathematics* (London: Williams & Norgate, 1911).

155   *met with approval from Walter White*   Of course, the reference is to the chemistry teacher turned drug kingpin on the remarkable television series *Breaking Bad*.

155   *I asked Benjamin Chan what would have happened*   Interview of the clinical pharmacist by the author, April 22, 2014.

155   *A study of Princeton undergraduates*   P. A. Mueller and D. M. Oppenheimer, "The Pen Is Mightier than the Keyboard: Advantages of Longhand over Laptop Note Taking," *Psychological Science* 25:1159–1168 (2014).

155   *Said Yale psychologist Paul Bloom*   Quoted in M. Konnikova, "What's Lost as Handwriting Fades," *New York Times*, June 2, 2014.

156   *The robot, installed in 2010 at a cost of $7 million*   For more on the robot, see K. Rush-Monroe, "New UCSF Robotic Pharmacy Aims to Improve Patient Safety," March 7, 2011, available at http://www.ucsf.edu/news/2011/03/9510/new-ucsf-robotic-pharmacy-aims-improve-patient-safety. A video of the robot at work can be found at https://www.youtube.com/watch?v=oumlYbwfAsI, which is also the source of the Laret quote.

156   *Yet, wrote anesthesiologist Alan Merry and novelist Alexander McCall Smith*   A. Merry and A. McCall Smith, *Errors, Medicine and the Law* (Cambridge, U.K.: Cambridge University Press, 2001).

## Chapter 18: The Nurse

159 *"Automation bias occurs when we place too much faith"* N. Carr, "All Can Be Lost: The Risk of Putting Our Knowledge in the Hands of Machines," *Atlantic*, October 23, 2013.

159 *Brooke Levitt had been on the nursing staff* Interview of the nurse (Brooke Levitt is a pseudonym) by the author, May 10, 2014.

161 *In some hospitals, nurses now mix or collect their medications* See S. Y. Li, M. Magrabi, and E. Coiera, "A Systematic Review of the Psychological Literature on Interruption and Its Patient Safety Implications," *Journal of the American Medical Informatics Association* 19:6–12 (2012); and J. Craig, F. Clanton, and M. Demeter, "Reducing Interruptions During Medication Administration: The White Vest Study," *Journal of Research in Nursing* 19: 248–261 (2014).

161 *One element of the TPS is known as "Stop the Line"* See C. Furman and R. Caplan, "Applying the Toyota Production System: Using a Patient Safety Alert System to Reduce Error," *Joint Commission Journal on Quality and Patient Safety* 33:376–386 (2007).

162 *In a seminal 1983 article, Lisanne Bainbridge* L. Bainbridge, "Ironies of Automation," *Automatica* 19:775–779 (1983).

162 *In a famous 1995 case, the cruise ship* Royal Majesty National Transportation Safety Board, *Grounding of the Panamanian Passenger Ship* Royal Majesty *on Rose and Crown Shoal Near Nantucket, Massachusetts, June 10, 1995* (Washington DC: National Transportation Safety Board, 1997).

162 *In a dramatic study illustrating the hazards* K. L. Mosier, L. J. Skitka, S. Heers, and M. Burdick, "Automation Bias: Decision Making and Performance in High-Tech Cockpits," *International Journal of Aviation Psychology* 8:47–63 (1998).

163 *most notably the crash of Air France 447* There are several accounts of this terrible crash. See, for example, W. Langewiesche, "The Human Factor," *Vanity Fair*, October 2014. For a description of the aviation industry's response, and of automation bias more generally, see also N. Carr, *The Glass Cage: Automation and Us* (New York: W. W. Norton, 2014).

163 *George Mason University psychologist Raja Parasuraman is working* Interview of Parasuraman by the author, June 3, 2014.

## Chapter 19: The Patient

165 *"Hospitals should be arranged in such a way"* A. W. Watts, *The Essential Alan Watts* (New York: Celestial Arts, 1977).

165 *Pablo Garcia was 16 years old* Interview of the patient (Pablo Garcia is a pseudonym) by the author, June 14, 2014.

165 *Pablo's mother, Blanca, is fiercely protective* Interview of the patient's mother (Blanca Garcia is a pseudonym) by the author, June 14, 2014.

166 *While many (including myself) are skeptical* See R. M. Wachter, "Can Patients Help Ensure Their Own Safety? More Importantly, Why Should They Have To?," *Wachter's World* blog, October 14, 2009, available at http://community.the-hospitalist.org/2009/10/14/can -patients-help-ensure-their-own-safety-more-importantly-why-should-they-have-to/.

166 *Levitt remembers thinking to herself* Interview of the nurse by the author, May 10, 2014.

## Chapter 20: OpenNotes

171 *"Each patient carries his own doctor inside him."* A. Schweitzer, as quoted in N. Cousins, *Anatomy of an Illness as Perceived by the Patient* (New York: W. W. Norton, 2005).

171 *In a 1996 episode of the iconic TV comedy* Seinfeld The episode is "The Package," first aired October 17, 1996, available at https://www.youtube.com/watch?v=pyossoHFDJg.

172 *Tom Delbanco is intellectual, bookish, worldly, and iconoclastic.* Interview of Delbanco by the author, July 14, 2014.

173  *In 1957, Goffman described the psychological distance*    E. Goffman, "Characteristics of Total Institutions" (1957), in E. Goffman, *Asylums: Essays on the Social Situation of Mental Patients and Other Inmates* (New York: Anchor Books, 1961).

173  *One memorable encounter transmuted Delbanco's general passion*    R. F. White, "Patient-Centered Care and Communication: An Expert Interview with Tom Delbanco, MD," *Medscape Psychiatry*, February 11, 2005, available at http://www.medscape.com/viewarticle/498177#vp_2.

174  *In 1973 . . . Yale's Budd Shenkin and David Warner argued*    B. N. Shenkin and D. C. Warner, "Giving the Patient His Medical Record: A Proposal to Improve the System," *New England Journal of Medicine* 289:688–692 (1973).

174  *In a letter to the editor, a former medical missionary*    F. F. Holmes, "Medical Records in Patients' Hands," *New England Journal of Medicine* 290:287–288 (1974).

174  *In 1980, Delbanco and his colleagues recruited 25 patients*    R. L. Fischbach, A. Sionelo-Bayog, A. Needle, and T. L. Delbanco, "The Patient and Practitioner as Co-authors of the Medical Record," *Patient Counseling and Health Education* 2:1–5 (1980).

175  *Delbanco and his main collaborator*    T. Delbanco and J. Walker, "Benefits from Destroying the Black Box (or Are We Opening Pandora's Box?)" *SGIM Forum* 35:1–2 (2012).

176  *In a 2004 study in which patients were surveyed*    J. B. Fowles, A.C. Kind, C. Craft, et al., "Patients' Interest in Reading Their Medical Record," *Archives of Internal Medicine* 164: 793–800 (2004).

176  *The study's results were astonishingly positive.*    T. Delbanco, J. Walker, S.K. Bell, et al. "Inviting Patients to Read Their Doctors' Notes: A Quasi-Experimental Study and a Look Ahead," *Annals of Internal Medicine* 157:461–470 (2012).

178  *This happens "all the time"*    Interview of Susan Edgman-Levitan by the author, July 25, 2014.

179  *In a 2010 article in* Wired *magazine*    S. Leckart, "The Blood Test Gets a Makeover," *Wired*, November 29, 2010.

180  *Rather, he said, "I think the doctor and patient will be talking*    Interview of Roni Zeiger by the author, March 14, 2014.

## Chapter 21: Personal Health Records and Patient Portals

183  *"When we try to pick out anything"*    R. H. Limbaugh and K. E. Lewis, eds., *The John Muir Papers, 1858–1957* (Stockton, CA: University of the Pacific, 1980).

183  *Mark Smith, the former CEO of the California HealthCare Foundation*    Interview of Smith by the author, July 24, 2014.

184  *Ted Eytan, a family physician*    Interview of Eytan by the author, July 22, 2014.

184  *The evidence that offering e-mail access to patients*    (footnote) The study that showed increased visits is T. E. Palen, C. Ross, J. D. Powers, and S. Xu, "Association of Online Patient Access to Clinicians and Medical Records with Use of Clinical Services," *Journal of the American Medical Association* 308:2012–2019 (2012). A prior study (from Kaiser's Northwest region) that showed a decrease in utilization is Y. Y. Zhou, T. Garrido, H. L, Chin, et al., "Patient Access to an Electronic Health Record with Secure Messaging: Impact on Primary Care Utilization," *American Journal of Managed Care* 13:418–424 (2007).

185  *Rereading a blog post I wrote in 2008*    R. M. Wachter, "Google Health: A View from the Inside," *Wachter's World* blog, May 22, 2008, available at http://community.the-hospitalist.org/2008/05/22/google-health-a-view-from-the-inside/.

186  *Roni Zeiger, Google Health's chief strategist*    Interview of Zeiger by the author, March 14, 2014.

186  *Missy Krasner, another member of the Google Health team*    Interview of Krasner by the author, August 7, 2014.

187   *Perhaps the most visible failure was in Santa Barbara*   A very useful and honest post mortem is R. H. Miller and B. S. Miller, "The Santa Barbara Country Care Data Exchange: What Happened?," *Health Affairs* 26:w568–w580 (2007).

188   *The hope is that these new models, called accountable care organizations*   The ACO concept was created by Elliott Fisher of Dartmouth in the mid-2000s, in an effort to promote value-driven healthcare while avoiding the problems that torpedoed the managed care/ HMO movement in the 1990s. See, for example, E. S. Fisher, S. M. Shortell, S. A. Kreindler, et al., "A Framework for Evaluating the Formation, Implementation, and Performance of Accountable Care Organizations," *Health Affairs* 31:2368–2378 (2012). As of this writing, ACOs have been implemented in a series of pilot programs, largely by Medicare and Medicaid, and the evidence of their effectiveness is mixed.

189   *"Halamka, Wachter—those are uncommon names"*   Interview of John Halamka by the author, August 12, 2014.

189   *Michael Blum, CIO at UCSF Medical Center, agrees*   Interview of Blum by the author, August 6, 2014.

189   *In December 2004, Halamka had a chip*   J. Halamka, "Straight from the Shoulder," *New England Journal of Medicine* 353:331–333 (2005).

190   *"I'm a rock climber, and I believe that if I fall off a cliff"*   7 On Call with Dr. Jay Adlersberg (television news report), September 16, 2007, available at https://www.youtube.com/ watch?v=j9deGVYSOqg.

190   *most commonly used patient identifier today is probably the social security number*   (footnote)   AHIMA, "Limiting the Use of the Social Security Number in Healthcare," *Journal of AHIMA* 82:52–56 (2011), available at http://library.ahima.org/xpedio/groups/public/ documents/ahima/bok1_049016.hcsp?dDocName=bok1_049016.

192   *In an October 2014 report*   D. McCallie and M. Tripathi, "JASON Report Task Force Final Report," October 15, 2014, available at http://www.healthit.gov/facas/sites/faca/files/Joint_ HIT_JTF_JTF%20HITPC%20Final%20Report%20Presentation%20v3_2014-10-15.pdf. It was developed in part as a response to calls from other experts and consulting groups for new, cloud-based solutions, such as so-called health record banks—W. A. Yasnoff, L. Sweeney, and E. H. Shortliffe, "Putting Health IT on the Path to Success," *Journal of the American Medical Association* 309:989–990 (2013)—as well as an earlier report from the JASON consulting group that called for a new infrastructure for record sharing: JASON, "A Robust Health Data Infrastructure," November 2013, available at http://healthit.gov/sites/ default/files/ptp13-700hhs_white.pdf.

## Chapter 22: A Community of Patients

195   *"Therein the patient"*   W. Shakespeare, *Macbeth* (Mineola, NY: Dover, 1993).

195   *I served as the program director*   I described this experience in R. M. Wachter, *The Fragile Coalition: Scientists, Activists, and AIDS* (New York: St. Martin's Press, 1991).

196   *My favorite example of the latter*   A video of the planning and the act itself, by the ACT-UP affinity group Treat Action Guerrillas, is available at https://www.youtube.com/ watch?v=TS-w4Pqvkuw.

196   *When I entered the Feldman home*   Interview of Neal and Judy Feldman by the author, July 23, 2014.

196   *that is now called Smart Patients*   www.smartpatients.com.

198   *Boston University researchers developed a computerized avatar*   S. Butterfield, "Computer Teaching Patients: Virtual Advocates Help with Medication Instruction, Post-discharge Care," *ACP Hospitalist*, March 2011. The quote is from B. Jack and T. Bickmore, "The Re-engineered Hospital Discharge Program to Decrease Rehospitalization," *Care Management*, December 2010–January 2011:12-15.

198   *Larry Fagan, the retired Stanford informatics professor*   Interview of Fagan by the author, August 7, 2014.

198 *Dave deBronkart, who has made a second career* Interview of deBronkart by the author, *AHRQ WebM&M*, June 2014, available at http://webmm.ahrq.gov/perspective.aspx ?perspectiveID=159.
199 *As Zeiger sees it* Interview of Roni Zeiger by the author, August 7, 2014.

# Chapter 23: Meaningful Use
205 *"Experience hath shewn"* T. Jefferson, Preamble to a bill for the more general diffusion of knowledge, fall 1778, in P. B. Kurland and R. Lerner, *The Founders' Constitution* (Chicago: University of Chicago Press, 1987).
205 *"I do not mean to say that this government is charged"* A. Lincoln, speech in Cincinnati, Ohio, September 17, 1859, in R. P. Basler, ed., *The Collected Works of Abraham Lincoln* (Springfield, IL: Abraham Lincoln Association, 1953).
206 *I met Blumenthal in his office at Harkness House* Interview of David Blumenthal by the author, July 16, 2014. The architectural descriptions of Harkness House are from P. Goldberger, *Harkness House* (New York: Commonwealth Fund, 1987), available at http://www.commonwealthfund.org/publications/other/2004/aug/harkness-house.
207 *The penetration of electronic health records* Statistics (both overall adoption and the incentive payments in the footnote) come from ONC report to Congress, October 2014, described in the note from the Preface.
207 *"David had a combination of extraordinary vision"* Interview of John Halamka by the author, August 12, 2014.
208 *Stage 2 . . . upped the ante considerably* "Stage 2," available at http://www.cms.gov/ Regulations-and-Guidance/Legislation/EHRIncentivePrograms/Stage_2.html.
209 *I tried explaining the view, download, and transmit* Interview with Bernice Wachter by her son (the author), September 17, 2014.
210 *"All the things in Meaningful Use were well meaning"* Interview of Christine Sinsky by the author, June 25, 2014.
211 *"A shaved-head, bow-tied bundle of enthusiasm"* R. Mitchell, "Farzad Mostashari: Man on a Digital Mission," Kaiser Health News, March 9, 2012, available at http://www .kaiserhealthnews.org/Stories/2012/March/09/Farzad-Mostashari-health-information -technology.aspx?p=1.
211 *"We knew what we believed in and were not shy"* Interview of Farzad Mostashari by the author, August 11, 2014.
211 *"I think there were things done in regulation"* Interview of Jacob Reider by the author, July 1, 2014.
212 *His answer was a categorical "no."* Interview of David Brailer by the author, June 18, 2014.
212 *Those who think that Stage 2 was a bridge too far* See K. Terry, "Critics Attack Meaningful Use Program, but Disagree on Solutions," *iHealthBeat*, June 30, 2014, available at http:// www.ihealthbeat.org/insight/2014/critics-attack-meaningful-use-program-but-disagree -on-solutions; and J. Halamka, "The Standards Committee Work Ahead," *Life as a Healthcare CIO* blog, October 1, 2014, available at http://geekdoctor.blogspot.com/2014/10/the -standards-committee-work-ahead.html.
212 *"is that people with vision problems should be able to transmit"* Meaningful Use 2 specifies the need to comply with the federal Web Content Accessibility Guidelines (WCAG) 2.0, which focus on making web content more accessible to people with disabilities. The guidelines can be found at http://www.w3.org/TR/WCAG20/.
213 *Carl Dvorak, Epic's president, believes that the HITECH money* Interview of Dvorak by the author, July 15, 2014.
214 *An August 2014 article in the* New York Times A. Hartocollis, "Baby Pictures at the Doctor's? Cute, Sure, but Illegal," *New York Times*, August 9, 2014.
215 *a proposal to create a federal health IT safety center* D. Tahir, "ONC Panel Backs Health IT Safety Center," *Modern Healthcare*, July 8, 2014.

216   *I asked MIT's Andy McAfee*   Interview of McAfee by the author, August 13, 2014.

217   *DeSalvo appears to be listening*   Interview of Karen DeSalvo by the author, July 23, 2014.

## Chapter 24: Epic and athena

219   *"Eschew the momumental. Shun the Epic."*   E. Hemingway, January 1932 letter, in C. Baker, ed., *Ernest Hemingway: Selected Letters, 1917–1961* (New York: Scribner, 1981).

219   *On a cool day in Verona, Wisconsin, in September 2014*   Account is from various media sources, including M. Ivey, "No Joke: Epic Systems CEO Judy Faulkner Humors Crowd at Annual Meeting," *Cap Times* (Madison, WI), September 17, 2014; and J. Grimes, "The Most Epic Tweets from Epic JGM 2014," *Healthcare IT Leaders*, September 18, 2014. Some facts confirmed in interviews with Carl Dvorak and Sasha TerMaat, September 29, 2014.

220   *Her humble start is the stuff of legends.*   See Z. Moukheiber, "Epic Systems' Tough Billionaire," *Forbes.com*, April 18, 2012, available at http://www.forbes.com/sites/zinamoukheiber/ 2012/04/18/epic-systems-tough-billionaire/; Z. Moukheiber, "An Interview with the Most Powerful Woman in Health Care," *Forbes.com*, May 15, 2013, available at http:// www.forbes.com/sites/zinamoukheiber/2013/05/15/a-chat-with-epic-systems-ceo -judy-faulkner/; and M. Freudenheim, "Digitizing Health Records, Before It Was Cool," *New York Times*, January 14, 2012, as well as author interviews.

221   *In July 2014, representative Phil Gingrey held hearings*   G. Pema, "Epic Grilled by GOP Lawmaker in Regulatory Hearing over Interoperability," *Healthcare Informatics*, July 18, 2014, available at http://www.healthcare-informatics.com/news-item/epic-grilled-gop -lawmaker-regulatory-hearing-over-interoperability.

221   *"I'm hugely introverted, not atypical of math majors"*   Moukheiber, "Interview with the Most Powerful Woman."

221   *Dvorak... told me that until relatively recently*   Interview of Dvorak by the author, September 29, 2014. The *Schoolhouse Rock* video, "How a Bill Becomes a Law," is at https://www .youtube.com/watch?v=2nKyihoV9z8.

221   *In 2014, the company hired its first Washington lobbyist*   D. Tahir, "Epic Hires Lobbyist to Repair Interoperability Image," *Modern Healthcare*, September 13, 2014.

222   *That Epic would find itself labeled a monopoly*   See R. Koppel and C. U. Lehmann, "Implications of an Emerging EHR Monoculture for Hospitals and Healthcare Systems," *Journal of the American Medical Informatics Association*, October 2014 [published online].

222   *Said David Bates, chief quality officer*   Interview of Bates by the author, July 28, 2014.

224   *"They were very honest about what they had"*   Quoted in Moukheiber, "Epic Systems' Tough Billionaire."

225   *while some media reports claim that Epic charges*   For example, J. Creswell, "Doctors Find Barriers to Sharing Digital Medical Records," *New York Times*, September 30, 2014. I found no evidence that this was true in discussions with Epic and several of its customers.

225   *"Developers have to work through a customer"*   Moukheiber, "Interview with the Most Powerful Woman."

226   *Epic and IBM have teamed up to bid*   K. McCaney, "DOD, at Last, Invited Bids for Electronic Health Records System," *Defense Systems*, August 26, 2014.

226   *and a social activist mom*   Faulkner's background is pieced together from the articles and interviews already cited. The obituary for Faulker's mother, Del Greenfield ("A Heroine of Our Time") can be found at http://action.psr.org/site/DocServer/spring07 .pdf?docID=4422.

226   *Jonathan Bush, age 45, is the cofounder*   Bush biography and quotes pieced together from various media reports and interviews, as well as his book, J. Bush and S. Baker, *Where Does It Hurt? An Entrepreneur's Guide to Fixing Health Care* (New York: Portfolio, 2014).

227   *"I mean, can you imagine"*   J. M. Donnelly, "Recovering Workaholic: Athenahealth Founder Jonathan Bush Finds Healthy Balance to Life," *Boston Business Journal*, June 17, 2011.

227 *I met Jonathan Bush on a bright autumn day*  Interview of Bush by the author, September 22, 2014.

228 *Said Brandon Hull, a venture capitalist*  E-mail from Hull to the author, September 24, 2014.

229 *Jacob Reider . . . told me that ONC was sensitive to the risk*  Interview of Reider by the author, July 1, 2014.

231 *Speaking in March of that year, athena's CFO*  L. Lopez and A. Penn, "Read David Einhorn's Brutal Presentation on Athenahealth That Had a Room Full of Investors Laughing Out Loud," *Business Insider*, May 7, 2014, available at http://www.businessinsider.com/einhorn-at-sohn-investment-conference-2014-5?op=1. Adams resigned from the company two months after making these comments.

231 *In February, 2015, athena and John Halamka's*  S. Mace. "Athenahealth, BIDMC Ink Development Deal," *HealthLeaders Media*, February 3, 2015.

232 *Don Berwick, former head of Medicare*  Quoted in A. Gawande, "The Velluvial Matrix," *New Yorker*, June 16, 2010.

232 *In May 2014, activist investor David Einhorn*  Lopez and Penn, "Read David Einhorn's Brutal Presentation." Bush rebutted Einhorn in J. Wieczner, "Bush vs. Einhorn: How athenahealth's CEO Met His Short-Seller," *Fortune*, May 28, 2014.

## Chapter 25: Silicon Valley Meets Healthcare

235 *"For thousands of years, guys like us"*  "Minimum Viable Product," *Silicon Valley* (television series), HBO, 2014.

235 *"Our investment convinced the IT world"*  Interview of David Blumenthal by the author, July 16, 2014.

236 *"Health IT Sees First Billion Dollar Quarter"*  A. Gold, *Politico Morning eHealth*, July 17, 2014, available at http://www.politico.com/morninghealth/0714/morninghealth14675.html.

237 *a . . . healthcare impresario named Matthew Holt*  Interview of Holt by the author, August 6, 2014.

237 *He became interested in technology as a kid*  Interview of Nate Gross by the author, August 6, 2014.

238 *One was Doximity*  www.doximity.com.

238 *The other was Rock Health*  www.rockhealth.com.

240 *The first is called Augmedix.*  www.augmedix.com. The company's deal with Dignity Health is described in H. Gregg, "Google Glass Startup Augmedix Strengthened with Dignity Health Partnership, Capital Infusion," *Becker's Health IT & CIO Review*, June 18, 2014.

240 *Another Rock Health company, Cellscope*  www.cellscope.com.

241 *Finally, he described a company called Lift Labs*  www.liftlabsdesign.com. The company's purchase by Google is described in C. Dougherty, "Google Buys Lift Labs in Further Biotech Push," *New York Times*, September 10, 2014.

## Chapter 26: The Productivity Paradox

243 *"You can see the computer age"*  R. M. Solow, review of *Manufacturing Matters: The Myth of the Post-Industrial Economy*, by S. Cohen and J. Zysman, *New York Times Book Review*, July 12, 1987.

243 *"I took my own medicine"*  Interview of David Blumenthal by the author, July 16, 2014.

244 *As the economist Paul Krugman has observed*  P. Krugman, *The Age of Diminished Expectations: U.S. Economic Policy in the 1990s* (Washington, DC: Washington Post Company, 1990).

244 *Information technology falls into the same category*  E. Brynjolfsson and A. McAfee, *The Second Machine Age: Work, Progress, and Prosperity in a Time of Brilliant Technologies* (New York: W. W. Norton, 2014).

244  *In a seminal 1993 article*  E. Brynjolfsson, "The Productivity Paradox of Information Technology," *Communications of the ACM* 36:66–77 (1993).
245  *after electricity replaced steam engines*  P. A. David, "The Dynamo and the Computer: An Historical Perspective on the Modern Productivity Paradox," *American Economic Review Papers and Proceedings* 1:355–361 (1990).
246  *Robert Wah . . . told me what happened*  Interview of Wah by the author, August 4, 2014.
246  *In 1995, the consulting group Gartner coined*  Gartner Hype Cycle, available at http://www.gartner.com/technology/research/methodologies/hype-cycle.jsp.
247  *One widely cited 2005 RAND study*  R. Hillestad, J. Bigelow, A. Bower, et al., "Can Electronic Medical Record Systems Transform Health Care? Potential Health Benefits, Savings, and Costs," *Health Affairs* 24:1103–1117 (2005).
247  *Bob Kocher, the Obama advisor*  Interview of Kocher by the author, June 19, 2014.
247  *President-elect Obama, who, in a January 2009 speech, declared*  Remarks of President-elect Barack Obama, January 8, 2009, available at http://change.gov/newsroom/entry/president-elect_obama_speaks_on_the_need_for_urgent_action_on_an_american_r/.
247  *In 2014 . . . another RAND team reviewed the literature*  S. S. Jones, R. S. Rudin, T. Perry, and P. G. Shekelle, "Health Information Technology: An Updated Systematic Review with a Focus on Meaningful Use," *Annals of Internal Medicine* 160:48–54 (2014).
248  *Julia Adler-Milstein, a professor at the University of Michigan*  Interview of Adler-Milstein by the author, June 27, 2014.
248  *Ashish Jha . . . recalled the cheerleading about efficiency*  Interview of Jha by the author, July 2, 2014.
248  *Spencer Jones and colleagues from RAND considered the IT productivity paradox*  S. S. Jones, P. S. Heaton, R. S. Rudin, and E. C. Schneider, "Unraveling the IT Productivity Paradox—Lessons for Health Care," *New England Journal of Medicine* 366:2243–2245 (2012).
249  *Peter Drucker . . . presciently described*  P. F. Drucker, "The Coming of the New Organization," *Harvard Business Review*, January 1988.
250  *"Organizational factors that unlock the value of IT"*  E. Brynjolfsson and L. M. Hitt, "Beyond the Productivity Paradox: Computers Are the Catalyst for Bigger Changes," *Communications of the ACM* 41:49–55 (1998).
250  *The business model of "creative destruction"*  J. Schumpeter, *Capitalism, Socialism, and Democracy* (New York: Harper & Row, 1942).
250  *In his 2012 book . . . Eric Topol*  E. Topol, *The Creative Destruction of Medicine: How the Digital Revolution Will Create Better Health Care* (New York: Basic Books, 2012).
252  *In my own division of 60 hospitalists*  http://hospitalmedicine.ucsf.edu/home/index.html.
253  *Today at UCSF, many specialty questions are answered*  R. Vesely, "Expanding Access to Specialty Care," University of California, July 30, 2014, available at http://www.universityofcalifornia.edu/news/expanding-access-specialty-care.

## Chapter 27: A Vision for Health Information Technology
257  *"The future is already here"*  W. Gibson, *Talk of the Nation*, NPR Radio, November 30, 1999.
260  *more like a Wikipedia page than today's static and siloed notes*  Several observers have suggested this. For example, see J. Halamka, "Rethinking Clinical Documentation," *Life as a Healthcare CIO* blog, April 5, 2010, available at http://geekdoctor.blogspot.com/2010/04/rethinking-clinical-documentation.html; and, by the same author, "Brainstorming About the Future of Clinical Documentation," December 18, 2012, available at http://geekdoctor.blogspot.com/2012/12/brainstorming-about-future-of-clinical.html.
260  *Color-coded digital dashboards*  An impressive version of this is being developed by Peter Pronovost and colleagues at Johns Hopkins, in collaboration with Michael Gropper and other colleagues at UCSF, funded by the Gordon and Betty Moore Foundation. Interviews of Peter Pronovost and Mark Romig by the author, July 22, 2014, and S. Rice, "Ambitious

Checklist App Comes as Hospitals Struggle with Basic Checklists," *Modern Healthcare*, June 21, 2014.

262 *There is no doubt, however, that the "Internet of Things"*    See S. Ferber, "How the Internet of Things Changes Everything," *HBR Blog Network*, May 7, 2013, available at http://blogs.hbr.org/2013/05/how-the-internet-of-things-cha/.

265 *Instead, most will be of outcomes*    Harvard's Michael Porter has been promoting this argument, such as here: M. E. Porter, "What Is Value in Health Care?" *New England Journal of Medicine* 363:2477–2481 (2010). I have favored retaining some process measures for now, because the state of case-mix adjustment is not uniformly advanced. Once it is, then a shift to outcome measurement makes sense.

## Chapter 28: The Nontechnological Side of Making Health IT Work

267 *"Ninety percent of this game is half mental"*    Y. Berra and D. Kaplan, *What Time Is It? You Mean Now? Advice for Life from the Zennest Master of Them All* (New York: Simon & Schuster, 2002).

268 *David Blumenthal recalls the training in note writing*    Interview of Blumenthal by the author, July 16, 2014.

269 *In a 2012 video discussing what healthcare can learn*    Boeing checklist video, Boeing Corp., 2012, intranet.

270 *As Captain Sullenberger told me*    Interview of Chesley "Sully" Sullenberger by the author, May 12, 2014.

## Chapter 29: Art and Science

271 *"The more questioningly we ponder"*    M. Heidegger, *The Question Concerning Technology* (New York: Harper & Row, 1977).

272 *There is a famous story about Franz Ingelfinger*    F. J. Ingelfinger, "Arrogance," *New England Journal of Medicine* 303:1507–1511 (1980). I wrote about this in R. M. Wachter, "The Question of the Future: When Do You Need to See a Doctor?," *Wall Street Journal*, September 19, 2014, available at http://online.wsj.com/articles/what-health-issues-will-millennials-face-that-their-parents-didnt-1411138828.

273 *Arnie Milstein seemed like a particularly good person to ask*    Interview of Milstein by the author, August 4, 2014.

275 *In his 2014 book,* The Glass Cage    N. Carr, *The Glass Cage: Automation and Us* (New York: W. W. Norton, 2014).

276 *"Any doctor who could be replaced"*    See the discussion in Chapter 9.

276 *or instance, when I asked MIT's Andy McAfee*    Interview of McAfee by the author, August 13, 2014.

276 *"greatly diminished in the face of* Moneyball*"*    M. Lewis, *Moneyball: The Art of Winning an Unfair Game* (New York: W. W. Norton, 2003).

276 *I asked my son Doug, who works in baseball analytics*    Interview of Douglas Wachter by the author (his dad), August 24, 2014.

276 *In his book* Smarter than You Think    C. Thompson, *Smarter than You Think: How Technology Is Changing Our Minds for the Better* (New York: Penguin Press, 2013).

277 *In 1957 . . . Popular Mechanics predicted that we'd be driving*    G. Genford and the Editors of *Popular Mechanics*, "Prediction 1957: Flying Fan Vehicle," 1957, available at http://www.popularmechanics.com/technology/engineering/future-that-never-was-personal-aviation#slide-39. Thanks to John Halamka, whom I first heard use this story and who permitted me to personalize it here.

# National Coordinators for Health Information Technology

David Brailer, 2004–2006

Robert Kolodner, 2006–2009

David Blumenthal, 2009–2011

Farzad Mostashari, 2011–2013

Karen DeSalvo, 2014–present[42]

---

[42] DeSalvo was named acting assistant secretary of the U.S. Department of Health and Human Services in October 2014, but retained her leadership role at the Office of the National Coordinator.

# People Interviewed

| Name | Title(s) at Time of Interview (Former Titles in Parentheses) |
|---|---|
| Julia Adler-Milstein, PhD | Assistant professor, School of Information and School of Public Health, University of Michigan |
| Ronald Arenson, MD | Chairman and Alexander R. Margulis Distinguished Professor, Department of Radiology, UCSF |
| Kyle Armbrester, MBA | Vice president of business development, athenahealth |
| David Avrin, MD, PhD | Professor and vice chair of informatics, Department of Radiology, UCSF |
| Sameer Badlani, MD | Chief medical information officer, University of Chicago Medical Center |
| Richard Baron, MD | President and CEO, American Board of Internal Medicine (lead physician, Greenhouse Internists; director, Seamless Care Models at the Innovation Center, Center for Medicare & Medicaid Services) |
| David Bates, MD, MSc | Professor, Harvard Medical School; senior vice president for quality and safety and chief of the Division of General Internal Medicine, Brigham & Women's Hospital |
| Ross Berning | Research and development, Epic |
| John Birkmeyer, MD | Executive vice president for enterprise support services, Dartmouth-Hitchcock Health System; founder and chief science officer, ArborMetrix |

| Name | Title(s) at Time of Interview (Former Titles in Parentheses) |
|------|-------------------------------------------------------------|
| Michael Blum, MD | Professor of medicine, UCSF; chief medical information officer, UCSF Health System; director, UCSF Center for Digital Health Innovation |
| David Blumenthal, MD, MPP | President and CEO, Commonwealth Fund (national coordinator for health information technology; professor of medicine, Harvard Medical School; chief health information and innovation officer, Partners HealthCare) |
| Kent Bottles, MD | Consultant and lecturer (president, Institute for Clinical Systems Improvement [ISCI]; chief medical officer, Iowa Health System) |
| David Brailer, MD, PhD | CEO, Health Evolution Partners (national coordinator for health information technology; founder and CEO, CareScience) |
| Eric Brown, PhD | Director of Watson Technologies, IBM |
| Matthew Burton, MD | Clinical informatician, Office of Knowledge and Information Management, Mayo Clinic |
| Jonathan Bush, MBA | President and CEO, athenahealth |
| Brian Clay, MD | Professor of medicine and chief medical information officer, University of California, San Diego |
| Enrico Coiera, PhD[a] | Professor, Faculty of Medicine and Computer Science, University of New South Wales, Australia; Director, Centre for Health Informatics, Australian Institute of Health Innovation |
| Patricia Conolly, MD | Associate executive director, Permanente Medical Group |
| Natalie Cronje | Technical services director, Isabel Healthcare |
| Russ Cucina, MD, MS | Associate professor of medicine, UCSF; associate chief medical information officer, UCSF Health System |
| David deBronkart[a] | Patient advocate, known as "e-Patient Dave" |
| Tom Delbanco, MD | Richard and Florence Koplow–James Tullis Professor of General Medicine and Primary Care, Harvard Medical School; codirector, OpenNotes Project |
| Karen DeSalvo, MD, MPH, MSc | National coordinator for health information technology[b] (health commissioner for New Orleans; professor and vice dean for community affairs and health policy, Tulane University School of Medicine) |
| Gurpreet Dhaliwal, MD | Professor of medicine, UCSF |
| Barbara Drew, RN, PhD | David Mortara Distinguished Professor in Physiological Nursing Research, UCSF |
| Carl Dvorak | President, Epic |

| Name | Title(s) at Time of Interview (Former Titles in Parentheses) |
| --- | --- |
| Shahram Ebadollahi, PhD | Vice president, health informatics research and chief science officer, IBM Healthcare |
| Susan Edgman-Levitan, PA | Executive director, John D. Stoeckle Center for Primary Care Innovation at Massachusetts General Hospital |
| Ezekiel Emanuel, MD, PhD | Vice provost for global initiatives; chair, department of medical ethics and health policy; Levy University; Professor, University of Pennsylvania |
| Ted Eytan, MD, MS, MPH | Physician director of the Kaiser Permanente Center for Total Health |
| Larry Fagan, PhD | Codirector, Stanford University Biomedical Informatics Training Program (retired) |
| Rollin (Terry) Fairbanks, MD, MS | Director, National Center for Human Factors in Healthcare and Simulation Training & Education Laboratory, MedStar Institute for Innovation; associate professor of emergency medicine, Georgetown University |
| Neil Feldman | Participant, Smart Patients |
| Mark Friedberg, MD, MPP | Senior natural scientist, RAND Corporation; professor, Pardee RAND Graduate School |
| Atul Gawande, MD, MPH | Professor, Harvard T.H. Chan School of Public Health and Harvard Medical School; executive director, Ariadne Labs; staff writer, *New Yorker*; author, most recently, of *Being Mortal* |
| Jody Hoffer Gittell, PhD | Professor of management, Heller School for Social Policy and Management, Brandeis University; executive director, Relational Coordination Research Collaborative |
| Nate Gross, MD, MBA | Cofounder and medical director, Rock Health; cofounder, Doximity |
| Barbara Grosz, PhD | Higgins Professor of Natural Sciences, School of Engineering and Applied Sciences, Harvard University |
| Paul Grundy, MD, MPH | Global director of healthcare transformation, IBM; founding president, Patient-Centered Primary Care Collaborative |
| John Halamka, MD, MS | Chief information officer, Beth Israel Deaconess Medical Center; chairman, New England Healthcare Exchange; professor of emergency medicine, Harvard Medical School |
| Dan Haley, JD | Vice president, government and regulatory affairs and assistant general counsel, athenahealth |
| Sean Hogan, MBA | Vice president, IBM Healthcare |

| Name | Title(s) at Time of Interview (Former Titles in Parentheses) |
|---|---|
| Matthew Holt, MS | Cochairman, Health 2.0; founder/author, *The Health Care Blog* |
| Joel Howell, MD, PhD | Victor Vaughan Professor of the History of Medicine and professor in the Departments of Medicine, History, and Health Management and Policy, University of Michigan |
| Jeanne Huddleston, MD, MS | Associate professor of medicine, Mayo School of Medicine; medical director, Health Systems Engineering, Mayo Clinic Kern Center for the Science of Health Care Delivery |
| Jason Hwang, MD, MBA | Cofounder and chief medical officer, PolkaDoc; coauthor of *The Innovator's Prescription* (executive director of healthcare, Clayton Christensen Institute for Disruptive Innovation) |
| Alan Jacobsen, PhD | Technical fellow in human factors, Boeing |
| Ashish Jha, MD, MPH | K. T. Li Professor of International Health and director, Harvard Global Health Institute, Harvard T. H. Chan School of Public Health |
| Vinod Khosla, MBA, MS | Founder and CEO, Khosla Ventures (founding CEO, Sun Microsystems) |
| Bob Kocher, MD | Partner, Venrock (special assistant to the president for healthcare and economic policy, National Economic Council) |
| Ross Koppel, PhD | Adjunct professor of sociology, University of Pennsylvania |
| Missy Krasner, MA | Managing director for healthcare and life sciences, Box, and special advisor for health IT, Canvas Venture Fund (founding member, Google Health; special assistant to the national coordinator for health information technology) |
| Barron Lerner, MD | Professor of medicine and medical humanities, New York University Langone Medical Center |
| Patrick Luetmer, MD | Associate professor of radiology, Mayo College of Medicine; chief, health information coordinating subcommittee, Midwest Specialty Care Clinical Practice Committee |
| Raghavendran Mani, MS | Research and development, Epic |
| Jason Maude | Founder and CEO, Isabel Healthcare |
| Andrew McAfee, DBA, MS | Associate director, Center for Digital Business at MIT Sloan School of Management; coauthor of *The Second Machine Age* |

| Name | Title(s) at Time of Interview (Former Titles in Parentheses) |
|---|---|
| Blackford Middleton, MD, MPH, MS | Professor of biomedical informatics and of medicine, and assistant vice chancellor for health affairs, Vanderbilt University School of Medicine; chairman of the board, American Medical Informatics Association |
| Arnold Milstein, MD, MPH | Professor of medicine and director, Clinical Excellence Research Center, Stanford University; medical director, Pacific Business Group on Health |
| Farzad Mostashari, MD, MSc | Founder and CEO, Aledade (national coordinator for health information technology; deputy commissioner, New York City Department of Health) |
| Robert Myers, MA | Chief flight deck engineer, Boeing |
| Mark Nikolic, PhD, MS | Flight deck human factors engineer, Boeing |
| Don Norman, PhD[a] | Director of the design lab, University of California, San Diego; author of *The Design of Everyday Things* |
| Raja Parasuraman, PhD | University professor and director of the graduate program in human factors and applied cognition, George Mason University |
| Steven Polevoi, MD | Professor and director of quality improvement, Department of Emergency Medicine, UCSF |
| Peter Pronovost, MD, PhD | Professor, Departments of Anesthesiology, Critical Care Medicine, and Surgery and Bloomberg School of Public Health; senior vice president for patient safety and quality; director of the Armstrong Institute for Patient Safety and Quality, Johns Hopkins Medicine |
| Sumit Rana | Chief technology officer, Epic |
| Rick Rasansky | Founder and CEO, Yorn |
| Raj Ratwani, PhD | Scientific director, National Center for Human Factors in Healthcare, MedStar Institute for Innovation |
| Jacob Reider, MD | Deputy national coordinator for health information technology[c] |
| Mark Romig, MD | Assistant professor of anesthesiology and critical care medicine, John Hopkins Medicine |
| Gordon Schiff, MD | Associate professor of medicine, Harvard Medical School; associate director, Brigham Center for Patient Safety Research and Practice |
| Bret Shillingstad, MD | Clinical informatics, Epic |
| Christine Sinsky, MD | Primary care physician, Medical Clinics Associates, Dubuque, Iowa; codirector, Sinsky Healthcare Innovations |

| Name | Title(s) at Time of Interview (Former Titles in Parentheses) |
| --- | --- |
| Dean Sittig, PhD | Professor, School of Biomedical Informatics, University of Texas Health Sciences Center at Houston |
| Warner Slack, MD | Professor, Harvard Medical School and cofounder, Division of Clinical Informatics, Beth Israel Deaconess Medical Center; author of *Cybermedicine* |
| Mark Smith, MD, MBA | Senior leadership fellow, Harvard T.H. Chan School of Public Health (president and CEO, California HealthCare Foundation) |
| Chesley "Sully" Sullenberger | Speaker and consultant (pilot, US Airways; "Miracle on the Hudson" pilot) |
| Peter Szolovits, PhD | Professor of computer science and engineering and head of the Clinical Decision-Making Group, Computer Science and Artificial Intelligence Laboratory, MIT |
| Sasha TerMaat | Operations, Epic |
| Amanda Tomlinson | Quality assurance director, Isabel Healthcare |
| Eric Topol, MD | Director, Scripps Translational Science Institute, Gary and Mary West Endowed Chair of Innovative Medicine, Scripps Research Institute; author of *The Creative Destruction of Medicine* and *The Patient Will See You Now* |
| Abraham Verghese, MD | Linda R. Meier and Joan F. Lane Provostial Professor and vice chair for the theory and practice of medicine, Stanford University School of Medicine; author, most recently, of *Cutting for Stone* |
| Douglas Wachter | Intern in baseball operations, Tampa Bay Rays (research and development intern, Baseball Info Solutions) |
| Robert Wah, MD | President, American Medical Association; chief medical officer, Computer Sciences Corporation (deputy, Office of the National Coordinator for Health Information Technology) |
| Michael Weiner, DO, MSM, MSIST | Director of healthcare strategic services, IBM (director of the Military Health System EHR Planning Office) |
| Michael Zalis, MD | Associate professor of radiology, Harvard Medical School; interventional radiologist, Massachusetts General Hospital; cofounder and product strategist, QPID Health |
| Roni Zeiger, MD, MS | Founder and CEO, Smart Patients (chief health strategist, Google) |
| Anonymous (Nurse)[d] | Pediatrics nurse, UCSF |

| Name | Title(s) at Time of Interview (Former Titles in Parentheses) |
|---|---|
| Anonymous (Physician)[d] | Resident in pediatrics, UCSF |
| Anonymous (Pharmacist)[d] | Pediatric clinical pharmacist, UCSF |
| Anonymous (Patient)[d] | 16-year-old student with NEMO syndrome |
| Anonymous (Mother of Patient)[d] | Mother of the patient who received the Septra overdose |

[a] Interview conducted by the author for AHRQ WebM&M (webmm.ahrq.gov).

[b] In October 2014, DeSalvo was named Acting Assistant Secretary for Health, with primary responsibility for the federal response to the Ebola epidemic. Lisa Lewis, ONC's chief operating officer, was named Acting National Coordinator for Health Information Technology. Although it appeared at first that DeSalvo was leaving the health IT world, a subsequent press release indicated that she remained in charge of ONC's policy initiatives.

[c] Reider resigned from ONC in November 2014.

[d] Names withheld at the request of the individuals (in the case of the clinicians) and for privacy (in the case of the patient and his mother). No clinically relevant details have been altered.

# Bibliography

Baker, S. *Final Jeopardy: Man vs. Machine and the Quest to Know Everything*. New York: Houghton Mifflin Harcourt, 2011.

Brynjolfsson, E., and A. McAfee. *The Second Machine Age: Work, Progress, and Prosperity in a Time of Brilliant Technologies*. New York: W. W. Norton, 2014.

Bush, J. and S. Baker. *Where Does It Hurt? An Entrepreneur's Guide to Fixing Health Care*. New York: Portfolio/Penguin, 2014.

Carr, N. *The Glass Cage: Automation and Us*. New York: W. W. Norton, 2014.

Christensen, C. M., J. H. Grossman, and J. Hwang. *The Innovator's Prescription: A Disruptive Solution for Health Care*. New York: McGraw-Hill, 2009.

Cole, T. R., N. Carlin, and R. A. Carson. *Medical Humanities: An Introduction*. Cambridge, U.K.: Cambridge University Press, 2014.

Fogg, B. J. *Persuasive Technology: Using Computers to Change What We Think and Do*. San Francisco: Morgan Kaufmann Publishers, 2003.

Hanson, W. *Smart Medicine: How the Changing Role of Doctors Will Revolutionize Health Care*. New York: Palgrave Macmillan, 2011.

Howell, J. D. *Technology in the Hospital: Transforming Patient Care in the Early Twentieth Century*. Baltimore: Johns Hopkins University Press, 1995.

Institute of Medicine. *Digital Infrastructure for the Learning Health System: The Foundation for Continuous Improvement in Health and Health Care* (Workshop Series Summary). Washington, DC: National Academies Press, 2011.

Institute of Medicine. *Health IT and Patient Safety: Building Safer Systems for Better Care*. Washington, DC: National Academies Press, 2012.

Institute of Medicine. *Best Care at Lowest Cost: The Path to Continuously Learning Health Care in America*. Washington, DC: National Academies Press, 2013.

Koppel, R., and S. Gordon, eds. *First Do Less Harm: Confronting the Inconvenient Problems of Patient Safety*. Ithaca, NY: Cornell University Press, 2012.

Lanier, J. *You Are Not a Gadget: A Manifesto*. New York: Vintage Books, 2010.

Ludmerer, K. M. *Let Me Heal: The Opportunity to Preserve Excellence in American Medicine*. Oxford, U.K.: Oxford University Press, 2014.

Millenson, M. L. *Demanding Medical Excellence: Doctors and Accountability in the Information Age* (with a new afterword). Chicago: University of Chicago Press, 1999.

Norman, D. *The Design of Everyday Things*, revised and expanded edition. New York: Basic Books, 2013.

Reiser, S. J. *Technological Medicine: The Changing World of Doctors and Patients*. New York: Cambridge University Press, 2009.

Shortliffe, E. H., and J. J. Cimino, eds. *Biomedical Informatics: Computer Applications in Health Care and Biomedicine*, 4th ed. London: Springer-Verlag, 2014.

Slack, W. V. *Cybermedicine: How Computing Empowers Doctors and Patients for Better Health Care*. San Francisco: Jossey-Bass, 1997.

Thompson, C. *Smarter than You Think: How Technology Is Changing Our Minds for the Better*. New York: Penguin, 2013.

Tillack, A. A. *Imaging Trust: Information Technologies and the Negotiation of Radiological Expertise in the Hospital*. PhD dissertation. San Francisco and Berkeley, CA: Department of Anthropology, History, and Social Medicine, University of California, San Francisco, and University of California, Berkeley, 2012.

Topol, E. *The Creative Destruction of Medicine: How the Digital Revolution Will Create Better Health Care*. New York: Basic Books, 2012.

Topol E. *The Patient Will See You Now: The Future of Medicine is in Your Hands*. New York: Basic Books, 2015.

Wachter, R. M., and K. J. Shojania. *Internal Bleeding: The Truth Behind America's Terrifying Epidemic of Medical Mistakes*. Updated. New York: Rugged Land, 2005.

West, E. M., and E. A. Miller. *Digital Medicine: Health Care in the Internet Era*. Washington, DC: Brookings Institution, 2009.

Zipperer, L., ed. *Patient Safety: Perspectives on Evidence, Information and Knowledge Transfer*. Surrey, U.K.: Gower, 2014.

# Illustration Credits

# Index

# About the Author

Robert Wachter is professor and associate chair of the Department of Medicine at the University of California, San Francisco, where he directs the 60-physician Division of Hospital Medicine. A practicing physician, he is also the author of 250 articles and five prior books. He coined the term *hospitalist* in 1996 and is generally considered the father of the hospitalist field, the fastest-growing specialty in the history of modern medicine. He is past president of the Society of Hospital Medicine and past chair of the American Board of Internal Medicine. In 2004, he received the John M. Eisenberg Award, the nation's top honor in patient safety. For the past seven years, *Modern Healthcare* magazine has named him one of the 50 most influential physician-executives in the United States; he is the only academic physician to receive this recognition. His blog, *Wachter's World*, is one of the nation's most popular healthcare blogs, and he contributes regularly to the *Wall Street Journal* as one of "The Experts." He lives in San Francisco with his wife, Katie Hafner. They are empty nesters but for their miniature poodle, Newman.

31901056335799